Prepping and Shooting Short Film

Focusing on the practical tools required to make your first student film, this book is a concise and accessible guide to film production. Demystifying the process of taking a film from concept through to production, author Rory Kelly covers all the key bases including: organizing your script, when and how to shoot, production budgeting, finding actors and locations, and roadmapping postproduction.

Featuring common problems and challenges producers and directors face throughout the production process and providing practical solutions, the book illustrates how to effectively create a film that can be successfully shot in a classroom or micro-budget environment. Filmmakers will be empowered to prioritize realistic goals, balance practical and creative demands, manage a budget, and schedule time to ensure concept translates to reality. Kelly brings together the creative process and practicalities of producing a student film. A concise and accessible guide written with the specific constraints of a student production in mind, this book will equip any filmmaker with the tools to produce an impactful short film.

Ideal for undergraduate and graduate students of filmmaking, amateur filmmakers, as well as students in high school, community-based, for-profit and summer filmmaking programs.

Additional downloadable online resources include a look-book with images and video clips, as well as printable budget templates, shooting schedule templates, block breakdown sheets, a digital workflow worksheet, timed shot list forms and templates for location agreements, appearance releases, crew deal memos and call sheets.

Rory Kelly teaches in UCLA's Department of Film, Television and Digital Media. His first feature, *Sleep with Me*, premiered as an Official Selection at Cannes, had a Gala Screening at Toronto and was distributed by MGM/UA. His second feature, *Some Girl*, garnered him the Best Director Award at the Los Angeles Film Festival. His most recent short, *Down to Nothing*, premiered at the Maryland International Film Festival and his first feature documentary, *To Someday Understand*, premiered at the Oakland International Film Festival. He has worked as a camera assistant, camera operator, sound designer and was co-executive producer on MTVU's *Sucks Less with Kevin Smith*. He is the recipient of a Distinguished Teaching Award and a published scholar.

Prepping and Shooting Your Student Short Film

A Brief Guide to Film Production

Rory Kelly

Routledge
Taylor & Francis Group

LONDON AND NEW YORK

First published 2023
by Routledge
4 Park Square, Milton Park, Abingdon, Oxon OX14 4RN

and by Routledge
605 Third Avenue, New York, NY 10158

Routledge is an imprint of the Taylor & Francis Group, an informa business

© 2023 Rory Kelly

British Library Cataloguing-in-Publication Data
A catalogue record for this book is available from the British Library

Library of Congress Cataloging-in-Publication Data
Names: Kelly, Rory, author.
Title: Prepping and shooting your student short film : a brief guide to film production / Rory Kelly.
Description: Abingdon, Oxon ; New York, NY : Routledge, 2022. | Includes bibliographical references and index.
Identifiers: LCCN 2021062442 (print) | LCCN 2021062443 (ebook) | ISBN 9780367771225 (hardback) | ISBN 9780367771201 (paperback) | ISBN 9781003169864 (ebook)
Subjects: LCSH: Short films–Production and direction–Handbooks, manuals, etc. | Low budget films–Production and direction–Handbooks, manuals, etc.
Classification: LCC PN1995.9.P7 K45 2022 (print) | LCC PN1995.9.P7 (ebook) | DDC 791.4302/3–dc23/eng/20220503
LC record available at https://lccn.loc.gov/2021062442
LC ebook record available at https://lccn.loc.gov/2021062443

ISBN: 978-0-367-77122-5 (hbk)
ISBN: 978-0-367-77120-1 (pbk)
ISBN: 978-1-003-16986-4 (ebk)

DOI: 10.4324/9781003169864

Typeset in Bembo
by Newgen Publishing UK

Access the Support Material: www.routledge.com/9780367771201

For Sarah
And for all my students, who have taught me
as much, or more, as I have taught them

Contents

Preface

Congratulations, you've gotten into film school! Now it's time to make your movie. This means you need actors, locations, wardrobe and set dressing. You need crew, equipment and insurance. You need a shooting schedule and budget. You need, in other words, to make it happen.

That's where this book comes in. It covers only the most essential information you need to successfully prep and shoot a student film, from breaking down and scheduling a shooting script to shot-listing it, budgeting it, casting it, rehearsing it and heading to set to shoot it.

The central argument is that the practical and the creative are one and the same thing. It is only when you exhaustively prep your project, and match its scope to your available resources, that you gain time to be imaginative and open to creative possibilities while directing, as opposed to simply hammering out a series of shots every day on set.

The focus, therefore, is on how to design films that can successfully be shot by student directors and student crews in the limited number of shooting days typically allowed by film programs and with the modest amount of money most students have available to spend. It is, in short, about how to design projects that you and your classmates can successfully make.

Since the focus is on student production, this book won't overwhelm you with matters that are only relevant to professional productions. Renting and setting up a production office, for example, is beyond the scope of what you are doing, as are things like securing a completion bond and negotiating salaries for rewrites. If you one day need to know how to do such things, you will learn them by way of on-the-job experience and from books that cover such topics.

But right now, you only need to shoot your student film. And that's what this book is about.

It is primarily addressed to student directors for the simple reason that they typically write the script and spend their own money to produce it. Therefore, it is first and foremost the director, beginning during the script-writing phase, who must understand that feasibility, which means prioritizing realistic goals over less realistic goals, leads to positive outcomes.

Moreover, a director who absents themselves from the logistical concerns of production learns very little about how movies are actually made, which puts them at a disadvantage. Take, for example, the amount of money that is allocated to wardrobe in a budget. That has creative repercussions. It is not simply a numbers game and a director with no knowledge of budgeting cannot productively work with a line producer to achieve their creative goals.

It is much the same with scheduling. Only the director knows which scenes in the script are most important, but without an understanding of what constitutes a feasible shooting schedule, they cannot help an AD appropriately prioritize those scenes in terms of shooting order.

As this suggests, this book is of equal value to student producers and assistant directors and also student cinematographers, who are all directly addressed in its pages as well. These three key collaborators are responsible for maintaining momentum during prep and production, so they must also understand how realistic goals lead to positive outcomes.

In sum, this book is a primer on student production in the broadest sense with all members of a production team being able to find solid and specific information and advice in its pages. But this still only works if the director, as team leader, brings reasonable and well-informed expectations to the table and knows how to effectively collaborate with their producer, AD and DP, and with all other department heads, from the production designer to the makeup artist, as well as actors.

All of these collaborations are covered in the pages that follow.

My recommendation is that you read each chapter in turn and then revisit specific chapters as needed. However, if, based on your interests and experience, you decide to read chapters out of order, you should still begin with Chapter 1. It is intended to ground student filmmakers in an achievable reality, making it the basis for every chapter that follows.

Finally, this is not a book about basic techniques of filmmaking; it is about how to prep and shoot a primary narrative film project in a college or university film program. Students in high school, community-based, for-profit and summer filmmaking programs should also find it useful. But it assumes that you and your classmates are receiving instruction in craft classes dedicated to camera, lighting, production sound, digital workflow, etc. It also assumes that you are being taught short-form screenwriting. And it assumes that your department has or will provide you with practical, *hands-on* safety training before you head to set. No book can substitute for that.

Chapter Outline

Chapter 1 (*Keep It Simple*) provides advice on how to develop a script that can actually be shot in the number of shooting days allowed by your department and with the amount of money you know you have available to spend. This includes matching the number of locations to the number of shoot days, prioritizing, in some cases, the number of scenes over the number of pages and writing for locations that won't break the bank.

Chapter 2 (*Organize Your Script*) is about how to create a shooting script, one that accurately represents the number of scenes and pages that need to be shot. This way, the amount of work that actually has to be completed each day on set can be planned for. The chapter also covers how to break down a script and how to use that breakdown as an opportunity to begin making creative choices about what will appear in the movie.

Chapter 3 (*Decide When to Shoot What*) provides step-by-step instructions on how to create a shooting schedule, one that is feasible in terms of the number of locations, scenes and pages planned for each shoot day. The goal, once again, is to allow time to be creative on set.

Chapter 4 (*Decide How to Shoot What*) is about how to develop shot lists that effectively and creatively manage how the audience will both attend to and understand the unfolding story. Standard coverage is explained, but alternatives to coverage are also considered.

Chapter 5 (*Settle on a Look*) covers how to create a look book that demonstrates how casting, wardrobe, production design, lighting, cinematography, editing and sound will be used to build the world of the story, to support that story, and to both reveal character and underscore theme.

Chapter 6 (*Don't Break the Bank*) explores the ways in which a budget is an essential creative tool insofar as the look and quality of a film is in large part the result of how funds are allocated to production design, costumes, locations, etc. It is stressed that developing a budget means making a multitude of creative decisions that are, in every case, linked to the intelligent distribution of funds. In this way, a budget becomes the blueprint for a film, a step-by-step guide to actually making it. It is the longest chapter because the thought process behind assigning funds to each and every line item is covered in detail.

Chapter 7 (*Find Crew*) covers how to find and choose key collaborators – cinematographer, production designer, costumer and producer – as well as how to recruit the rest of a crew.

Chapter 8 (*Find Places to Shoot*) provides straightforward advice on how to scout for locations along with practical and creative advice on how to choose locations. Permits and location agreements are also covered as are the advantages and disadvantages of building sets.

Chapter 9 (*Find Actors*) is a guide to successfully completing the casting process. Emphasis is on how to handle casting in an organized, creative and professional way that leads, in the first place, to finding talented actors and, in the second place, to inspiring confidence in those actors about the project, rather than uncertainty, concern or dismay.

Chapter 10 (*Collaborate and Communicate*) begins by covering the importance of creative meetings between the director, DP, production designer, costumer and other department heads. It then moves on to the necessity of production meetings, tech scouts, finalizing and timing out shot lists and establishing the digital workflow for a project. Proper equipment checkout is discussed, call sheets are explained and consideration is given to crafty, catering, transportation, parking, etc.

Chapter 11 (*Rehearse It Before You Shoot It*) covers script analysis, rehearsals and techniques for directing and blocking actors. While it is the penultimate chapter, you are advised to read it before you begin shot-listing and casting because, as is made clear in the chapters on those subjects (4 and 9), shots are typically inseparable from performance and blocking, and casting requires that you know how to talk to actors.

Chapter 12 (*Obey the Rules of Engagement*) brings you on set. Basic set protocols and the workflow in each department are broken down. A detailed description of a typical shoot day is provided, beginning with load-in and the staging and building of equipment, followed by the blocking, lighting and shooting of action, followed by wrap.

In the Afterword a brief overview of postproduction is provided, from dailies to final mix.

But primary focus is on prep and production because these are the first hurdles you face. There is no film to edit, color or mix until principal photography is complete. And that is what this book is about. Every author chooses their subject, and I have chosen this one because after more than two decades of teaching, I have found that it is while students are prepping and shooting a first film that they need the most support and advice.

Acknowledgments

I am grateful for the funding I received for this project from a Faculty Research Grant awarded by the UCLA Council on Research. I am also grateful to my former student, Karen Glienke, for allowing me to use her short script, *Orbiting*, as an example in several chapters. And for her many contributions to this book, from creating sample storyboards and floor plans to developing a look book for *Orbiting*, I thank my most excellent student assistant, Christine Auger-Zivic.

I would also like to thank my friends and colleagues Nancy Richardson, Becky Smith, William McDonald, Fabian Wagmister, Kristy Guevara-Flanagan, Liza Johnson and Gina Kim. Without what each of you has taught me about filmmaking and film teaching, I could not have written this book.

I am also grateful to Brian Kite and Steven Anderson for ensuring that I had the time I needed to write this book. Thanks, as well, to Karl Holmes for tirelessly ensuring that everyone at UCLA Film/TV – from faculty to staff to students – has the resources they need to get their work done.

For her guidance and patience, I am indebted to my editor, Claire Margerison, and her assistant, Sarah Pickles. Also, I deeply appreciate the many helpful criticisms I received from several anonymous reviewers who not only read and commented on the original proposal, but generously did the same for a number of chapters.

I would also like to acknowledge the following people, who all contributed to this book, whether they know it or not: Erma Acebo, Julia Angley, David Bordwell, Vittoria Campaner, Samuel Cumming, Alex Diaz, Gabriel Greenberg, Ryan Hamilton, Roger Hedden, Lisa Kohn, Katie Lemon, Stephanie Morrison, Kerry Schutt Nason, Marisa Ribisi, Andrew Rieger, Brie Shaffer, Ellen Scott, Gayle Seregi and Brooks Yang.

Above all, thank you Sarah for sustaining me through this process, for always cheering me on and for providing countless insightful suggestions that improved each and every chapter. You are my most perfect critic, supporter and life partner.

1 Keep It Simple

You're making a film. Now you need to prepare. This requires, in the first place, that you be realistic about what you're in for. It's going to be an uphill battle. That's part of what makes it worthwhile. But also, at times, very frustrating.

There may be days when it feels like nothing goes your way. The camera overheats. A fuse blows. A light burns out. An actor or crew member arrives late to set. Or not at all. A gardener arrives with a noisy lawn mower, making it impossible to record sound. A neighbor or passerby complains. Clouds block the sun. Rain falls. And who knows what else might happen to slow down or even bring your production to a grinding halt.

And this is only when you are on set. Before that there will be other difficulties. An actor you want is not available. The perfect location costs too much to rent. The perfect location doesn't exist. You can't find enough crew. You've already spent more than you planned. On and on.

And postproduction will provide its own difficulties.

As I like to tell my students, *God does not want you to make a movie.*

Now, these kinds of problems occur on professional and student shoots alike. But as a student you won't have the experience, the time and the money that professionals rely on to overcome or work around the endless setbacks that plague all productions. But even on professional shoots only so much is possible. Every production is constrained by finite resources of time, money, talent and expertise.

The most seasoned and talented director working with the most seasoned and talented cast and crew must still bow to the necessities of the shooting schedule and budget. Only so much can be done on any given shoot day, and only so much money will ever be available to do it.

In short, even under the best of circumstances only so much can be accomplished.

None of this is meant to discourage you. Movies get made. They get made all the time. Filmmakers prevail. It is foolish to focus only on the negative. The goal is problem solving, which is what this book is about. But do go into the process with your eyes open.

DOI: 10.4324/9781003169864-1

Given that you're probably going to have to shoot your film quickly, on a limited budget and with a student crew that, like yourself, has limited experience, *keep it simple*.

The more you try to do, the less you may accomplish.

Designing a film that can be made by you and your classmates in the number of shooting days allowed and with the money you know you have available, is not only the most practical course of action, it is one of the best creative decisions you can make. Every decision in filmmaking, whether it concerns the script, the budget, the shooting schedule or the performance of an actor, is a creative decision. The practical and the creative are one and the same thing.

Take the number of shots and scenes you try to complete each day. If your project requires that you get off a large number of shots and scenes each day, then you may get burned. If, on the other hand, you reasonably limit the number of shots and scenes you try to complete each day, your chances for success increase. This is because you give yourself the wiggle room you need when mishaps occur. And that wiggle room is what gives you the time you need to rehearse, light and shoot your film.

In other words, it gives you time to be creative.

If your project is too big, your production may become about simply finishing. And when that happens, the work suffers. And when finishing becomes the only grinding goal, no one involved learns anything, except that maybe they don't want to work with you again. Moreover, safety is compromised when film crews rush. People get hurt. People have died.

There should always be enough time on a student production for the director, cast and crew to work safely, creatively and at a pace that allows for at least some trial and error and reflection. You are all trying to learn, after all, which is why you are in school.

So, where do you begin? With the script. Everything begins with the script. It has to be doable. This is as true on a student film as it is on a Hollywood blockbuster. Again, every production is constrained by finite resources of time, money, talent and expertise. Therefore, as you go about the work of developing and writing your story – and only you know what story you want to tell – you are advised to keep the following in mind.

Number of Locations

Generally speaking, the number of locations your script requires should not exceed the number of days you have to shoot. This way you are not forced to make a company move in the middle of a shoot day.

Company Move. This is when an entire production packs up and moves to a new location. You can easily lose several hours of shooting when you make a company move during a shoot day. A shoot day is never longer than twelve hours (shorter if your department or instructor requires it) and the clock doesn't stop ticking when you move to a new location.

Ideally, you want to shoot all day at a single location then start at a new location the next day. If you can stay at the same location for several days, so much the better, especially if it is a location like a house or an apartment where you won't have to fully wrap at the end of each shoot day. This allows you to pick up every morning where you left off the day before, which significantly reduces setup time.

Setup Time. When you begin at a new location, setup time is often an hour to two hours. This includes not only blocking the action, lighting it and setting up and rehearsing the first shot, it also includes unloading gear, staging it and building it.[1] Even when shooting day exterior with only a few bounce boards to lessen contrast, you still have to get the camera and sound gear up and running.

When I was a camera assistant I would, whenever possible, bring the camera to set already built, but that didn't mean the director could just start shooting. The action still needed to be rehearsed, focus needed to be rehearsed, and camera moves, if there were any, also needed to be rehearsed.

Plus, the sound department needs setup time too. Not just wiring the actors but also rehearsing placement of the boom. And makeup and wardrobe have their work to do too. Not to mention grip and electrical. So, you're almost never going to get your first take off in less than an hour.

What all this means is that you should not pack your script with location changes. If, for example, you are allowed four days to complete principal photography, then don't include more than four locations in your script. This won't always work out. But it should be your goal.

Also, keep in mind that a location that is only good for one scene almost guarantees you will have to make a company move during a shoot day. The one exception is if you have a single complicated scene that is going to take all day to shoot. But in most cases, the best locations are ones where you can shoot more than one scene. How many? Let's turn to that question now.

Number of Scenes

As a general rule, you should not try to shoot more than three scenes per day. Shooting two scenes per day is ideal: one before lunch; one after lunch. Every new scene you shoot means starting over: first blocking the action, then lighting it, then shooting it. That is the structure of every production. Block. Light. Shoot. If you are not doing one of those three things, you are not making a movie.

When mishaps occur, or when you make a company move, then you are not blocking, lighting, or shooting. Company moves are within your control. Mishaps are not. And since there will be setbacks, perhaps many of them, it is a given that you won't always be blocking or lighting or shooting. The only way to account for that lost time is to limit how much you try to do each day, which includes limiting how many scenes you try to shoot.

Interior/Exterior. Day exteriors, which often, though not always, require minimal to no lighting, may allow you to get off four scenes. The same may be true if you are shooting all day in a single interior space, say a classroom, so long as you do not have significantly different lighting setups. Still, the more interior scenes you write into your script, especially night interiors, the more lighting you will have to do during production. Unless, of course, you're shooting in a location you can't or probably won't light, for example, a supermarket.

Night exterior scenes can be even more difficult. Crews are less efficient at night and significant lighting may be required. It is mostly only day exterior scenes that hold the promise of moving quickly without rushing. So, if possible, lean towards day exterior and away from interior and night exterior scenes.

Pre-Lighting. This can save some time, but pre-lighting is not always possible. It assumes you have access to the location and the crew to pull it off. Your classmates can't stay up until midnight lighting a scene and then return to set first thing in the morning. They have to sleep. Moreover, pre-lighting is not always desirable. If you haven't also blocked the action at the location in advance, then there is nothing to light.

If a scene is two people sitting or standing and having a conversation, then sure, light it in advance if you can. But if it is a scene with substantial blocking, and if you have not rehearsed that blocking in advance, then you may end up revising your pre-lighting, sometimes significantly, if the action doesn't turn out the way you planned. Actors have their own ideas, which can be better than your ideas, so don't expect them to simply walk on set and hit a bunch of marks you've taped on the floor. You can make them do that, but it may hurt the scene. Actors are your collaborators and not simply, or always, pieces on a chessboard.

Quick Scenes. Avoid falling into the trap of the quick scene. Be wary when someone says, "Oh, but that scene is only one shot." It often takes just as long to shoot a scene in one shot as it does to shoot it in three shots. This is because when you cover a scene in a single shot – a oner as it is called – you must get a take that works from start to finish. This doesn't matter much if the scene is only an actor exiting a room or, cliché of clichés, staring at their reflection in a mirror, but it applies in many cases.

For all these reasons, it is best to limit the number of scenes in your script. If, as in the example above, you have four days to shoot your film, then you should have no more than four locations and, as a general rule, none of those locations should be used for more than three scenes. This will give you the time you need to properly block, light and shoot the action. Again, the practical and the creative are one and the same thing. You don't want your production to become about simply finishing. Because of this, shooting two to three scenes per day is ideal.

Number of Pages

It may seem strange that I am covering the number of pages you are trying to shoot after I have covered the number of scenes but there is often a basic misunderstanding about this. Remember what I said above: every scene you shoot means starting over. First blocking the action, then lighting it, then shooting it. Because of this, the number of scenes you try to complete on any given day may often matter more than the number of pages.

Only focusing on the number of pages can undermine your chances for success.

Imagine, for example, that you have a three-page dialogue scene to shoot before lunch and a three-page dialogue scene to shoot after lunch. That is a well-planned shoot day which will allow you to knock off six pages so long as you don't go overboard with the number of shots you have planned (more on this in Chapter 10). Now imagine that you only have three pages to complete in the course of a day, except that in this instance you have six scenes to shoot, each of which is a half a page in length (technically 4/8ths of a page since scenes are measured in eighth-page increments to account for very short scenes, as short as 1/8th of a page). Despite being half as many pages, that's well over twice as much work, since you must, as I've been trying to impress upon you, start over again with each scene.

If all of your six scenes are in the same space at a single location that's one thing, but if you are moving from one space to another, say from a kitchen to a hallway to a bathroom to a bedroom, or if you are making a company move to a new location, that is another thing entirely. You very possibly won't finish or make your day as it is called. Or if you do finish, much of what you shoot may not be very good since you will be rushing.

Your goal isn't simply to make your day. Your goal is to make your movie.

The question, then, is how many pages should your script be?

Page Requirements. The answer to that question may not be entirely up to you. Currently, in my program, an undergraduate senior is permitted to shoot a 12-page script for their capstone project, but a first-year graduate student is expected to shoot a six-page script. Most likely there are page requirements in your department.

The purpose of page requirements is to limit the scope of student projects. Some of our first-year graduate students are making their first film ever so we want what they do to be manageable and not too costly. Moreover, since we require them to crew on seven projects in as many weeks, we have to limit each project to three shooting days, which means the scripts have to be short. (But once again, short is not enough; the number of scenes matters too.)[2]

Running Time. The other issue with page requirements is the running time of the finished film. Keeping a short film to 15 minutes or less is typically considered desirable. People don't want to watch films longer than that. Certainly not people in the industry. And festivals mostly won't program them.

The rule of thumb is that each script page equals one minute of screen time. Presumably, then, you want your script to be no longer than 15 pages. But the page-per-minute rule is only an estimate, and not a very accurate one. Dialogue scenes may run about a minute per page, but action scenes run longer, sometimes much longer. The famous car chase in *Bullitt* is about six pages in the script but runs almost 11 minutes onscreen. Even simple action can run long:

```
Ed drives down a street delivering newspapers.
```

It's certainly going to take longer for that to play on screen than it does to read it. So, if your script is action heavy, even when that action is simple, make it as short as possible. This is particularly important because action also often takes longer to shoot than dialogue. The car chase in *Bullitt* took three weeks to film.

Characters

Number of Roles. Be careful about how many speaking roles you include in your script. Ideally, it will have between two and four. There are several reasons for this. First and foremost is the issue of casting. As will be discussed in Chapter 9, finding actors appropriate to your parts can be a long and grueling process. Because of this, the more roles you have, the more difficult and time-consuming that process becomes.

Next is the problem of blocking, lighting and shooting. The more actors you have in a scene the longer it is going to take to shoot it, especially if you are planning a lot of coverage (two shots, over-the-shoulder shots, closeups, inserts, etc.). This will likely lead to you rushing on set, which will affect the quality of the film.

Finally, there is the issue of costs. Each role potentially increases wardrobe expenditures and every actor is another mouth to feed. There may also be additional expenditures, for example salaries. More on all of this in Chapter 6 on budgeting.

Age. Something else to think about with characters is age. Working with children is difficult. First, they can't work 12-hour days. Not even close. Second, you must also hire a studio teacher, at least in California where I teach, and unless you are shooting on a weekend, they must spend part of each day doing schoolwork. But even on weekends you may, depending on the age of the child, only end up having them on set for six hours or so.

Try to focus on characters between the ages of 18 and 35 and/or 65 and above. Here's why: there are many aspiring young actors looking to be in student films as well as many senior citizens who turn to acting as a second career or at least as a fulfilling activity after retirement, and many of them are quite good and also willing to be in student films. But with middle-aged actors, many of them are already established and work regularly at their craft and so don't need or want to do student films. Time and again when my students write characters into their scripts who are in their 40s and 50s, they get very few submissions when they post to casting sites, and that just makes the process more difficult and time consuming.

Talented actors of all ages are out there and ready to do student films, but some ages offer you more options than others, and if your main character is a child, that will significantly limit how many hours you can shoot each day. This is not to say that you should not tell a story about a child, but be prepared for the consequences in terms of shooting time.

Funding

Never try to make a film you don't have enough money to make.

While you won't be able to accurately budget your production until you have a shooting script, breakdown and shooting schedule, which are covered in the next two chapters, you still need to be thinking like a producer from the start. In fact, you should bring on a producer, typically one of your classmates who is adept at planning and organizing, as soon as possible. Someone needs to help you manage the logistics of your production within the limits of your budget (the role of the producer is covered in detail in Chapters 6 through 10 and in Chapter 12).

But your producer, no matter the extent of their organizational skills, and their ability to haggle with location owners and equipment rental houses, can only stretch your money so far. So, as you write your script, please also keep the following in mind.

Locations. Try to only include locations in your story that you know you have access to for free or that you can reasonably expect to rent or permit for not much money. As soon as you type INT. AIRPORT TERMINAL – DAY you are placing a strain on your budget. Even if you could secure such a location, in addition to any rental fee you would almost certainly have to pay for a monitor and/or security officer to be present during shooting. If your school is in or near a city where commercial production is common, you might be able to find a standing set (a mock airport terminal which is used for filming), but such sets are typically expensive to rent.

Restaurants, bars and stores can also be expensive to rent, especially if they have to close down during any part of the time you are shooting. Also, don't write multi-million-dollar homes into your story as these are hard to come by. Unless you know someone willing to give you access to their high-end property for little or no money, steer clear.

Building sets can also strain your budget. It depends on what you are trying to pull off. But as a general rule, it is difficult to build believable sets on a tight budget, so think twice before writing any location into your story that needs to be constructed (more on this in Chapter 8).

Also, try to avoid writing anything that requires out-of-town shooting since travel, lodging and living costs can be prohibitive. The main exception is if you are going to a place, your home town for example, where you know you have a strong support system in place. But when you take a cast and crew out of town, the onus is on you to put them up and feed them three meals a day.

One good option is to write for locations you know are available on your campus. These are almost always free for students. And college campuses offer many options: offices, classrooms, libraries, museum and/or gallery spaces, gardens, athletic fields, etc. Public spaces like city parks and sidewalks are also typically free, or require that you pay only a small permit fee. This won't be true in every case, though. One of my students, for example, had to pay for a lifeguard to be on set at a public beach because their actor went into the water.

Action. As the example just cited suggests, you should avoid writing scenes in which your characters engage in risky activities. This is especially true of scenes that include weapons, in particular guns. Your department may not allow the use of weapons in films – mine only allows them on advanced projects – but if your department does allow them beware: using weapons can be expensive.

You might be able to get a deal on renting prop guns but you will almost certainly have to pay for at least one police officer to be present in order to film anywhere outdoors with prop guns. This is also true at businesses. You can't, for example, shoot a liquor store holdup without police supervision because a passerby might misunderstand and call 911. The authorities need to be aware of what you are doing. And you may also need to hire a professional armorer to supervise gun safety on set (the staff person who handles production insurance in your department should be able to explain all of the requirements to you).

And if you intend to hold up traffic on a street while shooting, you will need to hire traffic officers. This may not be a rule in some places, as it is in Los Angeles, but do you really want to park one of your classmates in the middle of a street to stop cars? I hope not.

Fist fights, fire, explosions and the like also require that you hire safety personnel. So, my advice, once again, is to avoid, if you can, writing risky action into your script.

Genre. You should also be cognizant of genre. In my program genre films are rare. The one exception is sci-fi. But films set in the future can be costly. Your goal, if you want to do scifi, is to keep the story contained. In my experience, post-apocalyptic stories (which technically aren't always science fiction) work best because they do not, or at least need not, require building an elaborate future world. I had a student who used little more than a ransacked drug store to evoke the apocalypse. Another used the desert. It doesn't take much to convince an audience that civilization has come to an end.

There are similar issues with period pieces and the solution, once again, is to keep the story contained. I once saw a pretty good Civil War movie made by a student. They pulled it off because most of the action took place in the woods where two soldiers hide after fleeing a battle, which was depicted primarily by way of smoke and off-screen gunfire.

Rentals. In terms of equipment rentals, this may or may not be an option for you; it depends on where your school is located and what your department allows. But if renting equipment is an option, you should still, as much as possible, try to stick with the equipment your department can supply you with. This means not writing scenes – again night exterior scenes come to mind – that might require renting significant additional G&E gear (which will also take time to set up).

In sum, don't write a script you can't afford to make. And don't write a script you haven't got the time to make. Only so much can be done on any given shoot day, and only so much money will ever be available to do it.

The more you try to do, the less you may accomplish.

So, *keep it simple*. Make it doable. Set yourself up to beat the odds.

Notes

1 Blocking action means working out with the actors how, when and where they will move during a scene. As for staging equipment, this has to do with organizing it for easy access during shooting. Equipment can be staged on a truck, if you are renting one, or in a designated space at a location, or both.
2 Another reason film departments limit shoot days is to ensure availability of equipment for all students. Most departments supply equipment packages that include camera, sound and grip & electrical, or G&E, gear, but even the wealthiest department will have only so many of these packages to go around.

2 Organize Your Script

Once you've written your script and gone through several drafts while receiving notes from faculty and classmates, it's time to turn it into a shooting script and then break it down. Without a shooting script and breakdown, you can't schedule or budget a film.

Shooting Script

This is exactly what its name implies: the script you are going to shoot. It must meet certain requirements or it cannot be used to properly plan your production. Specifically, it must accurately represent the exact number of scenes and pages you have to shoot.

Identify Every Scene. In a shooting script, scenes are best thought of as lighting setups, and each must be slugged and numbered. A slug line is a scene heading, for example: INT. OFFICE - DAY

Let's say your script begins as follows:

```
INT. HOUSE - NIGHT

MARIE (30) enters and walks from the living room
into the kitchen where she finds a note on the
counter.
```

That's two lighting setups: one in the living room and one in the kitchen. Both rooms have to be lit. Thus each must be slugged and numbered:

```
1.   INT. LIVING ROOM - NIGHT

     MARIE (30) enters, crosses the room, and
     exits into:

2.   INT. KITCHEN - CONTINUOUS - NIGHT

     Where she finds a note on the counter.
```

DOI: 10.4324/9781003169864-2

Since the action is continuous, I used that word in the slug line for scene 2. This specifies, in the first place, that scene 2 has the same wardrobe, hair and makeup requirements as scene 1. You and your collaborators need to know that because the scenes may not be shot consecutively. The same is true of props. If Marie is, for instance, carrying flowers and a bottle of wine, then those props need to be available for both scenes.

Lastly, by indicating that scene 2 is continuous with scene 1, the script supervisor now knows to keep track of screen direction. If Marie exits screen-left from the living room then, ideally, she should still be moving screen-left when she enters the kitchen (I will have more to say about maintaining screen direction in Chapters 10 and 12, but my assumption is that it is being drilled into you by your production instructors).

Even continuous action in the same space may require separate lighting setups. This is typical of party scenes. The action may all take place in the same room at the same time, but you might have two characters talking on the couch, two talking by the fireplace and two more over by the front door. Each pairing is a separate lighting setup, with its own camera setups, so each must be slugged and numbered.

In this instance you wouldn't want to write out a full slug line for each setup; you might instead write OVER ON THE COUCH, AT THE FIRE PLACE, and BY THE FRONT DOOR. So long as each is numbered then each can be scheduled. This is additionally necessary because you may choose to shoot them out of script order.

But if you don't identify and slug every scene in your script, then you won't know how much work needs to be completed each day on set. At the same time, doing this also adds more scenes and, as I said in the previous chapter, you can only shoot so many scenes each day. Be aware of this and try to cut scenes as you go.

In the example above, you might ask yourself if the audience really needs to see Marie enter the house and walk through the living room into the kitchen. Perhaps it is enough to begin in the kitchen and simply have her enter. It may be enough to begin on the note as she picks it up. But if you cut the living room you cut a lighting setup which saves you time.

Most scripts contain extraneous scenes and it is while you are creating your shooting script that you should strenuously try to identify these.

I once made a film in which a man drives a hundred miles to visit an old flame from high school. We had a scene in the script in which he stops at a store to buy a single rose. This was meant to emphasize his romantic desire. But we decided it was enough for him to simply show up at her house with a rose. This change allowed us to cut a location and save maybe half a day of shooting because the store would have also required a company move.

When you write a script, you are constructing a *plot*. A plot is everything we see and hear in a film in the order that we see and hear it. It is the action as it is structured for us. That definition goes back to Aristotle. He defined plot as the arrangement of incidents. A *story*, on the other hand, is all that (the plot), plus everything that is not presented but which is implied or hinted at. That definition as well goes back to Aristotle. He defined story as the total action of the plot.[1]

Your goal, therefore, is to imply and hint at as much of the action as possible.

A good example of this can be found in *E. T. the Extra-Terrestrial* (1982), a movie that in my experience many students have seen. In the opening sequence, after the men chase E. T. through woods and he escapes, our last view of him is as he starts walking down a hillside towards the lights of a town. After that, we don't encounter E. T. again until Elliot tosses a baseball into a tool shed and the ball is tossed back. That event reveals that E. T. is now in the shed. And we know this without even having to see him. We fill in all of the blanks, which include E. T.'s full journey from the hillside to the town, his discovery of the shed, and his decision to seek shelter inside of it now that he no longer has access to his spaceship.

Our minds, in other words, do all the work, and none of the other action needed to be shot. It's possible that Spielberg did shoot those scenes and didn't use them, but it is always painful in the editing room to discover that you wasted precious time shooting scenes you don't need.

Don't overtell your story. Trust the audience to fill in the blanks. This will save you a lot of time and money. And that time and money can be used to properly shoot scenes you actually need. If you are uncertain about whether you can cut a scene, just cut it and have someone read the revised draft to see if it works for them.

When you can't cut, try to combine. In another movie I made a young woman drops by her boyfriend's house to find out if he is still interested in her. She discovers he is not. In the script this was followed by a scene of her alone in her parked car expressing frustration. Rather than shoot that, though, I ended the first scene, the one with the boyfriend, by having her turn away from him towards camera and silently express that frustration. Shooting her in the car might have only taken an hour, but I got that hour back to focus on the scene that mattered, the one in which she finds out that her boyfriend is no longer interested in her.[2]

In short, always avoid using multiple scenes to cover story beats that can be handled in a single scene. This is simply more efficient when you have limited time and money to shoot a film.

Page Count. Of equal importance is that your shooting script accurately represent how many pages your script truly is. Again, the rule of thumb is that each script page equals one minute of screen time, but it is quite common for, say, a 10-page script to come in at 15 minutes or even longer when it is edited together. Almost all films run longer than their script, at least in early cuts, but there are two rules you can follow to help minimize this discrepancy.

The first of these I have just discussed: breaking your script up into the exact number of scenes it actually contains. Don't fudge this. Every lighting setup is a scene and every slug line you add lengthens your script to reflect this.

The second rule might be called "the rule of empty space." A reader should see a great deal of blank, empty space on every page of your script. No paragraph describing action should take up more than three or at most four lines on a page (not sentences but lines), and often only one or two lines. Paragraphs that take up five or six or seven or more lines are a cheat. They allow you to cram too much action onto a page, giving you a false sense of length, and therefore a false sense of how much material actually needs to be shot.

Long paragraphs also make your script difficult to read. A script should read like a movie. It should draw the reader's attention in quick succession to each important narrative detail and event, using line breaks in between:

```
EXT. HOUSE - DAY

An upper-middle class suburban home.

MARTIN (64) stands looking out a window.

A DELIVERY TRUCK rolls down the street and parks.

Martin runs outside.

The DELIVERYWOMAN meets him, carrying a BOX.[3]
```

That reads like a movie. First, we see the house, establishing the locale. Next, in what is obviously a closer view, Martin is revealed in the window. After that we see the truck. Then we see Martin run outside, leading us to infer that he has been waiting for the truck. That inference is confirmed when he receives a box (the true object of his desire).

Because the events are broken into discrete units, the writing mimics how we would experience the flow of story information watching the film. It also more accurately reflects the amount of time it will take for those events to unfold on screen. Putting all of those events into a single paragraph would not do that. It would be a cheat.

When I teach production classes, the first thing I have each student do is break up all the long paragraphs in their script. Sometimes this lengthens their script by a page or more. If this pushes them over the page limit allowed for the course, then they must cut down their script. If they don't, then they may have more action than they can shoot in the number of days they are allowed for principal photography and/or their finished film may run long.

Here's the deal: if you are allowed, for example, a maximum of ten pages to tell your story, then come up with a story that can be told in ten pages. There is nothing odd about that. TV writers do it all the time. A half-hour show, to allow for commercials, is typically 21–22 minutes. So, the writers must write scripts that fit that requirement. That's just the way it is.

Finally, if I were to invoke a third rule, it would be this: don't narrow the margins in whatever screenwriting software you are using. The only reason to do that is to make your script appear shorter than it is, which, as I hope I've made plain, is a bad idea.

Description. A shooting script should not contain anything that can't be shot. If in the scene above it read, `MARTIN (64) has been waiting impatiently all morning for a package`, much of that story information can't be shot.

A shooting script, again, should only contain what we will see and hear in the movie in the order that we will see and hear it. This forces you to dramatize story information. If it is relevant that Martin has been waiting for a while, then you have to show that and not tell it. And I believe the scene as written does so. It does not have Martin step up to the window and look out; it begins with him already looking.

Here is a more obvious example to better illustrate the point. I once had a student submit a script about a young man who decides to quit smoking that began as follows:

```
EXT. PARKING LOT - DAY

VICTOR (20) screeches into a parking spot late
for class. He jumps out, running, as he fumbles
through his pockets for a cigarette.
```

There are several problems here. First, how is a viewer supposed to know that Victor is late for class, as opposed to, say, late for a meeting or dealing with an emergency? Moreover, how is a viewer supposed to know that he is looking for a cigarette, as opposed to, say, his phone or his sunglasses? And how is a viewer supposed to know that he wants a cigarette because being late to class is stressing him out?

The answer to each question is that if the scene were shot *as written* there would be no way for a viewer to apprehend any of those intentions. It was easy for the writer to spell out the character's intentions, but that is a cheat. None of them would make it onscreen. It's a rookie mistake.

For the sake of brevity, I'll focus only on the problem of the character searching for a cigarette. One way that story information could be dramatized is by having Victor find a pack of cigarettes only to discover it is empty. He could then crumple the empty pack in frustration and begin fumbling in his pockets again. But all that needs to be written into the script. It is not enough to tell the reader what Victor is looking for because *that can't be shot.*

The time to figure out how you are going to dramatize story information is while you are writing your script. And by the time you are preparing your shooting script it must be worked out.

Lastly, a shooting script should emphasize all important elements that will appear on screen. This is handled using `ALL CAPS`. When a character is first introduced, their name should be in capital letters:

```
MARTIN (64) stands looking out a window.
```

This applies to other important elements as well:

```
The DELIVERY WOMAN meets him, carrying a BOX.
```

Using all caps grabs the reader's attention but, more importantly, it spells out everything you need to shoot the scene. This helps you when you do your script breakdown.

Script Breakdown

A breakdown tells you who and what needs to be on set each day in order to shoot the film. Let's take the scene above in which Martin receives a box. That box would be listed in the breakdown. Martin would also be listed. And the deliverywoman. And her uniform. And the delivery truck. All of those elements need to be on set the day the scene is shot.

On a professional production the initial breakdown is overseen by the line producer because the other primary purpose of a breakdown is budgeting, which the line producer is in charge of (more on this in Chapter 6). In this case, the delivery truck may need to be rented. The uniform too (or it will have to be created). Even the box might have to be purchased. And if the actor playing Martin is getting paid a day rate, it is important to identify every scene he is in so as to determine how many days he is working.

The initial breakdown is only a starting point. In time each department head will create their own breakdown. For instance, you and your costumer might decide that an actor is going to wear a particular green dress in a certain scene. Since that green dress is not indicated in the script it wouldn't make it into the initial breakdown. But it must make it into the costume breakdown and at that point it is up to the costumer to ensure that the dress makes it to set.

Typically, you give your department heads a budget to work within. Oftentimes this plays into how you choose department heads. You tell a potential costumer, for instance, how much money you have to spend on wardrobe, and then they figure out if they can do it for that amount, usually by creating a breakdown. If they decide your wardrobe budget is too low, then you can interview someone else. But if you get the same response, you have two choices: up your wardrobe budget or simplify your script to align its wardrobe requirements with your available funds.

I suggest that as the director of your movie you do the initial breakdown. This will allow you to begin making creative choices about what will appear in your film, in particular production design and wardrobe. This is the starting point of your look book (Chapter 5). You can even begin searching for images of what you want. These can relate to everything from casting to props to hair. These images can be exact or merely representative.

This doesn't mean you shut out your department heads. In the end they will have to find or create everything you envision and more. That is their job and you have to let them do it. You should let them make as many choices as possible using their own judgment, creativity and taste. But you will have no guidance to offer them if you don't think through the elements in your film.

Elements. For each scene, these are the primary elements you are looking to identify:

Cast. This refers to speaking roles. Cast members are numbered. You can do this according to the order they appear in a script, but you should probably make your protagonist number 1, whether they enter the story first or not.

Extras - Silent Bits. These are actors who do not speak but interact with the principal cast, for example the parking attendant outside a restaurant. While they are still extras, they are listed separately because they often go through makeup and wardrobe. A parking attendant, after all, may wear a uniform, even it is only a white shirt and black vest.

Extras – Atmosphere. These are background extras, for example diners at a restaurant. Always list how many background extras you think you need for a scene. Since you will be working on a limited budget, these extras will bring their own wardrobe (you can ask them to provide choices) and they will handle their own makeup or forgo it altogether. There are exceptions, of course. If you are making a period piece, then you will likely have to dress all your extras. Or if your movie includes, let us say, zombies, then they will all have to go through makeup and wardrobe.

Props & Set Dressing. The word prop technically refers to objects that actors handle, for example a phone, a comb, a wallet. But in practice these are called hand props because prop shops also have everything from couches to juke boxes to curtains to wall art, most of which is set dressing unless it serves a specific story function.

Wardrobe. Your script may not mention any wardrobe choices or it may be full of descriptions of what characters are wearing. Probably it is somewhere in between. But any wardrobe that is described in the script or logically implied (e.g., a police uniform) must be listed.

Makeup & Hair. Indicate any special makeup that is needed, for example a scar or a bloody wound. Also, indicate any specific hair requirements, for example wigs or period hair styles or styles specific to a subculture you are portraying in your movie.

Vehicles. This refers to vehicles seen on screen. These are called picture vehicles and can include cars, trucks, motorcycles, whatever. Basically, if it is a means of transportation and is going to appear on screen then include it in this category, even if it is not going to move. For example, in the sample student script I am going to schedule and budget in Chapters 3 and 6, a character is seen standing beside his giant, luxury SUV, which is intended to show how successful he is.

Animals. There is an old saying: "Never work with children or animals." This is because they slow you down. They often require longer blocking sessions and extra takes. But if your film includes any animals, then they need to be listed in the breakdown.

Practical Effects. Maybe you need a fogger, a flame bar, or some other practical effect (one that is done on set and not created digitally). Be aware that certain effects like a flame bar may come with added costs, which can include additional insurance and a fire marshal to monitor safety.

Special Equipment. This refers to any significant piece of equipment that would not be needed every day of the shoot, for example a Steadicam.

Stunts. If your film has stunts you need a stunt coordinator for safety. Even something as simple as an actor tripping and falling down needs to be carefully choreographed for safety.

Production Notes. This is where you identify issues that might arise during production so that they can be dealt with prior to rather than during shooting.

Tagging Elements. A breakdown is done by first tagging elements in the script. This is the standard scheme for doing that:

Cast	Red
Silent Bits	Yellow
Atmosphere	Green
Props & Set Dressing	Purple
Wardrobe	Circle
Makeup & Hair	Asterisk
Vehicles & Animals	Pink
Special Equipment	Box
Special Effects	Blue
Stunts	Orange
Production Notes	Underline

Let's stick with our first example (refer to the list above for what would be the correct color of each shaded element):

EXT. HOUSE – DAY

An upper-middle class suburban home.

MARTIN (64) stands looking out a window.

A DELIVERY TRUCK rolls down the street and parks.

Martin runs outside.

The DELIVERYWOMAN meets him, carrying a BOX.

Breakdown Sheets. Once elements have been tagged, they are transferred to breakdown sheets:

FREE VIOLETTE

Breakdown Sheet: ___1___

Scene No.: ___1___   Scene: _____MARTIN'S HOUSE_____   I/E: _EXT_   D/N: _DAY_

Synopsis: _Martin receives a package_ _____

Pg. Count: ___2/8___   Script Pgs.: ___1___   Location: _____Los Angeles_____

CAST	EXTRAS - SILENT BITS	EXTRAS - ATMOSPHERE
1. Martin	Deliverywoman	

PROPS & SET DRESSING	WARDROBE	MAKEUP/HAIR
Box Clipboard Logo on truck	Driver's uniform	

VEHICLES & ANIMALS	SPECIAL EQUIPMENT	PRACTICAL EFFECTS/VFX
Delivery truck		

STUNTS	PRODUCTION NOTES
	Driver for delivery truck? (Insurance)

The sheet is fairly self-explanatory, but a few points:

First, the information at the top of the page is important because much of it will carry over to your shooting schedule. When you are scheduling, it matters a great deal whether a scene is interior or exterior and whether it is day or night. The synopsis is important because there may be several scenes in front of Martin's house and in the shooting schedule, they need to be clearly differentiated from each other by their action.

Finally, page count is important. Scenes, again, are measured in eighth-page increments so that short scenes can be identified, and it is short scenes in particular that you want to keep track of. This scene is only 2/8ths of a page but could easily take several hours or more to shoot (as we will see in Chapter 10). Again, the number of scenes you try to shoot each day can matter more than the number of pages.

Next, you may have noticed in the tagged script that the delivery truck is underlined in addition to being highlighted. This indicates a production note, which on the breakdown sheet is the question of who will drive the truck. If you rent a vehicle, it may be that not just anyone can drive it. If that is the case, the easiest solution would be to have a crew member who is insured to drive the vehicle play the delivery person. But the reason for having this production note is so that the issue is resolved prior to the day the scene is shot.

Lastly, I added props not mentioned in the script. A clipboard is low-tech, a tablet device would be better, but if you were to shoot this scene, Martin would sign for the package. Not because that is realistic necessarily, but because characters in movies always seem to have to sign for packages. It is a convention.

In this same vein, it only makes sense that the delivery truck, which for the sake of simplicity should probably be a van, would have the logo of a company on it. This is called signage and unless you can get a delivery company to lend or rent you one of its vehicles, your production designer would have to design a logo and create it. You could forgo this signage, but it would likely be apparent to the audience that you are cutting corners.

For this reason, it might be best to lose the vehicle and simply show the deliverywoman walking up to the house. The sound of an off-camera truck played over Martin looking out the window would do the trick. Such sleights of hand typically save both money and time. Because if the truck is dropped, it also doesn't need to be shot (at the same time, I am going to create a shot list for this scene in Chapter 4, and when I do that I am going to keep the truck; my only point for now is that, in a pinch, the scene could plausibly be shot without it).

Always look for workarounds like this as you are doing your breakdown. Whenever you come up against an expensive element, or one that could be difficult to procure, try to think of a way to lose it.

Once again, *keep it simple*.

Notes

1 Aristotle also defined story as the correct chronology of the plot, as when we take flashbacks and mentally put them back into their correct story order, but that distinction is not relevant to the current discussion.
2 I am going to return to this scene about the girlfriend who discovers that her that her boyfriend is no longer interested in her in Chapter 11 on rehearsals.
3 The sample scene (Martin receives a box) is adapted from *Free Violette* by Lisa Kohn.

3 Decide When to Shoot What

A feasible shooting schedule is essential to the success of your production. But what makes a shooting schedule feasible? Think back to what was discussed in the first chapter.

I said that the number of locations your project requires should not exceed the number of days you have to shoot. This way you don't get stuck with company moves during shoot days. I also said that each location should work for at least two scenes, else you may also get stuck with company moves, the exception being a single difficult scene that will take all day to shoot.

I also advised you not to shoot more than three scenes per day because every new scene you shoot means starting over: first blocking the action, then lighting it, then shooting it. And I encouraged you to write as short a script as possible. Whatever maximum page limit is imposed on you, there is no rule stating your script can't be shorter.

In sum, a shooting schedule must be feasible in terms of locations, scenes and pages.

The amount of time it takes to light each scene, and the number of shots you try to pull off each day, matter as well, but if you limit your locations, scenes and pages, then you gain more time to block, light and shoot. Because of this, one thing you may learn when you first schedule your production is that your script needs to be condensed. Cutting and combining scenes, as discussed in the previous chapter, can help. But rethinking where scenes take place can also help.

In a film I made, two characters had a dialogue scene at work and another dialogue scene at a bar. The problem, though, was that each scene was the only scene at its location. All that mattered for the story was that the first scene take place at the start of the day and the second at the end of the day. With a few small tweaks to the script we were able to have both scenes take place at work. The bar was dropped, saving us a company move and also a location rental fee.

DOI: 10.4324/9781003169864-3

To schedule a film, the first thing you need is a numbered shooting script (Chapter 2). For this exercise, we are going to schedule *Orbiting* (Appendix I), written by a former student of mine, Karen Glienke. Please read it before you read the rest of this chapter.

Second, you need to know how many days you are permitted to shoot. Karen had four days, from Thursday through Sunday. As will become clear, on very short productions, less than a week, it is especially important to know the exact days of the week you will be shooting.

Next, you don't need scheduling software. If your school provides access to such software, by all means use it because it will make your schedule look professional. But there is no reason to buy it. You can, as I do in this chapter, use word processing software (you wouldn't want to do this on a feature, but shorts require you to input much less information).

Finally, while you should make a first pass at the schedule yourself, never go into production with a schedule that hasn't been approved by your AD and DP. They are primarily responsible for maintaining momentum during production, so they have a strong incentive to ensure that a reasonable amount of work is scheduled on each shoot day. They want to succeed, and their success is your success.

Step 1 – List All Numbered Scenes in the Script

List them in order and for each scene include the following information from the breakdown: scene number, location, synopsis, day/night, actor role numbers and page count. Additionally, you can list each scene on an index card. This will make it easier to move them around as you schedule each shoot day.

For the sake of clarity, the roles in *Orbiting* are numbered as follows in the breakdown:

1. Trevor
2. Dad
3. Mom
4. Wendy (cashier #1)
5. Linda (cashier #2)
6. Store Manager
7. Scott
8. Amber

And here are all the scenes in order (those in bold are discussed below), and though I am not using column headings, I think the format is clear:

1	INT. TREVOR'S ROOM	D	Trevor writes, parents argue off-screen, Dad enters Actors: 1,2	1 2/8 pgs.
2	INT. LIVING ROOM	D	Mom and Dad send Trevor to the store Actors: 1,2,3	2 1/8 pgs.
3	EXT. RESIDENTIAL STREET	D	Trevor forlornly walks to the store Actors: 1	2/8 pgs.
4	**INT. DRUG STORE AISLE**	D	Trevor grabs two boxes of Starlight Ultra Actors: 1	1/8 pgs.
5	**INT. DRUG STORE - REGISTER 1**	D	Trevor discovers that he no longer has the coupon Actors: 1,4,5	1 1/8 pgs.
6	**INT. DRUG STORE AISLE**	D	Trevor searches the floor for the coupon Actors: 1	2/8 pgs.
7	**INT. DRUG STORE - REGISTER 2**	D	Trevor tries again to buy the two boxes of Starlight Ultra Actors 1,4,5,6	7/8 pgs.
8	EXT. BOULEVARD	D	Trevor runs from store manager Actors: 1,6	2/8 pgs.
9	EXT. RESIDENTIAL STREET	D	Trevor bumps into Scott and Amber Actors: 1,7,8	1 pgs.
10	**EXT. ALLEY**	D	Trevor smashes a Starlight Ultra box on a fence Actors: 1	1/8 pgs.
11	INT. LIVING ROOM	D	Trevor throws the Starlight Ultra boxes at mom's desk Actors: 1	1/8 pgs.
12	INT. TREVOR'S ROOM	D	Trevor packs a suitcase while he watches TV Actors: 1	3/8 pgs.
13	**INT. TREVOR'S ROOM**	N	Trevor has fallen asleep in front of the TV Actors: 1	1/8 pgs.
14	INT. LIVING ROOM	N	Mom and Dad return and find the boxes on the floor Actors: 2,3	4/8 pgs.

The six scenes in bold were added to the shooting script. In earlier drafts the store was treated as a single scene: INT. STORE - DAY. But it is really four scenes: two in the aisle and two at the cash registers. As I said in the previous chapter, each lighting setup is a scene. In the case of a brightly lit store, lighting may be minimal, but the aisle and two registers are still distinct areas within the store, each with its own unique blocking and camera setups. We might call them locations within a location. So, each must be slugged and numbered.

In the case of scene 10, prior to the shooting draft the script simply stated that Trevor "ducks into an alley." But an alley is not the same as a residential street (scene 9), and since we may not find those two locations adjacent to each other, and may in fact shoot them on different days, it is best to slug and number both.

Finally, scene 13 had to be added because in the transition from Trevor packing to Trevor sleeping, it changes from day to night. Originally, Karen treated this as a single scene, only inserting the word "Later," but these are different lighting setups. Again, a shooting script must accurately reflect the amount of work that has to be completed each day.

One last thing to note is that each scene synopsis I have provided is succinct but detailed. There are, for example, three scenes in the living room and in the final schedule, each of those scenes must be easily identifiable by its action.

Step 2 – Determine Common Locations

Be precise. In *Orbiting*, all scenes in the house belong together, but the action in the house is not confined to a single room. There is Trevor's bedroom and there is the living room. As with the store, these are locations within a location. Therefore, the scenes in each of those rooms will be kept together.

The reason is this: during production it wouldn't make sense to move back and forth between the two rooms. The goal would be to shoot every scene in the bedroom, then shoot every scene in the living room. Or *vice versa*. But jumping back and forth would be a waste of time and energy.

I am therefore going to keep all scenes that take place in the same space together. When I do that, the locations break down as follows:

Trevor's bedroom

1	INT. TREVOR'S ROOM	D	Trevor writes, parents argue off-screen, Dad enters Actors: 1,2	1 2/8 pgs.
12	INT. TREVOR'S ROOM	D	Trevor packs a suitcase while he watches TV Actors: 1	3/8 pgs.
13	INT. TREVOR'S ROOM	N	Trevor has fallen asleep in front of the TV Actors: 1	1/8 pgs.

Living room

2	INT. LIVING ROOM	D	Mom and Dad send Trevor to the store Actors: 1,2,3	2 1/8 pgs.
11	INT. LIVING ROOM	D	Trevor throws the Starlight Ultra boxes at mom's desk Actors: 1	1/8 pgs.
14	INT. LIVING ROOM	N	Mom and Dad return and find the boxes on the floor Actors: 2,3	4/8 pgs.

Street Exteriors

3	EXT. RESIDENTIAL STREET	D	Trevor forlornly walks to the store Actors: 1	2/8 pgs.
9	EXT. RESIDENTIAL STREET	D	Trevor bumps into Scott and Amber Actors: 1,7,8	1 pgs.
8	EXT. BOULEVARD	D	Trevor runs from store manager Actors: 1,6	2/8 pgs.
10	EXT. ALLEY	D	Trevor smashes a Starlight Ultra box on a fence Actors: 1	1/8 pgs.

Drug Store

4	INT. DRUG STORE AISLE	D	Trevor grabs two boxes of Starlight Ultra Actors: 1	1/8 pgs.
6	INT. DRUG STORE AISLE	D	Trevor searches the floor for the coupon Actors: 1	2/8 pgs.
5	INT. DRUG STORE - REGISTER 1	D	Trevor discovers that he no longer has the coupon Actors: 1,4,5	1 1/8 pgs.
7	INT. DRUG STORE - REGISTER 2	D	Trevor tries again to buy the two boxes of Starlight Ultra Actors 1,4,5,6	7/8 pgs.

Once scenes are organized in this way, it is easy to determine if the number of locations exceeds the number of shoot days. *Orbiting* breaks down nicely. So long as the street exteriors are very close to each other, we basically have four locations for four days of shooting. It is concerning that there are four scenes in the store, but we may yet cut or combine. One way or another, though, we are going to have to deal with that.

Step 3 – Decide the Shooting Order of Locations

There are a number of issues to consider.

Availability. If you want to shoot in a classroom, for instance, it may only be available on the weekend when school is not in session. There is also the issue of actor availability. Actors, even non-professional actors, have busy schedules like the rest of us and you may, in part, have to organize the order of your locations according to one or more of their schedules. There are limits, of course. Either an actor is available to be in your film or they are not. More on this in Chapter 9 on casting.

Difficulty. The number of scenes and pages you have to shoot at a location matters too. Despite your best efforts you may still wind up with a difficult day. If you do, it's best not to put that day at the start of the schedule. Every production needs time to get into a rhythm and crews and directors become more efficient as time goes by. This is true even on shoots of only two to three days.

Day/Night. It also matters whether a location is being used for day scenes or night scenes or some combination of the two. Usually, night shoots go at the end of a production. Otherwise, you have to take a day off before you can return to day shoots. This has to do with what is called turnaround time. Between one shoot day and the next your cast and crew must be given 12 hours off. For this reason, if you were to wrap a night shoot at, say, 5:00am, and if you wanted to return to shooting days, you would have to allow for something in the area of 24 hours of turnaround time, which your department could count as a shoot day since you would be holding on to equipment. It would also increase equipment rental costs if you are renting gear by the day.

It logically follows from this that locations with night scenes are scheduled last so that once you move to nights you can stay on nights. An ideal structure for a shooting schedule is to move from days to split days to nights. A split day consists of both day and night scenes. You might begin, for instance, at 1:00pm and wrap by 1:00am. Split days, which aren't always necessary, or possible, are nonetheless useful because they ease your cast and crew from day shoots to night shoots by providing an actual transition rather than an abrupt jump.

On longer shoots it is easier to move back and forth between days and nights because there are days off built into the schedule. In principle, a lengthy production could begin each week shooting days and end each week shooting nights because the cast and crew get a day off, if not two, at the end of each week. This would not be an ideal schedule, but it could be done.

Sound. Always take sound into account when ordering locations. I wanted to shoot once in a house that was across the street from a grade school. Shooting there during the week would not have been possible due to noise. Saturday and Sunday were the only options.

Given all these considerations, here is a plausible shooting order for the locations in *Orbiting*:

Day #1 Thursday – Street Exteriors
Day #2 Friday – Living Room
Day #3 Saturday – Trevor's Bedroom
Day #4 Sunday – Drug Store

The reason to begin with day exteriors is because every production, as I've said, needs time to get its sea legs. As a general rule, it is best to begin with a shoot day that has a high probability for success. Even with four scenes, the day exteriors will be easier to shoot than any of the interiors. This will get the production off to a good start. Barring any big problems, by the end of the first day, everyone involved should, in theory, have a positive, optimistic feeling about shooting the project.

As to putting the drug store last on Sunday, Karen used the student store as her location and we are going to do the same. The store allows filming after hours but on weekdays is only closed between 9:00pm and 8:00am, which is less than 12 hours. On Saturdays and Sundays, though, it closes at 6:00pm, allowing plenty of time to squeeze in 12 hours. But given that this means shooting at night, Saturday won't work and the store must be placed at the end of the schedule on Sunday.

This leaves the living room and bedroom for Friday and Saturday. This is fortuitous because we want to shoot at the house on consecutive days. It should give us the luxury of not having to fully wrap equipment at the end of Friday.

And since wrap is part of our 12 hours, then if we gain this extra time, it will allow us to get off a few more shots. That's why the living room is scheduled first. The scene in there with Trevor and his parents (scene 2) is complex and will likely take half a day to shoot. Therefore, every second counts.

Step 4 – Decide the Shooting Order of Each Scene

There are, again, several issues to consider.

Important Scenes Go First. Schedule important scenes at the start of a day and less important scenes at the end. When you find yourself rushing it will almost always be during the second half of a shoot day, in particular the final two to three hours. In every film some scenes need to work better than others and those are the ones you don't want to rush.

Avoid Actor Downtime. Keep each actor's scenes back-to-back. In *Orbiting* there are two scenes in the living room that include the parents and one scene of Trevor alone. What we don't want to do is sandwich Trevor's scene between the two scenes with the parents. If we do that, the actors playing the parents will have to sit around and wait for no good reason, which may annoy them. And at that point we have created on-set conflict that could have been avoided.

Day/Night. Finally, as already stressed, keep day scenes with day scenes and night scenes with night scenes. There is no plausible way to move back and forth between the two.

When we apply all of this to *Orbiting*, here is the first day:

Day #1 – Thursday (6:00am – 6:00pm)

8	EXT. BOULEVARD	D	Trevor runs from store manager Actors: 1,6	2/8 pgs.
9	EXT. RESIDENTIAL STREET	D	Trevor bumps into Scott and Amber Actors: 1,7,8	1 pgs.
3	EXT. RESIDENTIAL STREET	D	Trevor forlornly walks to the store Actors: 1	2/8 pgs.
10	EXT. ALLEY	D	Trevor smashes a Starlight Ultra box on a fence Actors: 1	1/8 pgs.

Scenes 8 and 9 are important, which is why they are at the start of the day. Scene 9 is perhaps most important because it provides at least part of the motivation for Trevor to go home and start packing. But scene 8 is scheduled first to give us the opportunity to take advantage of rush-hour traffic on whatever city street we use. This will provide some hustle and bustle behind the action. Traffic always adds production value.

Scene 10 is scheduled last because it is least important. We don't need to see Trevor duck into an alley to hide his frustration from Scott and Amber. He can hide it by secretly crushing the box in his hand as he walks away from them. If we shoot him from the front the audience will see this action but Scott and Amber won't.

Scene 3 is scheduled third because while it provides a nice transition from the house to the store, it is not essential. The point of scene 3 is that Trevor feels humiliated. But that story beat can be played at the store. He can forlornly take the boxes from the shelf and/or he can forlornly walk up to the register with them. This doesn't mean scene 3 should be cut: it will provide options in the editing room, but that said, even if we only manage to complete scenes 8 and 9, we will still have shot everything we need to tell the story. All of this makes Day 1 very doable.

As to call time, let's assume we are shooting in early March when Karen did. At that time of year in Los Angeles the sun rises just after 6:00am. An hour or so after that there is enough light to shoot. Our call time, then, will give us ample setup time.

When shooting day exteriors, it is important to take maximum advantage of daylight hours, which means being ready to shoot as soon as there is sufficient light to get off a first take. For this reason, setup begins before the sun is up. This is especially critical in this instance because in early March in LA the sun sets before 6:00pm. There are fewer than 12 hours of usable daylight. By 5:00pm it will probably be too dark to shoot. In all we'll have about nine and a half hours of usable daylight minus lunch, minus the time it takes to move from the boulevard to the residential street and possibly also to an alley.

This is why we are going to cut scene 10 in the alley and fold its action into the end of scene 9 when Trevor walks away from Scott and Amber. Doing so will allow us to focus our efforts on scenes 8 and 9, and give us more time to shoot scene 3. It will also give us another advantage: if we finish early, we can move to the house and start lighting the living room for the next day's shoot. This means that whatever street locations are used, they would have to be near the house, but that would provide yet another advantage: the house could be used as a base camp, or center of operations. Cast and crew could eat there and have access to a bathroom. This will mean renting the house for an extra day, but as I said in the first chapter, don't write homes into your script that you don't have access to for free. This is what Karen did. So, my assumption is that all of this is possible.

Applying the same principles to Day 2, we end up with this:

Day #2 – Friday (7:00am – 7:00pm)

11	INT. LIVING ROOM	D	Trevor throws the Starlight Ultra boxes at mom's desk Actors: 1	1/8 pgs.
2	INT. LIVING ROOM	D	Mom and Dad send Trevor to the store Actors: 1,2,3	2 1/8 pgs.
14	INT. LIVING ROOM	N	Mom and Dad return and find the boxes on the floor Actors: 2,3	4/8 pgs.

While scene 2 with the parents is more important than scene 11, putting the latter at the start of the day not only allows us to keep the parents' scenes back-to-back, it affords us the opportunity to shoot scene 14, which is a night scene, at night. Hence the later call time this day. We could push call time even further to accommodate scene 14, but then we'd be throwing away daylight hours we need for the first two scenes, in particular scene 2, which includes the inciting incident for the story. We need to dedicate a significant portion of the day to shooting that scene.

A 7:00am start time will only give us about an hour of darkness or near darkness before we have to start wrap, but if we start rehearsing and lighting scene 14 before the sun goes down, we can aim to get it in a single shot. Perhaps a low angle view with the dented boxes in the foreground as the parents enter through the front door in the background. Shooting it this way would require minimal lighting. The living room could be mostly dark except for a rim light or kicker to highlight the edges of the boxes and the parents could be backlit by a single source from outside.

Now, I am aware that in the first chapter I said that shooting a scene in a single shot can take as long as shooting it in three shots. But I also said that when the action is simple, as it is in this case, the rule does not apply (the parents only have to walk in the door with the mother moving forward to inspect the boxes). Alternatively, we could shoot day for night by blacking out windows and by not providing a direct view of the front door, but those strategies would make the scene look flat. Blacked-out windows look odd because even at night we are accustomed to ambient light coming through windows.

We could get around this by rigging duvetyne tents outside the windows, which would allow us to put lights outside, but that is labor intensive and takes time.[1] A quicker solution would be to put weed netting over the windows (relatively cheap weed netting can be purchased at any nursery). This allows only a small amount of sunlight to pass through, creating the effect of ambient street light, but this still leaves us with the problem of not being able to show the front door. For this reason, in my opinion, it's almost always best to shoot night interiors at night if possible.

But whichever way we decide to capture scene 14, the principle is this: the time you have available on set always affects how you block, light and shoot. Therefore, scheduling requires that you begin considering how you might shoot certain scenes.

Turning to Day 3, it looks like this:

Day #3 – Saturday (7:30am – 7:30pm)

1	INT. TREVOR'S ROOM	D	Trevor writes, parents argue off-screen, Dad enters Actors: 1,2	1 2/8 pgs.
12	INT. TREVOR'S ROOM	D	Trevor packs a suitcase while he watches TV Actors: 1	3/8 pgs.
13	INT. TREVOR'S ROOM	N	Trevor has fallen asleep in front of the TV Actors: 1	1/8 pgs.

Scene 1 is up first because it is most important. It's our introduction to Trevor. It will also be the opening scene in the movie. For this reason, it needs to be especially well executed. No viewer is going to have faith in a movie that begins badly. It's unfortunate that we have to bring the actor playing the Dad back for a second day since we may be paying him. Also, he's one more moving part in the scene that might necessitate additional coverage. We could cut the Dad and only use his off-screen voice – "Trevor, we need you in the living room" – but then we would lose the moment when he finds Trevor hiding behind his bedroom door, which is a good gag. So, we're keeping the dad. But it's good to think things like this through just in case there are ways to simplify.

One element we should cut from the scene, though, is the cat. The cat sauntering in will almost certainly not work, or work well, unless we get a trained cat, which requires a trainer, all of which is too much money. The alternative, trying to get someone's house cat to hit a mark, would be a crap shoot. We don't want to waste time. So, the cat goes.

Scene 13 is last because it is a night scene and we want to shoot it at night. Again, we'll only have a short period of darkness, but the later call time extends this by a half hour and Trevor waking up could, like scene 14 in the living room, be handled in a single shot that is set up and lit before it gets dark. The action is simple enough to allow for this (he wakes up, looks around, end of scene).

Alternatively, we could place the bed where we wouldn't see any windows, in which case blocking out any sunlight would not be a problem. The issue, however, is that windows add depth to a scene. So too do open doorways. They provide excellent backgrounds for shots. So, let's assume we want a window in the shot and are going to shoot the scene after dark, and that we'll likely put a light outside the window. This assumes we'll be on the first floor, but even if the location is two stories and there are no bedrooms on the first floor, we can dress another room downstairs to be a bedroom. So long as this happens in advance of shooting, we're fine. On many productions, the art department works at night and then the crew comes in to shoot during the day. Or *vice versa*. In this case, though, since we plan to use the house for three days, Art could set dress both the living room and the bedroom while the street scenes are being shot.[2]

Turning, finally, to Day 4, it looks like this:

Day #4 – Sunday (6:00pm – 6:00am)

5	INT. STORE - REGISTER #1	D	Trevor discovers that he no longer has the coupon Actors: 1,4,5	1 1/8 pgs.
7	INT. STORE - REGISTER #2	D	Trevor tries again to buy the two boxes of Starlight Ultra Actors 1,4,5,6	7/8 pgs.
6	INT. STORE AISLE	D	Trevor searches the floor for the coupon Actors: 1	2/8 pgs.
4	INT. STORE AISLE	D	Trevor grabs two boxes of Starlight Ultra Actors: 1	1/8 pgs.

Scenes 5 and 7 are first because the action at the registers is most central to the story. Imagine for a moment that we never see Trevor take the two boxes of Starlight Ultra from the shelf but only see him walk up to the first register with them. And imagine for a moment that we never see Trevor return to the aisle in search of the coupon, but only see him show up at the second register to take another crack at purchasing them.

These cuts are not great, what happens in the aisle is fun, especially Trevor's futile search for the coupon, but these cuts are plausible and would not seriously affect the story. So, we're going to shoot at the registers first and then move on to shooting scene 6 in the aisle – Trevor looking for the coupon – because it is more important, and more fun, than scene 4. Another good reason to schedule the registers first is that there are four actors total in those scenes and it's smarter to bring them all in at the start of the day and then send everyone but the actor playing Trevor home early.

Step 5 – Create the Final Schedule

With every location and scene ordered, the schedule is now complete. Scene 10 will remain, but be marked as omitted. The same will be indicated in the shooting script. This way we won't have to keep renumbering scenes – in the script, in the breakdown, in the schedule – every time we cut something. If we were to add a scene at this point, we wouldn't renumber either. Let's say we were to slip in a scene between scenes 6 and 7; we'd designate it either 6A or A7. The latter makes more sense, though, given how shots are numbered on slates during production, which is covered in Chapter 12.

Finally, if I were to distribute this schedule, I would color code each scene according to industry convention, which is as follows:

Day Exterior	Yellow
Day Interior	White
Night Interior	Blue
Night Exterior	Green

A color-coded version is included in the online resources for this book. I encourage you to look at it. In the meantime, here is the final schedule not coded (note that it includes a page total for each shoot day which, as I've stressed, is information you want to keep track of):

ORBITING FINAL SHOOTING SCHEDULE

Day #1 – Thursday (6:00am – 6:00pm)

8	EXT. BOULEVARD	D	Trevor runs from store manager Actors: 1,6	2/8 pgs.
9	EXT. RESIDENTIAL STREET	D	Trevor bumps into Scott and Amber Actors: 1,7,8	1 pgs.
3	EXT. RESIDENTIAL STREET	D	Trevor forlornly walks to the store Actors: 1	2/8 pgs.
10	OMITTED			

End Day #1 – Total Pages: 1 4/8

Day #2 – Friday (7:00am – 7:00pm)

11	INT. LIVING ROOM	D	Trevor throws the Starlight Ultra boxes at mom's desk Actors: 1	1/8 pgs.
2	INT. LIVING ROOM	D	Mom and Dad send Trevor to the store Actors: 1,2,3	2 1/8 pgs.
14	INT. LIVING ROOM	N	Mom and Dad return and find the boxes on the floor Actors: 2,3	4/8 pgs.

End Day #2 – Total Pages: 2 6/8

Day #3 – Saturday (7:30am – 7:30pm)

1	INT. TREVOR'S ROOM	D	Trevor writes, parents argue off-screen, Dad enters Actors: 1,2	1 2/8 pgs.
12	INT. TREVOR'S ROOM	D	Trevor packs a suitcase while he watches TV Actors: 1	3/8 pgs.
13	INT. TREVOR'S ROOM	N	Trevor has fallen asleep in front of the TV Actors: 1	1/8 pgs.

End Day #3 – Total Pages: 1 6/8

Day #4 – Sunday (6:00pm – 6:00am)

5	INT. STORE - REGISTER #1	D	Trevor discovers that he no longer has the coupon Actors: 1,4,5	1 1/8 pgs.
7	INT. STORE - REGISTER #2	D	Trevor tries again to buy the two boxes of Starlight Ultra Actors 1,4,5,6	7/8 pgs.
6	INT. STORE AISLE	D	Trevor searches the floor for the coupon Actors: 1	2/8 pgs.
4	INT. STORE AISLE	D	Trevor grabs two boxes of Starlight Ultra Actors: 1	1/8 pgs.

End Day #4 – Total Pages: 2 3/8

Notes

1 Talk to your cinematography instructor about tenting windows, but it is a way to block sunlight while also creating an enclosed space where lights can be positioned on the exterior side of a window.

2 Another reason we wouldn't want to shoot in a second-floor bedroom is because we would have to lug all the equipment, and props and set dressing, up the stairs.

4 Decide How to Shoot What

You should begin thinking about how you might shoot your film as early as possible. Once you get deep into preproduction – location scouting, casting, production meetings, etc. – you may find that you don't have much time left over to think about shots.

You will, of course, have creative meetings with your DP once preproduction commences (see Chapter 10), and these meetings will include shot-listing sessions, but you should still develop preliminary shot lists on your own. Treat these as a first step only, though. You don't want to walk into your first meeting with your DP and say, "Here are the shots, this is how we are shooting the film." That would shut them out of the creative process.

People who work on your film want a creative stake in it and you should give them that. Film is a collaborative art form and as such it gives you the opportunity to mine the creativity of others. The ideas that other people bring to the table will in most cases only make your film better. So, always be open to what your collaborators have to contribute.

Still, it is up to you, as director, to tell the story, and shots are a big part of that. In most cases, especially in mainstream films, shots serve to direct the viewer's attention to important narrative details and events. We are all familiar with this. If while watching a film there is, for instance, a cut to an insert shot of a ring on a character's finger, then we will assume the ring is important and seek meaning in it that contributes to our understanding of the story.

One way to begin shot-listing, then, is to simply tell yourself the story in pictures, as if you are watching your own movie. This will allow you to determine what you want the audience to see, at what size (whether in a wide shot or a closeup, for example), and in what order. Flexibility about the latter is required once you get to the editing room, but if you tell yourself the story in pictures, as if you already have footage and are editing it together, then you will end up with a workable shot list.

To see what I mean, let's return, as promised, to our example from Chapter 2:

```
EXT. HOUSE - DAY

An upper-middle class suburban home.
```

DOI: 10.4324/9781003169864-4

```
MARTIN (64) stands looking out a window.

A DELIVERY TRUCK rolls down the street and parks.

Martin runs outside.

The DELIVERYWOMAN meets him, carrying a BOX.
```

One way to imagine that as an edited series of shots is as follows (note the repetitions):

1. Wide Master: Martin's house
2. Medium Shot: Martin standing in the window waiting
3. Reverse Wide: Truck pulls up
4. Closeup: Martin becomes excited and steps away from window
5. Medium Wide: Front door as Martin hurries outside
3. Reverse Wide: Martin and deliverywoman walk towards each other
6. Two Shot (profile): Martin meets deliverywoman and receives the box
1. Wide Master: Martin heads back to his house as the driver returns to the truck

The fact that I am assigning shots to specific actions does not mean that on set I would use those shots to only cover those actions. Shots 2 and 4, for example, both cover Martin in the window, so on set I would use both shots to cover all of his action in the window: waiting, becoming excited, then exiting frame. If I didn't do that, then I would limit my options in the editing room.

Likewise, the wide master, shot 1, would be used to cover all the action of the scene even though in my hypothetical edit I am only using it at the start and at the end of the scene.[1] The same is true of the reverse wide, shot 3, which can be used to cover almost everything that happens outside the house. Shots 5 and 6, though, focus on specific actions. The latter, the two shot, only works for the moment when Martin and the deliverywoman meet up and he accepts the box. The former, the medium wide, only covers Martin coming out of the house. In the edited scene it could be used to allow time for the deliverywoman to exit the truck and retrieve the box off-screen, which are actions not worth dwelling on. It could also be used to cover Martin going back inside the house, which would provide yet another option in the editing room.

At the same time, if I hadn't, as a first step, created a hypothetical edit, I might have missed certain shots. For instance, the reason I have two different sized shots of Martin in the window is because, as I told myself the story in pictures, it became apparent that his excitement about the truck's arrival deserves more emphasis than the moment when he is simply waiting for the truck.

Again, shots typically direct the audience's attention by determining what they see, when they see it and at what size. As to the box Martin receives, I need to consider how much emphasis it deserves. It is clearly important because it is what he has been waiting for.

My first instinct, though, as I told myself the story in pictures, was not to give it any special emphasis. The reason is this: it's going to be a rather big box (it contains, as we find out in the next scene, a shooting gallery with a laser rifle and little green monsters that can be shot down) so the size of the box, which will make it difficult for Martin to even carry it, will by itself grab the audience's attention and pique their curiosity. So, the box doesn't need its own shot.

Likewise, the reason I included no singles for Martin and the deliverywoman is because the deliverywoman is not important. The unwieldy box is important, and the profile two shot will make Martin's efforts to hold the box visible (as will both masters).

But the shots I have selected create a clear pathway for the audience's attention. This becomes even more apparent if I lay them out as storyboards, which I advise you to do because it is not always easy to *see* shots in a shot list:

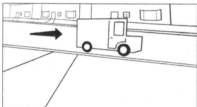

1. Wide Master: Martin's house

2. Medium Shot: Martin waiting

3. Reverse Wide: Truck arrives

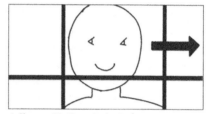

4. Closeup: Martin excited, exits frame

5. Medium Wide: Martin rushes out front door

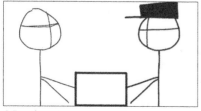

3. Reverse Wide: Martin meets driver

6. Two shot: Martin receives box

1. Wide Master: Martin heads back to house

Again, this is not meant to suggest that the shots would be cut together in this exact order. But what these storyboards do reveal is that if I shoot the action this way, I will have all the material I need to cut the scene together. And with that knowledge, I can now simplify the shot list by removing the repetitions and clearly indicating what action each shot will cover:

1. Establishing Shot: Martin's house – entire scene
2. Medium Shot: Martin in window waiting, reacts to truck arriving, exits frame
3. Reverse Wide: Truck arrives, driver retrieves box and meets Martin who exits back to the house as the driver returns to the truck and drives away
4. Closeup: Martin in window waiting, reacts to truck arriving, exits frame
5. Medium Wide: Front door - Martin hurries outside / Martin goes back inside
6. Two Shot (profile): Martin meets deliverywoman, receives the box, both enter and exit frame

But this remains only a preliminary shot list. In the first place, it is still in something like story order while the final version will be in shooting order. Shots 2 and 4, again, which cover Martin in the window, are the same camera setup, so on set they would be shot consecutively, probably by switching to a longer lens for shot 4 and not by moving the camera closer. But shooting order will be determined later with the DP and AD, as discussed in Chapter 10.

Next, because shot 4 will likely require swapping lenses, as it is called, this raises the issue of focal length. The final shot list will also include information about that, whether a wide, normal or long lens will be used for any given shot, but that information will be added later in consultation with the DP. Typically, though, when you pop in for a closer shot like this, you switch to a longer focal length because the increased magnification, shallower depth of field and compressed perspective of long lenses draw attention to actors' faces and their performances.[2]

Finally, this series of shots represents only one possible way to shoot the scene, and maybe not the best way. For this reason, some shots are likely to change once the DP provides input. So, it would be a waste of time and effort to finalize the shot list now. What I have created, though, provides a solid starting point for a discussion with a DP.

Coverage

This refers to breaking down a scene into closer views, what I just did above. Typically, you begin by shooting a wide shot, called a master, that reveals where the scene is taking place and who is there, and which usually covers the entire scene. After that, you shoot closer shots of the same action. In the case of a dialogue scene, for instance, these closer shots might include over-the-shoulders, closeups, inserts, etc.

When you shoot coverage, you give yourself options in the editing room. These include not only what you can draw the audience's attention to and when, but if you also shoot multiple takes of each shot, then in the editing room you get to use only the best material from each take. In most cases, this means picking the strongest performance moments, but you also gain the ability to work around problems with focus, framing, lighting, sound, continuity, etc.

Moreover, coverage gives you control over the pace of a scene. When you shoot a scene in a oner, the pace is baked into the shot. But if you have multiple shots of the same action, then depending on when you cut into any one of those shots, you can usually speed up the action or slow it down (perhaps by adding or removing a pause before an actor delivers a line of dialogue or, as in the example above, using the medium wide of Martin exiting the house to elide some of the time it will take for the deliverywoman to exit the truck and retrieve the box).

Coverage also allows you to delete material from a scene if you later decide you don't need it. With singles, for example, you can easily remove lines of dialogue when you edit those singles together. In the case of a oner, though, everything in the scene, both action and dialogue, stays in the scene, unless you are willing to use jump cuts to excise the moments you don't want.

This is why editors advise directors to shoot cutaways to supplement a oner. These are typically insert shots of various details in the action, though a director may also strategically shoot a single of one or more actors. These additional shots not only allow the action to be trimmed, they also provide a means for changing takes. You can, for example, get out of one take of a oner by using a cutaway, say an insert shot of a character's nervously fidgeting hands, and then when you return to the oner, you can come back to it using a different take, one that includes better material for the remainder of the scene than the take you were previously using.

Another common strategy is to include cut points in a oner. If, for example, you have an actor briefly block the camera's view of the action, then you can hide a cut, and thus change takes, as they wipe through the foreground of the frame. With a moving camera, foreground objects that wipe through frame, from furniture to trees, can serve the same purpose. So too can whip pans.

Still, oners are always tricky, making coverage an attractive shooting strategy. At the same time, if you shoot coverage for everything, then you lose some control over managing the audience's attention because if you are always using closer shots, especially closeups, then it becomes difficult to give additional visual emphasis to specific moments that deserve it.

Camera movement can provide one remedy for this. For example, a push-in on a character at an important moment will signal its significance to the audience. Shooting different sized coverage shots is another way around this problem. If you cover a conversation in, say, a two shot, over-the-shoulders, medium closeups and head-and-shoulder closeups (or even tighter than that), then you give yourself more control over managing the audience's attention because you can, when you edit the scene, shrewdly use your tightest shots for the most significant moments.

But there is a problem here too: shooting that much coverage is time consuming. If you haven't limited the scope of your project in all the ways I've discussed in previous chapters, then you may not have time to do this. And if you choose to do it anyway and rush through a bunch of shots, then you potentially undermine the advantages coverage is supposed to provide. You may end up with a lot of shots, but the performances in them may not be very good, lighting and framing may only be adequate, and you may discover continuity problems that were overlooked on set because no one had time to attend to them.

Again, the more you try to do, the less you may accomplish.

Additionally, when you shoot a scene in the way I just described, what you end up with can seem visually generic. Filmmakers have found all sorts of workarounds for this problem – for example shooting handheld, relying on Steadicams to keep the camera moving even during closeups, using unusual framings, cutting rapidly and even jumping the 180-degree line, sometimes repeatedly – but even those strategies have by now become commonplace. This is not to say you shouldn't use such techniques, but endless coverage, no matter how much you dress it up, can sometimes seem rote and uninspired.

At the same time, shooting oners is difficult and time consuming, especially if actor and/or camera movement is involved, which is often the case. After all, if a scene is covered in a single shot, then movement becomes an effective way to refocus the audience's attention. The camera might, for example, leave one actor to pick up another actor, or one actor might walk closer to camera while another actor walks farther away, or the camera might simply move in on an important detail. The possibilities are endless.

One solution to the problem of coverage sometimes seeming routine and oners often being difficult to pull off is to find a happy medium between the two, even within the same scene. Again, this is a matter of emphasis. You could, for example, identify the action that carries the most narrative/dramatic weight in a scene, only shoot coverage of that, and then devise an interesting but simple long take to cover what is less important in that scene.

This approach is sometimes called cutting in your head, which is said to be risky because it limits your options in the editing room. But if you cover every scene the same way – master, two shot, closeup, closeup – then every scene in your movie will look the same. It is definitely true that when you cut in your head you limit your options while editing, but that is not, in and of itself, a bad thing. It simply presents you with certain challenges that, by the way, untold numbers of filmmakers have successfully faced down.[3]

Selectively Using Coverage

Let's take a scene from my first feature, which I reshot to include in an online directing course. In the film it takes place on a beach and beneath a pier. For the reshoot, I used two locations on my campus: a walkway and a reflecting pool. It will become clearer as we go along why the scene should be divided like this. For the sake of simplicity, I'm going to focus only on the version I shot as a demonstration for my students. I will use it to provide one example of how coverage can be used for specific purposes, and not simply as a general shooting strategy.

The scene is about two close friends, Frank and Sarah, who have wandered away from Sarah's wedding rehearsal party because her husband-to-be, Joseph, has gotten drunk and embarrassed himself and her. As the scene begins, then, Sarah is upset, but not overly so because Joseph often plays the fool at parties. Still, now that they are about to get married, it seems that his antics are becoming less amusing to her. This is why she escapes. And she invites Frank to come along.

EXT. PATH - DAY

Sarah and Frank walk together.

> SARAH
> Haven't seen much of you lately.
> Got a girl?

> FRANK
> A couple.

> SARAH
> Oh, a couple. Do they know that?

> FRANK
> I'm pretty obvious.

Sarah smirks as they walk on.

> FRANK
> I've been thinking about moving
> back east.

> SARAH
> Why?

> FRANK
> I don't know. Things are just. I
> get headaches out here.

> SARAH
> Everybody gets headaches. It's the
> smog.

They continue on until they come to:

EXT. REFLECTING POOL - CONTINUOUS - DAY

Sarah impulsively jumps up onto the ledge of the
pool. She does a little spin for Frank, her dress
twirling. Frank grins and jumps up too. They walk
the ledge. Sarah turns inward for a moment.

                    SARAH
          You know that first time Joe and
          I broke up?

                    FRANK
          Which first time?

                    SARAH
          Which? The *first* first time.

Frank laughs.

                    SARAH
          What are you laughing at? The *first*
          first time.

                    FRANK
          Oh, the *first* first time.

                    SARAH
          Yeah.

                    FRANK
          I'm sorry.

                    SARAH
          Anyway. That *first* first time Joe
          and I broke up, I almost went
          after you.

                    FRANK
          Get outta here.

                    SARAH
          I did. I did.

                    FRANK
          You mean after me after me?

                    SARAH
          After you.

                    FRANK
     I guess it's lucky I was shy.
     I mean, it would be pretty
     uncomfortable now, wouldn't it?

                    SARAH
     We would have gotten over it. Joe
     would have thought it was all
     about him and once we got back
     together, he would have used it
     to get off the hook for whoever
     he'd been screwing with.

                    FRANK
     But what about me?

                    SARA
     Yeah. He would have tried to
     punch you. But then you both
     would have gone off together and
     gotten drunk.

Frank laughs again.

                    FRANK
     You're probably right.

                    SARAH
     Yep. I know my men.

                    FRANK
     What about you and me?

                    SARAH
     Us? Oh. We would have been fine.

                    FRANK
     You sure?

                    SARAH
     Frank. Come here.

She kisses him. Long and lingering. She breaks
the kiss.

                    SARAH
     See? We're still friends.

Essentially, the scene (written by my friend and collaborator Roger Hedden) is an extended walk and talk. Two or more characters, in this case Frank and Sarah, walk while they talk.

Their dialogue in the first section is brief but important, though not earth-shattering. We learn, first of all, that Sarah hasn't seen Frank for a while. Why not? Well, if we want to read between the lines, Frank is pulling away from Joseph and Sarah now that they are getting married. In the film's opening scene, which takes place before they are engaged, the three of them are driving back together from a weekend in Las Vegas. We discover that they are the three musketeers and have been best friends for years. Now, however, Frank is odd-man out. And if we want to further read between the lines, he's always had a thing for Sarah (which he admits to after this scene).

We also learn that Frank is at a crossroads. He's thinking about moving back east. This startles Sarah, causing her to ask why, and while Frank almost admits that it's because he is unhappy, he quickly backpedals and feebly offers up that he gets headaches in LA. Clearly, he can't tell her the real reason he's unhappy, which is that he feels he's losing her. Whether or not Sarah understands that, and I think she does, she certainly registers that he is melancholy and angsty.

This sets up for the next part of the scene when Sarah jumps up onto the ledge of the pool and Frank, following her lead, does the same. She's goofing around, trying to make things fun, which is a way to make herself feel better, and Frank too. And because she's having fun with Frank and not Joseph, and because she probably suspects why Frank is unhappy, this puts her in a certain mood, or state of mind, that leads her to admit she almost went after him once. And that takes us into to the heart of the scene, which culminates with Sarah kissing Frank.

As this outline reveals, everything prior to Sarah's revelation, and her assurances that she really did once consider going after Frank, while important, primarily serves as setup for the conversation that leads to the kiss. And that conversation doesn't begin in earnest until Frank asks, "But what about me?" With that question he is asking about what might have been, so it initiates a major turning point in the action.

One way to shoot this scene, then, is to hold off using coverage, at least singles, until the third and final section. That's how I did it when I reshot the scene for my class. The first time I shot it, I held off on shooting coverage until the moment Sarah says she almost went after Frank, but even then, I only used a fairly wide two shot to get closer to the action. As I said, though, I'm going to focus on the reshoot.

We can, as suggested, think of the scene as being in three parts, which I will name as follows:

1. Haven't Seen You in Awhile
2. I Almost Went After You
3. We're Still Friends

Haven't Seen You in Awhile

To cover this first part of the scene I decided on a dolly shot that would track with them as they walked, in part because I had access to a dolly, but also because it would make for a more dynamic shot since it was going to be a oner.

However, at the urging of the DP, I decided to cover myself and shoot the shot at two sizes: a head-to-toe wide shot and a medium shot from the thigh or waist up. In other words, the second shot would be close enough that I could pop into it from the wide shot if I needed to, perhaps at the moment when Sarah asks Frank why he wants to move back east because the audience needs to register her concern, but not so close that it would put too much emphasis on the preliminary action that unfolds in this opening section.[4]

At the same time, a dolly shot can always be made more interesting, so I wanted to find a location where we could have some foreground elements wipe through the moving frame. Luckily, the DP and I found a walkway bordered by a row of trees where it was possible to put those trees between the camera and the actors (it is always productive to location scout with your DP or to at least shot-list on location with them when possible). This made the shot even more dynamic and, as discussed above, the trees could potentially provide hidden cut points.

I further decided that Sarah should stop walking when she asks Frank why he wants to move back east. Again, I think she is startled when she hears what he is considering because she doesn't want to lose him either (another reason she later tells him she almost went after him), and so by having Sarah stop, the camera could also pause, and both those breaks in the flow of the action would draw attention to her emotion and her question.

As it turned out, we used all these elements in the editing room, so I'm glad the DP encouraged me to shoot a tighter frame (Figures 1–5). Note that in both shots – the wide and the medium – the emphasis is on Sarah. She is driving the scene. That's why when I named each section, I used her dialogue for the titles. There is no point in drawing too much attention to Frank until the turning point that leads to the kiss.

I Almost Went After You

For the second part of the scene, the DP and I decided we would also use the dolly for a oner. However, as in the first section, there is a significant moment in this section as well – when Sarah tells Frank she almost went after him – so I needed to find a way to draw attention to that, but again without cutting into singles since I was saving those for the last part of the scene when the intimacy of closeups would be most effective. But there are always ways to direct the audience's attention without cutting.

One way to do that is by changing focus during a shot, which is what I did. I already knew we were going to use the reflecting pool for our second location because I thought it would be fun if the characters walked around its ledge as they talked. Again, Sarah is being playful and trying to cheer up herself and Frank (Figure 6). So, I decided to have the actors walk up opposite sides of the rectangular pool, as opposed to walk up the same side. This allowed me to keep the emphasis on Sarah by placing her in the foreground of the shot with Frank out of focus in the background. This is called staging or blocking in depth. Then, at the moment Sarah admits her past feelings for him, we racked focus to Frank for his stunned reaction (Figures 7–9).[5]

Next, I decided that Frank's reaction should motivate Sarah to escape and head back the way she came as a way to dissipate the tension her admission creates. As she did this, we returned focus to her in the foreground in order to reveal that despite her retreat, she is nonetheless still thinking about what might have been (Figure 10). In this way, I maintained the tension created by her admission and also provided myself with a transition to the third part of the scene.

We're Still Friends

At this point, I needed to get Sarah and Frank together again for the kiss. But having them return to the other end of the pool for this seemed bland. As luck would have it, there is an island in the middle of the pool with a statue on it and I decided it would be fun if Sarah, as part of her retreat, stepped into the water and walked out to it. This would provide a way for her to lighten the mood again and, since it would motivate Frank to jump out to the island to be with her, it would also mark the transition to the scene's climax. To further underscore this, we used a new wide shot to cover Sarah's journey through the water, which also served to finally reveal the pool (Figure 11).

However, their dialogue in this part – Frank says it was lucky he was shy and Sarah explains they would have gotten over it – is important because Sarah takes it for granted that she and Joseph would have gotten back together, which stings Frank, so in the editing room we quickly cut back to the previous shot to see Frank's reaction. Still, that shot is fairly wide, so I was careful to have both actors, once they reached the island, open up or play towards camera, as it is called, in order to provide access to their performances (Figure 12).

As this suggests, it was time to get into tighter shots for the scene's climax. My goal was to use Frank's question, "What about me?", to motivate a cut to a closeup of him, and this worked out in the editing room (Figure 13). It's as if he insists that the visual emphasis switch to him in that moment. And from there, the scene plays out in over-the-shoulders, singles and a tight two shot.

However, to keep it interesting I exploited the statue as an opportunity to keep both actors moving. When in response to Frank's question Sarah jokes that Joseph would have punched him, she is deflecting or avoiding. Frank, after all, is not asking about Joseph. So, as part of her deflection, I had Sarah circle around the statue to escape again. Because of this, Frank's coverage shots now became Sarah's coverage shots, and *vice versa* (Figures 14–17). Stand-and-deliver blocking, as it's called, which is when actors stand and deliver lines, can sometimes feel static, so having Sarah and Frank switch sides was a way to avoid that and mix things up a bit.

In the edit, we used the two shot for the kiss (Figure 18) because when characters kiss in over-the-shoulders and singles, oftentimes only the backs of their heads are visible. Then, to end the scene, I had Sarah circle behind the statue again, giving her one more opportunity to escape, but to also give the audience a moment alone with Frank to consider his reaction (Figure 19). After that, in the final shot, which retreats from the action, the statue becomes a barrier as each character, alone in their own world, reflects on what has just happened (Figure 20).

Here is how it all breaks down:

1. Frank and Sarah walk and talk.

2. A tree enters frame in the foreground.

3. As the tree wipes through frame, it provides a cut point to the medium shot.

4. Once they clear the tree, Sarah stops, concerned, to ask Frank why he wants to move back east.

5. Then, as Sarah dismisses Frank's explanation, they both exit frame.

6. Sarah lightens the mood once they reach the pool.

7. Because Sarah is both in focus and in the foreground, she draws our attention as she considers telling Frank about her past feelings for him.

8. Frank, however, draws our eye to him in those moments when he teases Sarah, even as he remains out of focus.

9. But when they reach the far side of the pool , focus racks to Frank as he stops and reacts to Sarah's admission.

10. Focus returns to Sarah as she retreats, revealing that despite her hesitancy, she is thinking about what might have been.

11. Sarah crosses to the island, marking the transition to the third and final part of the scene.

12. Once both actors reach the island, they play towards camera to provide access to their performances.

13. Then, there is a cut to a CU of Frank for his line "But what. about me?" A long lens is used to throw the background out of focus so as to draw attention to his face.

14. Likewise, a long lens is used to cover Sarah as she turns to Frank and deflects his question by joking that Joseph would have punched him.

15. This deflection motivates Sarah to retreat again, which is covered in a two shot that helps to keep the spatial relationships clear.

16. When Sarah appears on the opposite side, adding some variety to the stand-and-deliver blocking, it is clear that they have changed sides.

17. Once Sarah and Frank have swapped positions, his previous coverage shot becomes her shot.

18. The kiss takes place in the two shot to provide the best view.

19. Then Sarah retreats once more as the camera, in what was previously her coverage shot, holds on Frank for his reaction.

20. In the final shot, the statue serves to place each character in their own world as they reflect on what has just happened.

As I hope this extended example makes plain, shots are not merely containers for the action; they help to define the audience's understanding of the action. That is your goal as you go about the process of shot-listing your own film.

What I also hope you noticed is that shots are inseparable from blocking. I will have more to say about blocking in Chapter 11 on rehearsals, but for now do be aware that it should function meaningfully. In this scene, it is mostly linked to the characters' shifting emotions, as when Sarah repeatedly retreats from Frank. However, this is not true in every case. For instance, my decision to have Frank walk up the opposite side of the pool was determined by technical and aesthetic considerations. The actor's first instinct was to follow Sarah up the same side, but if he did that, I wouldn't have gotten my shot (Figures 7–10).

Thus, blocking is always about juggling the motivations of characters and the motivations of the director.

Lastly, keep track of your options as you shot-list. These include:

- Shot Size
- Angle
- Camera Height
- Framing
- Focal Length
- Focus
- Depth
- Movement – whether camera or actor movement or both

In the scene above, I very meticulously managed shot size, focus, depth and camera and actor movement. For any given scene or shot in your film, consider the techniques you most want to exploit in order to manage the audience's understanding of the unfolding story.

One final note: don't go overboard when you shot list. There are only so many shots you can shoot each day (discussed in Chapter 10). Think back to the first example in this chapter: Martin receives a box. When I decided not to include an insert of the box or singles of Martin and the deliverywoman I was, in effect, increasing the time that would be available on set to properly shoot the shots that actually tell the story. When you cover everything (a somewhat mindless activity), you certainly gain lots of options in the editing room, but giving yourself options you don't need is a waste of time during production and will likely only put you behind schedule.

Notes

1 Using a master at the start and end of a scene is a common, but by no means universal, editing strategy, sometimes called advance and retreat. You start wide, move into your closer shots, then conclude by returning to the wide shot again.
2 Again, as stated in the Preface, it is assumed that you and your classmates are receiving instruction in craft classes dedicated to camera, lighting, sound, etc. This should include instruction on how focal length affects an image. Still, for an excellent primer on the subject along with a discussion of how to creatively use different focal lengths, see director Sidney Lumet's chapter on the camera in his book, *Making Movies* (Vintage, 2010).
3 Ubiquitous coverage did not become commonplace in films, or at least sound films, until the 1980s. Prior to that, filmmakers, for various aesthetic, technological and economic reasons, tended to use it judiciously or not at all, and many filmmakers still use it sparingly. For a discussion of changing shooting practices, at least in Hollywood movies, see David Bordwell's essay, "Intensified continuity: Visual style in contemporary American film" (2002).
4 When you cut from a wide shot to a closer shot of the same subject, the difference in size needs to be significant enough to justify the cut. So, if the medium two shot

of Frank and Sarah for the first walk and talk were too loose, that is to say, too close
in size to the wide shot, I wouldn't have been able to use it.

5 A rack focus is an abrupt change in focus during a shot, from one subject to another.
It is meant to redirect the audience's attention. It is different from a focus pull, which
is a gradual and usually imperceptible change in focus intended to keep a subject
sharp when the distance between that subject and the camera's focal plane is changing, either because the subject, the camera or both are moving.

5   Settle on a Look

One reason people, even when they are strangers to each other, can come together and effectively and efficiently collaborate on a film, is that they all share an assumption about how style is supposed to work: its job is to support the story. Costumes and production design should reveal character, lighting and music should set the mood and, as was discussed in the previous chapter, shots and editing should clearly delineate the unfolding action.

Of course, in practice, this is not always the case. Glamorous costumes and makeup, opulent and eye-catching sets, spectacular action sequences, and *tour-de-force* camera moves can all sometimes be examples, at least in part, of style for its own sake. And in what we call art cinema, style may intentionally work against the story or function in purely formal ways that are divorced from the needs of the story.

You are therefore free to use style however you wish to. What follows, though, is a discussion of style in service of story since that is how it is typically used. At the same time, you may think beyond this approach, at least occasionally, if you feel inclined to do so.

Still, most filmmakers harness style to *depict* or *portray* characters, settings and events in specific ways that contribute to the audience's understanding of the narrative (this character is lonely, that character is cruel, this house is scary, on and on). Casting, production design and set dressing, wardrobe, makeup & hair, lighting, cinematography, editing and sound are the basic materials we have to work with, along with performance (discussed in Chapters 9 and 11).

You are encouraged, therefore, to create a look book, which is a presentation that shows how you intend to exploit these techniques to tell your story. You can use existing media to do this (frame grabs, images and videos from the web), as well as location photos, headshots, etc. Two useful websites for finding existing media are Shotdeck and Filmgrab. It is also a good idea to include some text that explains the meanings of your choices.

When you create a look book, your goal is to help people to see and even hear your film and to give them a sense of what it would feel like to watch it. Keep in mind, though, that most films don't try to sustain a single feeling or mood. One scene may be funny, the next one sad and the one after that frightening. In your look book, then, you want to capture all of the moods in

DOI: 10.4324/9781003169864-5

your script. This may mean, for example, that you want low-key lighting in some scenes, high-key lighting in other scenes, and less extreme lighting ratios in still other scenes.

My point is this: style is rarely static. It changes in concert with your story, and your look book should reflect those changes, and so should your film.

As discussed in Chapter 2, your script breakdown can begin the process of creating a look book. As you identify elements that will appear in your film, you can begin to collect images of what you want. These can relate to everything from casting to props to wardrobe to hair. At some point, though, you just need to sit down and create your look book.

However, as I said about preliminary shot lists, don't be precious about your look book. Your collaborators will have ideas of their own, and these may be better than your ideas. When you interview potential production designers and costumers, for example, they may arrive with a mood board or pitch deck illustrating how they see your story and its characters. And some actors who audition for you may arrive dressed "in character." And your DP will likely have very specific ideas about what kind of images they would like to create. Be grateful for this and open to everyone's ideas.

There are different ways to structure a look book. You can simply break it down according to the categories listed above or you can have it unfold scene by scene, which is easy to do with a short script since, as I've stressed, a short script should not have too many scenes in it. Or you can use some combination of these two approaches. So long as your look book helps people to see and even hear your film, and gives them a sense of what it would feel like to watch it, then you have succeeded. It may also be that your instructor has a specific way they want a look book to be organized, in which case follow their template.

What follows is not meant to suggest a structure, or to comprehensively cover all possibilities. It is simply intended to spark your imagination. So too is the sample look book for *Orbiting*, which is included in the online resources for this book.

Also, you are not required to cover choices in every category. If, for example, you are not planning to use makeup and hair in particularly salient ways, then don't cover them. And if you plan to use editing and sound in unobtrusive ways, you can skip those as well. But a look book should at least cover casting, wardrobe, production design, lighting and cinematography.

Casting

Include your *ideal* casting choice for each character. These can be images of anyone, but feel free to think in terms of well-known actors. If, for example, you want Tessa Thompson in your film, then so be it. She's not going to be in your film, but that isn't the point; the point is to *show* your characters.

But do explain why Tessa Thompson is perfect for the role. And yes, her appearance matters. As will be discussed in Chapter 9 on casting, actors have headshots so that casting directors and directors know what they look like.

But in the case of well-known actors, they may also bring a certain persona to their roles based on previous characters they've played, the genres they work within and their style of acting, and you can consider those issues as well since doing so may help to clarify your thoughts about each character in your story.

In the case of *Orbiting*, Trevor, for example, probably shouldn't be played by a leading-man type. He's Kevin Hart and not Michael B. Jordan.

Wardrobe

For each character, include images of how they would/could/should be dressed. Keep in mind that characters typically have costume changes, so unless a character has a specific look or style, for example they always wear khakis and a polo shirt, then try to capture those changes.

This is especially important if a character's wardrobe is going to meaningfully change over the course of the story, say to reflect character change. For example, in *If Beale Street Could Talk* (2018), to visually underscore Trish's transition to being matriarch of her own family, she begins wearing a different sweater, one that previously we have only seen her mother wearing.

A more obvious example can be found in *The Godfather* (1972). Michael begins the film wearing Oxford button-downs and corduroy blazers ("A nice college boy," as Sonny says), but by the end of the film he is wearing silk suits and Homburg hats (the uniform of a gangster).

In *The Devil Wears Prada* (2006), the process is threefold. Anne Hathaway's character, Andy, initially dresses down, then she transitions to wearing designer outfits once she becomes seduced by the world of high fashion, and finally she returns to a more authentic version of herself, again reflected in her wardrobe.

In the case of *Orbiting*, there are no costume changes since the film takes place over the course of a single day. Moreover, while Trevor is presented with an opportunity to change, he chooses not to (he can own up to his incompetence in the store, as an adult would, but instead he chooses to steal the Starlight Ultra products, which demonstrates that he will, for the time being anyway, remain a child). So, in terms of Trevor's wardrobe, it is simply a matter of portraying him as an out-of-work sci-fi enthusiast. Worn out sneakers and jeans and an old T-shirt with a sci-fi logo on it would likely do the trick.

Makeup & Hair

If relevant, you can include images relating to makeup and hair. Such external character traits can be quite expressive. In Brian DePalma's *Carrie* (1978), for example, the title character's hair is often limp and frizzy, but when she goes to the prom, her coming out, as it were, it has a shiny, blow-dried look. It's a simple choice, but an effective one, since it demonstrates her conscious decision to rebel against her mother's pious religious values, which require that she repress her sexuality.

Returning to *The Godfather*, Michael's hair is initially boyish: parted on the side and drooping over his forehead. But later, once he becomes Godfather, it is slicked back and shiny. Moreover, makeup is used to play up his disfigured jaw (the physical mark of his transition to killer), and makeup is also used, at least in some later scenes, to give the impression of bags under his eyes (heavy is the head that wears the crown).

And Anne Hathaway's costume changes in *The Devil Wears Prada* also include changes in how she wears her hair and does her makeup.

As for *Orbiting*, Trevor probably doesn't shave often. Or spend much, if anything, on haircuts. And he probably stays up late watching TV. So, in terms of makeup and hair, the goal would be to turn the actor into a tired and scruffy but loveable *schlub*.

Production Design

Show your ideal locations and how you would use production design and set dressing to build the world of your story, to support the narrative's progression and to underscore character and theme. Keep in mind that production design often works in concert with wardrobe. In *Chinatown* (1974), for example, which is a fictional account of the water wars in California, the costumes and set design both lean towards tans, browns and grays: the colors of a drought.

As this suggests, color is important. Films often have specific palettes. In *Beale Street*, Trish and Fonny, from childhood through early adulthood, are both associated with yellow and blue, which is used both in their costumes and in the spaces they inhabit. These colors underscore the bond between them, and perhaps even their innocence, but they also foreshadow what will keep them apart: the jail where Fonny is held has quite distinct yellow tiles on the walls and the mostly faceless police officers, who seem to loom everywhere, are all in blue.

Also, keep in mind, as will be discussed in Chapter 12, that movie sets are typically busy with set dressing, which makes images more interesting and complex. So, unless you are specifically going for a minimalist aesthetic, think about how you will pack your sets with décor.

One thing you can do is go to a prop shop and walk around, which may generate ideas about the types of set dressing and props you want in your film. Visiting thrift stores can be useful too. On my last short, I stumbled upon several inexpensive props in thrift stores that I turned over to Art once preproduction began.

In the case of *Orbiting*, Trevor has a specific passion, science fiction, so filling his bedroom with items which reflect that would be half the fun of dressing his room. He is also a man living in a boy's room, so his bedroom should be dressed accordingly: single bed, functional dresser and desk, childhood memorabilia, etc.

It's not the case, though, that every choice must be meaningful. Some choices are purely visual. For example, characters in movies rarely inhabit rooms with white walls. Their houses are more colorful than that simply because white walls are uninteresting and, moreover, they bounce light all over the place, making it difficult for the DP to control where light goes in a scene.

This is not to say that such choices can't also be meaningful – think of my example above from *Beale Street* – but it remains the case that some types of décor simply photograph better than other types. Again, movie sets are typically packed with set dressing, some of which simply serves to fill in what would otherwise be empty or blank spaces in a set.

Lighting

Show how you want each scene in your film to be lit. Think in terms of lighting ratios, quality (hard or soft light), direction, coverage, etc. Also think in terms of source. Are the characters lit by natural or artificial light or some combination of the two in any given scene?

Lighting is also used to manage the audience's attention: it can both reveal and conceal elements in a frame. It can draw attention to a character's eyes, for example, or it can leave them shrouded in darkness. It can reveal a set or keep it in shadow. It can hide a character or keep them in silhouette until they step into light.

A primary consideration is mood. Is a scene romantic, happy, sad, whatever? As mentioned, few films try to sustain a single mood or feeling from scene to scene, so including images for how each scene should or could be lit is important in this respect.

Keep in mind, though, that film techniques, rarely, if ever, have fixed meanings. Low-key lighting, for instance, can, depending on narrative context, support any number of moods, from romance to mystery to sadness to horror. In *Casablanca* (1942), for example, the scene in which Rick drunkenly hits rock bottom after Ilsa reenters his life has a low-key lighting ratio almost identical to another scene, presented in a flashback, in which the two of them dance, happy and in love.

Likewise, the effects of high-key lighting are also dependent on narrative context. It is said that high-key lighting is typical of comedies but not, for example, in many Coen Brother's comedies. And in some science-fiction films, it is used to create an antiseptic future world, as is the case in *2001* (1968) and *THX 1138* (1971). In Alfred Hitchcock's *Psycho* (1960), it is used in the most horrific scene, Marion's murder in the shower.

Of course, high-key lighting was in some sense forced on Hitchcock for that scene by realistic considerations – bathrooms typically have flat, even lighting – but at the same time, he was intentionally playing against viewer expectations concerning the genre. After all, he chose to stage the murder in a bathroom. At the same time, there is a huge cheat in the lighting when Norman enters the bathroom, knife in hand, dressed as his mother: he is rather improbably lit in silhouette to hide his true identity from the audience.

So, don't be schematic when you think about lighting or about any film techniques for that matter. Context is typically everything. Take the opening sequence of *E. T.*, mentioned in Chapter 2. The men chasing E. T. are lit from behind, which prevents us from seeing their faces. This makes them appear menacing, but only because they are behaving in a menacing way. In later scenes, when E. T. is only lit from behind, this serves to make him appear more mysterious and otherworldly.

In the case of *Orbiting*, it would probably be best to use low-key lighting in Trevor's bedroom, not because those scenes are mysterious or romantic or frightening or even sad, but because Trevor is probably not someone who seeks out sunlight. He sits alone in a dark room all day watching TV while he toils away on a novel that he will likely never complete.

Finally, consider color temperature. There are actually a number of conventions concerning this. In many silent films, for example, night exterior scenes were tinted blue, and this technique, in modified form, remains in force today with moonlight often rendered as blue light. Likewise, winter scenes often have a cool blueish hue and summer scenes a warm orange hue. And when characters return home for the holidays, there is often a scene after they get out of the cab when they stand outside their childhood home in cold blue moonlight while they stare through a window at their family, who are almost invariably bathed in a warm orange glow.

There are numerous possible variations on this. Returning to *Beale Street*, when Trish reveals to her family that she is pregnant, which is received as joyful news, the many practical lamps in the scene give off a warm glow (practical lamps are lights that appear in the scene). But after Trish's mother invites Fonny's family over so they can share the news, the color temperature of the lamps appears more neutral to underscore the negative reaction Fonny's pious and judgmental mother and sisters have to the news.

Some of this is dependent upon color grading in post, but it remains the case that in terms of lighting, warm color temperatures are typically assumed to be inviting whereas cooler color temperatures are not. This is often quite apparent in horror films. In *The Shining* (1980), for instance, the main lobby of the Overlook Hotel, where Jack slowly goes insane, typically has a blue cast from the cold winter sunlight coming through the large windows, whereas other locations in the hotel are often lit more neutrally.

In any case, you need not follow these color conventions, which may or may not be based on actual biases in our visual system and cognitive makeup, but you should be aware of them.

Cinematography

This is where your look book can shine. You can include images and clips that illustrate shooting strategies you would employ and in which scenes you would use them. In the case of clips, you can think holistically, which means you can also bring in issues related to blocking and editing.

My advice, though, is not to focus too much on shot size and framing since those are covered in your shot lists and storyboards, but don't ignore those issues either, especially if you are considering using unusual framings, say canted angles, or perhaps frames within the frame as when shooting through doorways, archways, windows, etc. Still, you should give primary emphasis to other aspects of the image: camera movement, focal length, depth of field, focus, aspect ratio, exposure and color-grading techniques (including black & white), etc.

In *Beale Street*, for example, camera movement is sometimes used to link characters. This is the case when, after Trish and Fonny finally find a landlord willing to rent to a Black couple, they celebrate in the street by whooping and hollering as they walk. Throughout this, the camera mostly pans back and forth between them, rather than cutting, which visually unites them until the camera finally tilts down to reveal the moment when their hands slip apart. This is significant because immediately following this scene they will have their first encounter with the police officer who will ultimately separate them by sending Fonny to jail for a crime he did not commit.

Beale Street also uses depth of field and focus in interesting and meaningful ways. Once Fonny goes to jail, for example, Trish visits him a number of times. In their final meeting, right before he takes a plea deal and is sentenced, the depth of field in each of their singles is extremely shallow. As discussed in the previous chapter, this is a typical strategy, except that the background in each of their shots is so soft that I suspect the effect was digitally enhanced in post. This not only draws attention to their pain, isolation and disorientation (the rest of the world is just a blur), it also creates a quite striking effect when Fonny, broken and defeated, stands up to leave and focus does not shift with him. He is, at least in this moment, lost to Trish, and he becomes, from her perspective, an ethereal figure with no distinct shape or presence.

So, do think about ways you can use techniques of cinematography mean-ingfully, and include your own examples in your look book.

The kind of poetic uses of cinematography in *Beale Street* would be out of place in *Orbiting*, but techniques of cinematography can be used in many ways. For instance, for some of the coverage shots at the registers in the store, using canted angles, perhaps in concert with the distortion of wide-angle lenses, would play up Trevor's sense of disorientation and anxiety.

Editing

Beyond ensuring on set that continuity is maintained and that the action is adequately covered, filmmakers often don't think much about editing before they get to post. But thinking beyond such basic considerations can be productive.

In the comedy *American Pickle* (2021), for example, there is a scene in which a gang of Cossacks level an entire village in less than 15 seconds as the camera mostly holds on the faces of two characters watching the devastation unfold. It is quite common to use cutaways and reaction shots to elide small bits of story time so that certain actions, say a character crossing a room (or exiting a truck, as in the previous chapter), can more quickly progress off-screen, but this scene takes that strategy to the extreme, and the editing was almost certainly planned in advance.

Editing was also planned in advance for a striking courtroom scene in season 5 of *Better Call Saul*. The title character is defending a brutal murderer as the victim's mother sits crying behind him in the gallery. In a closeup, as he is seated beside the defendant, Saul undergoes a crisis of conscience. He looks miserable as the sounds of the courtroom become muted and echoey, suggesting that his mind is far away. But then the booming voice of the judge breaks through, addressing him. This motivates a cut to a medium wide of Saul, except now he is standing as he responds to the judge. Time has clearly elapsed across this cut; long enough for Saul to get to his feet. The audiovisual metaphor is this: Saul has become disconnected from what is going on around him, including the passage of time, such that the judge's voice penetrates to the past where his mind still lingers, and this hauls him back to the present where he finally acts.

As both these examples reveal, editing provides a great deal of control over story time. But thinking about how to exploit that prior to shooting, rather than simply using it as a way to tighten scenes in the editing room, can lead to quite creative results.

Other things to think about are jump cuts, crosscutting and, as discussed in the previous chapter, whether or not you will orchestrate hidden cut points in long takes or even just use them to change shot size, as I did in the first walk and talk with Frank and Sarah by having a tree wipe through frame. Probably the most famous example of this technique is in *Jaws* (1975). Chief Brody is on the beach nervously scanning the water and in order to amplify the tension, there is a hidden cut to a tighter shot of him every time a beachgoer wipes through the frame. At the same time, not hiding such cuts can be effective too. In *Ménilmontant* (1926), a character discovers that her parents have been murdered and to play up her shock there are five rapid cuts that take us by increments from a medium closeup of her to an extreme closeup of her eyes.

Something else to consider are scene transitions. A common transition is known as a dialogue hook. This is when the last line of dialogue in one scene directly connects to the first thing we see in the next scene. You are certainly familiar with this: a demanding boss is in the middle of a crisis at work and they scream out for their assistant, then there is a cut to their assistant at home dealing with a family emergency. Such hooks can also be used ironically. In *Bottle Rocket* (1996), Owen Wilson's character at one point confidently announces that he's going to rent "the best room in the house," then there is a cut to him and two other characters in a motel room so small that there is no space at all between their beds.

Transitions can also be purely visual. In *Bodies, Rest and Motion* (1993), the camera in one scene tilts down from a night sky and as it moves past a street lamp to reveal a house, there is a cut to a similar tilt down from a floor lamp to a character on a couch. This match cut, also called a graphic match, links the exterior of the house to its interior.

You might also think about how much you even want to edit. It is not unusual for studio films today to have 3000 to 4000 cuts in them, but prior to 1960 the average number of cuts in a sound film was between 300 and 700.[1] Clearly the overall pace of editing in films has sped up over time. But you are free to edit at whatever pace you want.

What is sometimes called slow cinema is a genre unto itself, which relies, by necessity, on long takes and few cuts. The most cited example of slow cinema is probably Chantal Akerman's 1975 film, *Jeanne Dielman, 23 quai du Commerce, 1080 Bruxelles*, but the strategy remains viable today. For example, *Days* (2021), a two-hour feature by Tsai Ming-liang, has, by one reviewer's count, only 60 cuts in it. Again, long takes are difficult to pull off, but not impossible.

Clearly, many filmmakers think about how they will (and won't) use editing prior to shooting, and you can do the same and include clips in your look book which reflect the approaches you intend to employ, even if only in certain scenes.

Sound

Thinking back to the example from *Better Call Saul*, audio plays a significant role in capturing Saul's subjectivity, his inward turn as he grapples with his conscience, and the muted, echoey courtroom sounds were certainly not an afterthought in the editing room (though their exact execution was of course decided upon in post). As this suggests, thinking beyond the need to properly record dialogue tracks during production can lead to interesting results.

One aspect of sound you can certainly think about is music. My students sometimes create sizzle reels for their films, which are essentially look books set to music. Sizzle reels can sometimes be misleading – for one thing, the quick pace of the editing in them often bears no relationship to how the film will actually be edited – but they do provide an opportunity to choose music that captures the tone and perhaps the over-arching mood of a film.

You are not required to create a sizzle reel. As the name suggests, its purpose is to generate "heat" or interest in a project which, unless you are trying to raise money, may not be necessary. But you should include at least one music clip in your look book. Ideally, it will be something that captures what could be a central theme in the film's score. Most, scores have recognizable motifs or melodies that are returned to again and again, though they are often performed in different ways to underscore different moods in the story.

In *Last of the Mohicans* (1992), for example, an instrumental piece, "The Gael," by Scottish folk musician Dougie MacLean, became the central theme in the score composed by Trevor Jones. It returns throughout the film, including as source music (performed by a fiddler inside a fort). But as score it is orchestrated and performed in varying ways to be, by turns, romantic, melancholy and thrilling, as when it is used over the film's final, climactic action sequence.

You can also think in terms of character. It is not uncommon for musical themes to be composed for specific characters. In *Moonlight* (2016), for example, which follows its protagonist through three stages of his life, a rhythmic and haunting melody, first titled "Little's Theme," then "Chiron's Theme," then "Black's Theme," weaves its way through each section, though with some variation in performance and even instrumentation each time it occurs (in one instance, "Chiron's Theme" is even remixed in the chopped and screwed style of Southern rap).

Of course, the score for your film won't be composed until you lock picture (though some composers, especially those working in episodic television, begin composing as soon as they receive a script), but incorporating some music in your look book, including songs, can be very effective and helpful later when you start working with a composer.

Look Book Checklist

Once you've made a first pass at your look book, ask yourself these questions:

1. Does my look book comprehensively address creative choices in the areas outlined above? This means including casting and wardrobe choices for every character and including, at minimum, production design, lighting and cinematography choices for every scene. There is no need to go overboard. Providing a long laundry list of choices about, say, cinematography, is not necessarily better than focusing on a few specific techniques that you will use in truly meaningful ways. This applies to all the categories.
2. Are the meanings and functions of your creative choices clearly, *concisely* and cogently communicated? Why, for example, do you want shallow depth of field in a certain scene, or high-key lighting in one scene and low-key lighting in another? What are these choices meant to communicate to an audience? What ideas, narrative and/or thematic, do you expect them to convey and/or what emotions are they intended to support? What are you trying to impart about your characters, their subjectivity, their situation, whatever?
3. Is your presentation well organized? Does it manifest a sense of design? Taken as a whole, does it provide an engaging mix of image, audio and text that together reveal your vision for how you will realize your film?

As to how much text is necessary to explain the meanings of your creative choices, the answer is as little as possible. If you revisit my examples above, you'll see that I don't say much about the techniques I cover. This is because their meanings and intended effects are straightforward and easily explained. This should be true of your explanations as well. Be precise but concise.

Finally, avoid focusing on meanings your script can't support. If you say, for example, that your protagonist will always wear their deceased mother's favorite necklace to demonstrate how much they miss her, that is meaningless if nowhere in the script do we learn the origin of the necklace or that the character misses their mother or that their mother is even dead.

In other words, don't assign arbitrary traits or psychological states to characters that relate to backstory which is not covered in your script and only exists in *your* mind. A look book should reveal how you will use film techniques to support the story your script actually tells. In short, don't go down a rabbit hole covering meanings that won't be relevant to an audience.

At the same time, many writers and directors like to create complex biographies for characters that stretch back into their childhoods and you may want to do the same. But remember this: anything in a character biography that is not also in the script is something the audience will never know. So, if while writing a character biography you hit on something you think the audience should know, then find a way to get it into the script: otherwise, you are only talking to yourself. And at that point, once it's in the script, you can refer to it in your look book.

Again, a sample look book for *Orbiting* is included in the online resources for this book. You can use it as a starting point for your own look book.

Note

1 For a discussion of average shot length and increased editing in contemporary films, I refer you again to David Bordwell's essay, "Intensified continuity: Visual style in contemporary American film" (2002).

6 Don't Break the Bank

As I said at the outset, the practical and the creative are one and the same thing. We have seen how this applies to creating a shooting script, a breakdown, a schedule and shot lists. We are now going to see how a budget is an essential creative tool. The amount of funding allocated to production design, costumes, locations etc., has a direct effect on the look and quality of a film.

What this means is that developing a budget entails making a multitude of creative decisions and, in every case, linking those decisions to the intelligent distribution of funds. In this way, a budget becomes the blueprint for your film, a step-by-step guide to actually making it. This will become clearer as we go along.

On a professional production, the budget is in some sense written in stone. Financiers typically do not provide an open line of credit. If a micro-budget feature raises, let us say, $500,000, then the film must be made for that amount of money. Cost overruns in one department, say Camera, must be covered by cuts in other departments, say Wardrobe or Art. This is because going back to the financiers, hat in hand, for additional funding, is rarely an option.[1]

Student productions often, and unfortunately, work a bit differently because in many cases no one exerts that kind of control over the purse strings. Rather than move funds around to deal with overages, students often opt to dig deeper into their pockets. But doing that is problematic, especially when it means taking out another student loan and/or racking up credit card debt.

To avoid this, it is important to have a feasible budget, one you actually stick to.

For this reason, the first step in creating a budget is determining how much money you have to spend. I strongly encourage you to set an upper limit and work within your means. To effectively do that, though, your script, as discussed in the first chapter, must match your funding. Expensive locations, out-of-town shooting, risky action and the kind of elaborate world building inherent to certain genres can all potentially overstrain your budget.

But as we are about to discover, you can spend too much on almost anything.

Before you budget you must break down your script and schedule it. You need to know what elements you need, and for how many days you need them, in order to project certain costs. Since we've already done a schedule

DOI: 10.4324/9781003169864-6

(Chapter 3) and breakdown (Appendix II) for *Orbiting*, we are going to budget it as well. Finally, as with scheduling, you don't need professional software. You can use any software that is designed to create spreadsheets.

Budgets are typically divided into three sections:

Above-the-Line expenses
Production expenses
Postproduction expenses

While the last two are self-explanatory, the first one requires brief explanation. Key creative personnel on a professional production are designated as above-the-line. These include cast members, writers, directors and producers. Their salaries and related costs (story rights, travel and living, etc.) are above-the-line expenses. All other expenses are below-the-line. However, on a student film there is no point in making such a distinction. There are production costs and there are postproduction costs.

While this book provides a brief overview of postproduction in the Afterword, it is primarily about getting your film shot or "in the can" as it used to be called.[2] I am not minimizing post, but as mentioned in the Preface, production is the first and most daunting hurdle you face, and you are primarily on your own while doing it. Shooting almost always takes place outside of class time, often on weekends, leaving you to figure out a great deal of it on your own.

Picture editing, on the other hand, is often highly supervised in classes where students screen cuts and receive notes and advice from the instructor and their classmates. Moreover, instruction on how to manage footage – from ingesting it, to adding a LUT, to organizing it for editing – is also typically provided in such classes (or in companion classes or workshops).

Most departments also offer post-sound classes in which students complete the dialogue edit, ADR, foley, and sound effects for their films. These classes also typically prepare them to deal with music and the final mix. And in some departments, students can specialize in sound, in which case they may do this work for the directing students.

Likewise, final color, visual effects and the creation of a DCP, or digital cinema package, which contains all of a film's final visual and audio files are also often handled in dedicated classes or supervised by staff with expertise in those areas. It is also common to hire vendors to handle some or all of these highly technical aspects of post.

Moreover, a great deal of knowledge about postproduction circulates among students, with those further along helping those just starting out. In my program we assign three graduate students each year as postproduction teaching assistants. Along with instructors and staff they help guide their classmates through the process of completing their films, both picture and sound.

In any case, the time to start planning for postproduction is during prep and production, as will be discussed in Chapter 10. But to return to projected post costs, a budget must contain these because exhausting all of your available funds during production only to have to find more money to complete a film is a bad idea. You may find that to raise that extra money you will have to go further into debt. Or worse, you won't finish your film beyond reaching a fine cut and doing a rudimentary sound mix and color pass in whatever picture-editing software you are using. Your film deserves better than that.

The way to save money in post, as suggested above, is to do as much of it yourself as you can. Enroll in the relevant classes and be your own picture editor, dialogue editor, sound editor, etc. Or in every case work with classmates who are willing to help you for free (or for a nominal fee) or who are required to help you because they are receiving course credit.

Accounts

Budgets comprise accounts, or departments, and line items within those accounts. Each account is numbered. For our purposes, they range as follows:

Above-the-line	1000–1900
Production	2000–4900
Postproduction	5000–5900

While we are not making a distinction between above-the-line and below-the-line expenses, we are still going number our Cast accounts accordingly. Here are the most common accounts:

Account	Department
1000	Cast
1100	Cast Travel & Living
2000	Production Staff
2100	Extras
2200	Art
2300	Wardrobe
2400	Makeup & Hair
2500	Grip & Electrical
2600	Production Visual Effects
2700	Camera
2800	Production Sound
2900	Transportation
3000	Locations & Catering
3100	Stunts & Weapons
3200	Practical Effects
3300	Animals
3400	Crew Travel and Living
3500	General Production Expenses
5000	Editorial
5100	Score and Music Rights
5200	Postproduction Sound
5300	Postproduction Visual Effects
5400	Color and DCP

Not all of these accounts will be relevant to your movie. *Orbiting* has no costs related to travel and living, stunts, weapons, practical effects (for example, fire or rain), animals or visual effects. So, we're not going to include those accounts in our budget.

The absence of these elements is, in fact, what makes *Orbiting* a good project for a first film. That's why I'm using it as my primary example: to encourage you to as well not include such elements in your own film. As I've already discussed, they can be expensive, time consuming and in some cases dangerous. As mentioned, something as simple as an actor tripping and falling requires supervision by a stunt coordinator, guns require the presence of police officers and also an armorer, animals often require trainers and fire usually requires a pyrotechnics expert. I add here that some visual effects require an experienced VFX Supervisor.

Simple VFX, which are primarily handled in post, as when a student of mine added falling snow to a scene, or when I once added a noisy, stuttering video effect to some footage, are relatively easy to pull off if you or a classmate know how to use the relevant software.

But in the case of complex VFX, as when a student of mine planned to have huge flying animals in her thesis film that transported people on their backs, those must be meticulously planned and require special equipment during production, as when shooting green screens. As indicated in the list of accounts above, Production Visual Effects is its own department with its own crew and costs. If you have effects like this, you are advised to hire a VFX Supervisor for prep, production and post unless you truly have the requisite expertise.

Do keep in mind that complex VFX often take a great deal of time to complete in post. Unless you are doing them yourself, expect to pay someone. If someone tells you they will do your VFX for free, they may be making a promise they can't keep due to the time commitment. I tell you this because it has happened more than once to students in my program that their unpaid VFX Supervisor had to back out before completing the work.

If your film does include elements not found in *Orbiting*, from weapons to animals to VFX, you must fully research all related costs so that you can appropriately budget for them. Talk to your instructors, to professionals, to classmates who have already done similar work and to the staff person in your department who handles production insurance because some of these elements may require additional coverage.

Percentages

It is best to think in terms of percentages. You can expect to dedicate 65–70% of your funds to production, 20–25% to postproduction and then hold back 10% as a contingency. You need this contingency because unexpected expenses, by which I mean *expenses you truly cannot predict*, almost always arise during prep, production and post. But unless you have exceptional post costs, say VFX or music rights, then these percentages are fairly consistent across student films, making them a good rule of thumb.

With that in mind, let's say that by way of some combination of personal funds, student loans and awards, grants and scholarships, we are able to set an upper limit of $15,000 to make *Orbiting*. You may not want to spend anywhere near that amount on your own movie. I encourage you not to. But since I have students who make shorts for several thousand dollars and other students who spend upwards of $30,000, I'm picking a number in the middle.

I'll begin by allowing the maximum percentage for production costs and the minimum percentage for postproduction costs. This may not work out, but it gives us a starting point:

Production (70%)	$10,500
Postproduction (20%)	$3000
Contingency (10%)	$1500[3]

Distribution of Funds

Next, we need to allocate funds. We are going to do this account by account, starting with Cast and ending with Color. This means that once we finish, we will likely have to revisit certain accounts. After all, we only have so much money to spend and we are going to work within our means, adhering, a least roughly, to the percentages above.

But the reason we want to do it this way is because it's always best, I think, to begin a budget by simply assigning to each account the amount of funding we hope we can assign to it. Then, once we have an overall picture of the budget, we can make changes to our production and postproduction plans as needed.

If after our first pass at the budget, for example, production costs exceed 70% of our funding, then we will have to rethink our approach to shooting the film. This is why I am allowing the maximum percentage at the start: it provides a line in the sand that we almost certainly can't cross. There is always some wiggle room, but we need to be cautious.

We are going to budget for shooting in Los Angeles where I teach and where Karen shot the film. This means that some of what I cover may not apply to where you are shooting. For example, shooting permits are handled differently in different cities, meaning costs vary, and in some places, for example rural areas, permits may not be required at all. I will try to make such distinctions when I can. But in the end, you will have to research the rules and laws governing film production in your area and seek advice from your instructors.

Finally, I'm going to introduce as many different production scenarios as possible, especially as this relates to hiring certain crew versus recruiting classmates for those positions. You can absolutely make a student film with an entirely student crew where no one is paid except by way of reciprocal labor (when someone crews on your film you crew on their film in return). But there can be distinct advantages to bringing on more experienced crew in certain departments, for example Art and Makeup, and I'm going to cover those scenarios. The result will be that our final budget will represent only one possible way to make *Orbiting*.

Because of this, you are encouraged, as an exercise, to budget alternative ways of making the film. A budget, once again, is a blueprint, a step-by-step guide to how you will make a movie.

As to the question of how you find crew who are not students, the answer is to ask classmates who've already shot films. In my program, the advanced graduate students who are assigned as teaching assistants to the first-year MFA students and undergraduates compile contact lists of reliable and talented professionals they have worked with. These lists, which include costumers, production designers, makeup artists, production sound mixers, etc., are an invaluable resource. There are also online resources for finding crew, for example Mandy.com.

I Production Costs

Account 1000 – Cast

As we know from the breakdown, there are eight speaking roles in *Orbiting*. That is a large number. As I said in the first chapter, you should aim for between two and four speaking roles. There are, again, several reasons for this. First, the more roles you have, the more difficult and time consuming casting will be. Second, the more actors you have, the more coverage you may have to shoot. Finally, each role potentially increases wardrobe expenditures and every actor is another mouth to feed.

Moreover, I mentioned that there might be additional costs for salaries. If you cast actors who are members of the Screen Actors Guild (SAG), the student agreement includes deferred salaries, but it has become common, at least in Los Angeles where I teach, to give actors some money up front. This money is not an advance on deferred wages; it is in addition to those deferred wages.[4]

When my students compensate an actor, they typically pay them $125/day. This is not significantly less than SAG wages, but since they don't have to engage a payroll company or contribute to SAG's pension and health fund, they come out ahead. Still, such salaries add up fast. If we were, for example, to give every actor in *Orbiting* $125/day, that would cost $1500, or 10% of our total funding, which is not feasible.

That said, let's allocate funds for the actor playing Trevor because he works four days. He may have a job and need to take unpaid leave to be in the film, plus we want to entice the best actor to accept the role. Trevor is the lead, after all, and the film lives or dies by his performance. And if it turns out the actor doesn't expect compensation, we can reallocate the funds (or pocket them).

But any cast member can come with costs. An actor may want to be reimbursed for gas, or they may want us to cover a parking ticket they received while working on set (this happens more than you think, and we can certainly refuse, but that may cost us in goodwill), or we may just want to do something nice, like buy an actor a small gift for being a trooper on a difficult shoot day. In our budget we are going to call these expenses Perks and Adjustments.

With all this is mind, here are our projected Cast costs:

Acct	Description	Amount	Units	X	Rate	Subtotal	Total
1000	**CAST**						
1002	Principal Cast						
	Trevor	4	Days		125	500	
	Dad					0	
	Mom					0	
	Wendy					0	
	Linda					0	
	Store Manager					0	
	Scott					0	
	Amber					0	500
1004	Perks & Adjustments		Allow		150	150	150
						Total 1000	**650**

Note that all eight speaking roles are listed. Our budget should contain every element we need to make *Orbiting*, including elements we expect to get for free. Also, if it turns out we have to compensate another actor, we can easily update the budget using this format.[5]

Note as well that I assigned an even number to each line item. I am going to do this in every account. The reason is this: if we later need to insert an additional line item into the middle of any account, we can do so using an odd number, which means we won't have to renumber everything. This will be helpful as the producer updates the cost report, which is an ongoing tally of what is being spent on each line item in every account. If the producer doesn't update the cost report, they won't know when to start moving funds around in the event of an overage.

Lastly, I am *allowing* $150 for Perks and Adjustments. It is not possible to exactly predict certain expenditures. All you can do is estimate them. My experience tells me that $150 is a good guess-estimate for this line item given the large number of actors.

Total funds assigned to production so far: **$650**

Account 2000 – Production Staff

On a student film, production staff includes the combined position of line producer/production manager, the assistant director and production assistants, or PAs. PAs are gofers: they go for this; they go for that. They run errands, drive people to set, set up food, etc. I will discuss the role of the AD in Chapters 10 and 12, but let's take a moment now to consider the combined role of line producer/production manager. On a student film, this person is typically called the producer.

On a professional production, a line producer manages the budget, what we are doing now. They oversee all aspects of preproduction, from the shooting schedule to location scouting to hiring crew to securing equipment rentals, and they do all of this within the limits of the budget. They are given a dollar amount to work with and that amount is what remains for below-the-line expenses after all above-the-line expenses have been negotiated. Hence the title line producer.

The production manager, on the other hand, supervises the day-to-day production process once shooting commences. This might include pulling shooting permits, maintaining a cost report and a daily production report and ensuring that proper releases have been secured from cast, crew and location owners. They are often designated the UPM, or unit production manager, because a professional production can, for example, have a second unit that is responsible for shooting action which does not include the principal cast. All of those wide shots you see in films of landscapes and the protagonist's car cruising down desert highways are often filmed by a second unit crew with its own UPM, director and cinematographer.

A student producer is responsible for all these tasks. They also organize, schedule and participate in auditions and tech scouts. They negotiate rental costs with location owners. They schedule catering. They provide script notes and weigh in on casting. They help monitor safety and ensure that all applicable labor laws are adhered to. This might include preparing timesheets for actors if the production is SAG signatory (even though salaries are deferred) and hiring a studio teacher if minors are involved (a salary that can't be deferred).[6] It is a tough and grinding job with a time commitment equal to, if not exceeding, that of the director, at least during prep and production.

I will have more to say about picking a producer in the next chapter, and will elaborate on their job duties in Chapters 8 through 10; the issue now is costs. While we won't be paying our student producer, free is almost never free. There may be related costs. We might, for example, reimburse our producer for gas, parking and meals. Just as we feed crew on set (more on catering below), we feed them during prep. Not all the time, but if our producer is running around town making the movie happen, then lunch may be on us. Gas too. And any parking fees.

Let me give an example. On a short film I made in Los Angeles, I had two far-flung locations: a house in Northridge in the San Fernando Valley and a newspaper loading dock in Palmdale in the Antelope Valley. Once I found each location, I did not approach the owners because I am not a good negotiator. So, I gave the producer the addresses and she went out instead (one quality a producer should have is a fondness for haggling). She drove almost 40 miles round trip to the house and over 110 miles round trip to the newspaper production plant. Therefore, gas was on me as was lunch on the day she went to Palmdale.[7]

So, here are our projected costs for Production Staff:

Acct	Description	Amount	Units	X	Rate	Subtotal	Total
2000	**PRODUCTION STAFF**						
2002	Producer						0
2004	Assistant Director						0
2006	Production Assistants						0
2008	Misc. Costs - gas, food, parking		Allow		100	100	100
						Total 2000	**100**

Note that I have again included all personnel, even though they are working for free. This is standard practice and we are going to continue to adhere to it. And, once again, I am only guess-estimating certain costs, in this case reimbursements to our producer. $100 may seem high, but a single $10 lunch plus $20 in gas plus a $5 parking fee is already $35. Expenses add up fast. So, it is always better to be safe than sorry. If we assign the bare minimum of funds to every account, we're likely going to come up short once we start spending money.

Total funds assigned to production so far: **$750**

Account 2100 – Extras

For *Orbiting* we need extras in the store. They are written into the script for the scenes at the registers, but we'll also want people wandering the aisles for atmosphere. We can recycle some if not all of the extras for both purposes, but there is no getting around having them.

The way to get extras for free is by recruiting friends and family. These are people who, for the most part, you can count on to actually show up, though don't be surprised when even some of your friends and family bail on you. People are busy and all of us sometimes make promises that we can't reasonably expect to keep. Count this as a warning if your film requires extras.

Crew members can also serve as extras if they are not working during takes. But keep in mind that having a bunch of twenty-somethings as atmosphere won't always make sense (as it would not make sense in *Orbiting*). If you have older classmates, great, but you may not.

One solution is to post for extras on casting sites (see Chapter 9), but unless you offer a day rate, don't expect to get many submissions or that anyone who does submit will actually show up. You can also reach out to actors who auditioned for your film and weren't cast, but they will almost certainly expect to be compensated for the demotion. There are also casting agencies that specialize in extras. This is called extras casting and if commercial production is common where you are shooting, then just search for such agencies online. But extras casting can be expensive and you shouldn't even consider going that route unless you are shooting something that requires a great deal of atmosphere, say a classroom or party scene.

For *Orbiting*, let's assume we need a dozen extras. We can put one or two of them in the aisle with Trevor, place others in the backgrounds of shots, then choose a select number of them, perhaps four and four, to stand in each checkout line at the two registers. Assuming we can get half of them for free (friends and/or family plus crew), we should budget for hiring six. Since it's a night shoot, I don't see how we can offer less than $75/day. That looks like this:

Acct	Description	Amount	Units	X	Rate	Subtotal	Total
2100	**EXTRAS**						
2102	Featured Extras/Bit Parts						0
2104	Atmosphere						
	Shoppers at drug store	1	Days	6	75	450	450
						Total 2100	**450**

Note that there is not a line item for each extra. We simply need six extras for one day (although we are shooting at night a shoot day is never called a shoot night; it's simply the case that some shoot days are night shoots).

Total funds assigned to production so far: **$1200**.

Account 2200 – Art

Never skimp on production design. It contributes a great deal to the look and quality of a film. We tend to give too much credit to the camera. We think that if we pour funds into renting an expensive camera and a set of high-end lenses it will make a film look great. But if the sets and set dressing are crap, no camera or set of lenses can fix that.

For this reason, assigning up to 15% of total funding to Art is not out of the question. We won't need that much for *Orbiting* since we only have two sets to dress – Trevor's bedroom and the living room – but we will have to spend something on those. The drug store will largely take care of itself, as will the street scenes with the exception of Scott's SUV, which will be handled by Art since we won't have a transportation department to procure picture vehicles.

To truly save money on Art, you have to write a script that doesn't require it. I had two students who collaborated to make a successful low-budget feature by making the story about a scavenger hunt. Almost every scene was day exterior – mostly in parks and on streets – with much of the rest of the action taking place in cars as the characters' search took them from one location to the next. They not only had minimal production design, they also had very little lighting to do. Again, you have to write for the funding and the available time you have.

Regarding the house in *Orbiting*, let's assume that the living room already has most of the required decor. After all, as portrayed in our look book, it need only establish that the family is solidly and conventionally middle class. Props and set dressing, then, will mostly consist of the mother's work table, bulletin board, oversized calendar and the file boxes she fills with coupons. None of that should cost much. The most expensive item, the mother's work table, which should be a craft table and not some cheap folding table, could be purchased and then resold online after shooting, allowing us to recoup a significant portion of that money.

Students also often return items purchased for set dressing once shooting wraps. But you should only return items you don't use. After you've used something, you own it. But a typical approach to set dressing is to have a lot of items on hand to use. This gives you choices. Then you return whatever wasn't used during production and resell the rest. So, I am going to assign $150 in net costs for the living room. This includes funds for window dressing, which is discussed below under G&E. And our production designer is going to encourage everyone to save those coupon flyers we all receive in the mail so they can be cut up to fill the file boxes.

This leaves Trevor's bedroom. As discussed in the previous chapter, and as portrayed in the look book, he is a man living in a boy's room with a specific passion: science fiction. So, our PD will likely need to rent items from a prop shop. I'll allow $250 for that. The goal, again, is to have choices on set. This means that as the PD wanders the prop shop and items present themselves, they will need sufficient funds to give us those choices.

As to the store, we have to solve the problem of the Starlight Ultra boxes. One option would be to use an existing product while hiding the company's logo. Filmmakers do this all the time. A character sips a soda but the label on the can is turned away from camera. Another option would be to get permission from a company to use their product in our movie for free. This is not impossible. It's a matter of going to the company's website, clicking the Contact link, and going from there. The process might drag out for several weeks, but I have more than once secured the right to use a commercial product in a short film.

At the same time, there are companies, easily found online, that sell custom packaging of various sizes with full-color printing. In that case, our production designer would create original artwork to be printed on the boxes. The number of boxes we order would be a creative decision. Do we want to fill a store shelf or only worry about the boxes Trevor brings to the register? Let's assume that for the sake of having fun artwork we want to create our own boxes, and that we want to fill a shelf with them. Since budgets should be as accurate as possible, we need an exact quote. The quote I received for an appropriately sized box was $4.72 each, including tax and shipping. If we order 50 boxes, that comes to $236.

As to Scott's SUV, it needs to be a sleek, shiny behemoth so that Trevor feels small in the presence of Scott and Amber's success. Since it's not likely that anyone involved in the film will own such a vehicle, we'll want to budget for renting one from a commercial car rental company. A good guess-estimate for this, based on an online search I did, is $125/day. This includes purchasing full collision coverage from the rental company, which is a good idea because it comes with no deductible if the vehicle gets dinged. To limit this to a one-day rental, we'd pick it up the afternoon before and return it right after the scene has been shot.

As for paying a production designer, or PD, this is sometimes the case on student films, especially if the PD is going to have to put in a great deal of time and effort, perhaps building sets and/or dressing many sets from scratch. But even when a PD doesn't expect a fee (they will, after all, gain footage for their reel), they may still want funds to pay key members of their crew because those people often have no compelling reason to work for free.

The people who crew on your film as grips, electricians, camera assistants etc. will typically be other film students who will expect you, as I've said, to crew on their projects. But the Art Department needs people who are creatively attuned to the craft, and those people won't always be other film students. If they are not, then you may not be able to compensate them by providing labor in return for their labor. So, let's assume that we may have to pay at least one key crew member, say the art director, a nominal fee for their time. I'll budget $250 for that.

On a student film there is often only need for an art director because what mostly needs to be handled is set dressing. On a professional film or TV show the PD designs the world of the story and the art director executes that vision, contributing their own ideas and expertise along the way. But such world building is much less common on student films which often rely exclusively on practical locations (i.e., ones that don't have to be built) which are then enhanced with additional items of décor. But it is still typical to have both a PD and art director so that they can divide the labor. For example, the art director might serve as the on-set dresser. On a professional production, this is the person who, during shooting, moves props and set dressing around so that they are actually visible in each shot.

Finally, since Art will have to head out to a prop shop to find and then reserve or tag items, as it is called, and since they have a load-in day at the house, we'll again have to cover meals and gas.

A reasonable budget for Art, then, is this:

Acct	Description	Amount	Units	X	Rate	Subtotal	Total
2200	**ART DEPARTMENT**						
2202	Production Designer						
	Prep, Shoot, Wrap						0
2204	Art Director/Set Dresser						
	Prep, Shoot, Wrap		Flat		250	250	250
2208	Purchases and Rentals						
	Starlight Ultra boxes	50	Boxes		4.72	236	
	Scott's SUV	1	Days		125	125	
	Trevor's bedroom		Allow		250	250	
	Living room		Allow		150	150	761
2210	Meals – prep		Allow		50	50	50
2212	Gas – prep		Allow		25	25	25
2214	Loss & Damage		Allow		50	50	50
						Total 2200	**1,136**

In all, we are allocating about 8% of our total funding to Art, which is quite reasonable. Our PD probably won't spend the funds exactly as I have broken them down, but what we can tell them, based on this first pass, is that they have about $1100 to design the film.

As to allocating funds for Loss & Damage, this is standard whenever rentals are involved. Stuff gets lost. Stuff gets broken. We'll have insurance, but the deductible will be high, so we must anticipate going out of pocket for Loss & Damage.

Finally, the art director's salary is a flat rate because they are not receiving a day rate or an hourly rate, but simply a lump sum for all of their work. It is a gesture of goodwill, to express our appreciation for all the effort they will put in.

Total funds assigned to production so far: **$2336**.

Account 2300 – Wardrobe

Orbiting is the type of project where many of the actors should be able to supply most of their own wardrobe. This is called going into an actor's closet. The big advantage of doing this is that it saves money. One of my students spent less than $100 on wardrobe for his film, despite having five central characters, because it was about college students with all the roles played by college students from the Theater Department. As he told me, "I just raided their closets."

A quick word of advice: when an actor uses their own clothes, don't rely on them to bring those clothes to set. They may forget or instead bring something that you and they and the costumer did not agree upon. Once anything from an actor's own wardrobe becomes part of a costume, it should be commandeered so that the costumer can ensure it arrives to set.

As we know from the look book, Trevor is a sci-fi T-shirt, jeans and sneakers guy and it is likely that the actor can provide all of that except for the T-shirt. We can't, for example, have him wear a Star Trek T-shirt without getting the rights, but our costumer could design something fun for a sci-fi franchise that doesn't exist. They could develop several possibilities and, after we chose one, that artwork could be printed on a T-shirt for not much money. The shirt would need to be distressed, as it is called, so that it doesn't appear new – Trevor likely has no money to spend on clothes – but costumers have many methods for doing that. Let's allow $50 for all this.

The dad, as we know, is a dress shirt, slacks and loafers type. And even if we had to buy all of those items, they could probably be purchased at thrift stores and off clearance racks. Still, the actor playing the dad should be able to provide at least some of their wardrobe. So, I'll assign only $50 for dressing him as well.

As for the mom, we decided she is kooky but practical and budget conscious. This is why she hoards coupons and pinches pennies. So, she shouldn't seem too put together. That wouldn't be her style. Thus, we might have to procure most or all of her wardrobe. I'll allow $150 for this with the knowledge that anything the costumer needs to purchase could likely be found at lower-end retail stores.

In terms of the cashiers, there is no reason the costumer won't be able to find everything they need in the actors' closets. The only expenses will be for their name tags and the ugly retail vests those tags will be pinned to. I'll allow $25 for each actress for those items.

Turning to the store manager, we decided on a classic middle-management look: short sleeve dress shirt, tie and slacks, all of which could be purchased at thrift stores or off clearance racks, or in part be provided by the actor. So again, I'll assign only a small amount of funds, $50.

This leaves Scott and Amber, the conventional power couple. And just as we can't skimp on their SUV, we can't skimp on their look. They must be dressed for success. Again, Trevor must feel inadequate in their presence. At the same time, significantly going out of pocket for their wardrobe would not be worth it. It is enough that we are already renting a vehicle for them.

The reason is this: Scott and Amber provide an additional reason for Trevor to feel humiliated and, by way of contrast, they play up his own lack of ambition and success, but they are not essential to the story. They are only icing on the cake.

Trevor's most potent moment of humiliation takes place at the store when Linda gets on the PA system. And it is at the store where he decides to steal the Starlight Ultra products so that his parents won't discover his utter incompetence. This proves, as I've said, that he is still a child. But rather than blame himself, he blames his parents, as if they are the reason that he is immature and inept. This is why he angrily hurls the douches at his mom's desk and makes the "adult" decision to leave home, which of course he has no means to do. It's pure theater.

As should be plain, Scott and Amber have little to do with any of that. This is not to say we should cut them. I suspect that doubly humiliating Trevor will be fun for the audience, but given that the story would work without Scott and Amber, we shouldn't spend any more money on them than we absolutely have to. So, a requirement for both roles will be that the actors we cast must provide the requisite wardrobe. We can even ask actors who read for the parts to come to their audition in costume. In the case of Amber, who only has one line, we might not even read anyone and could simply assign the role to someone we know who owns a smart enough outfit.

Thus, we have no wardrobe costs for Scott and Amber. Nor do we have any costs for dressing the extras, who will, as mentioned, provide their own wardrobe, but bring us choices.

In terms of finding a costumer, my student directors sometimes take on this position themselves. They enjoy dressing their characters. But dividing up labor is always more efficient. Plus, costuming is a craft. At my school, we have one of the best costume design programs in the country. So, it's not simply a matter of putting clothes on actors.

Let's assume, therefore, that we are going to hire someone with some experience, perhaps a recent graduate of a costume program who is just starting out. As with Art, we likely won't be able to repay this person's labor with our own labor. However, we need not hire them for the length of production. On my second feature, the costumer only worked for two weeks during prep, then once all the costumes were set, a wardrobe supervisor took charge on set.

We can do something similar: hire someone for, let us say, four days. During that time, they can come up with a design for Trevor's T-shirt, meet with the actors to get their measurements and/or go through their closets, and then select and purchase everything that is needed. After that we can assign a PA to supervise costumes on set, hopefully someone who can deal with small issues – a missing button, a broken zipper – as they come up. Some costumers might not agree to this, but there are others who will. It's a matter of finding the right person.

Our wardrobe budget, then, looks like this:

Acct	Description	Amount	Units	X	Rate	Subtotal	Total
2300	**WARDROBE**						
2302	Costumer						
	Prep only	4	Days		100	400	400
2304	Purchases & Rentals						
	Trevor		Allow		50	50	
	Mom		Allow		150	150	
	Dad		Allow		50	50	
	Wendy		Allow		25	25	
	Linda		Allow		25	25	
	Store Manager		Allow		50	50	
	Scott					0	
	Amber					0	350
2306	Meals	4	Meals		10	40	40
2308	Gas		Allow		25	25	25
2310	Cleaning & Repairs						0
						Total 2300	815

The day rate for the costumer is low, but we are looking for someone primarily interested in gaining experience. And if they come in under budget, we'll let them keep the difference (we can do this with Art as well). As with the PD, we are not telling the costumer exactly how to spend funds, only how much funding they have available based on our best guess-estimates. The amount may change, of course, once we complete our first pass of the budget, but what we have is a good starting point.

Finally, I am again assigning funds for meals and gas because the costumer will be running around town visiting actors and possibly shopping at clothing stores. As to Cleaning & Repairs, I added this line item even though it is not relevant to *Orbiting* because I want you to be aware that when you rent costumes, you are responsible for the costs of dry cleaning and any repairs. Items must be returned to costume shops in the same condition they were received.

Total funds assigned to production so far: **$3151**

Account 2400 – Makeup & Hair

At first glance, *Orbiting* has no special makeup & hair requirements. It would seem that each actor only needs to be made "camera ready." This doesn't mean, though, that each actor can handle their own makeup. Perhaps we can have a classmate handle makeup, but high-definition video sees everything, especially in closeups, so making actors camera ready requires some experience and finesse.

For this reason, and because there are so many actors on *Orbiting*, we are not going to forgo hiring someone with training to handle makeup & hair. These are separate crafts, but it is typical on a student film to hire a single person for both. Currently, my students are able to hire a competent makeup artist for $150/day. If there are special requirements, say a wound or a scar, they also have to pay for any materials needed to pull those off. But a makeup artist always depletes their makeup supplies when they work on a film, so they usually charge a kit fee.

Here, then, is our makeup budget:

Acct	Description	Amount	Units	X	Rate	Subtotal	Total
2400	**MAKEUP & HAIR**						
2402	Makeup Artist	4	Days		150	600	600
2404	Kit Fee		Flat		50	50	50
						Total 2400	**650**

A word of advice: if there were special makeup requirements for *Orbiting*, we would want to add a prep day for the makeup artist. Never wait until the day you are shooting a scene with special effects makeup to try out those effects for the first time. If you do, you may lose a lot of time on set revising and finessing them. Test everything beforehand. This means hiring the makeup artist for a day during prep.

Total funds assigned to production so far: **$3801**

Account 2500 – Grip & Electrical

In terms of your own film, my advice is to primarily rely on the G&E gear your department provides. In my program, the equipment office publishes a list of every item included in its packages, from the exact number of stingers, apple boxes, sandbags, C–stands, flags and nets, to the exact number and types of lighting units. This way students can plan their projects accordingly. They need not write any action or location into their script that will require more equipment than they can get from the department for free.

Since *Orbiting* is a simple script, a standard equipment package from school should suffice. We won't be lighting the street scenes, at least with lights, and we won't be lighting the store beyond maybe using some small floor units to add a key, fill or backlight as needed in the coverage. Our only equipment-heavy days will be in the house. The living room potentially presents the biggest problem because it may be a large room with a lot of windows. But we need not show the entire room and we can dress the windows with gauzy curtains and let them burn out. As mentioned above, this is called window dressing and it is important that Art always have some on hand.

As to lighting the living room, if we do limit how much of the room we see, then our DP's goal would likely be to bounce light into the scene, which won't require big units. Neither will Trevor's bedroom. So, we shouldn't need to rent any lights. Still, I will allow $200 for G&E rentals to be safe. As will be discussed in Chapter 10, the DP submits an equipment list to the producer and we need to be prepared for any essential items on that list which are not included in the equipment package from school.

We must also consider expendables: gaffer's tape, gels, clothespins (C47s), bounce boards, etc. The way to save money on expendables is to recycle them from shoot to shoot. You and your classmates who are also shooting can chip in to buy a basic cache of expendables for every production. But since we don't know yet if we can do that, and since every production has its own requirements, I'm going to allow $100 for expendables.

Finally, there is the issue of crew. As I will discuss in the next chapter, G&E should be populated with students. Only hire professionals – if your department even allows that – when you truly have difficult shoot days with a large number of camera and lighting setups. Thankfully, that is not the case on *Orbiting*. We have two tough days at the house, but we can solve that problem by bringing on an extra student in G&E both days.

Here, then, is our proposed G&E budget:

Acct	Description	Amount	Units	X	Rate	Subtotal	Total
2500	**GRIP & ELECTRICAL**						
2502	Gaffer						
	Prep	1	Days			0	
	Shoot	4	Days			0	
	Wrap	1	Days			0	0
2504	Key Grip						
	Prep	1	Days			0	

Acct	Description	Amount	Units	X	Rate	Subtotal	Total
2500	**GRIP & ELECTRICAL Cont'd**						
	Shoot	4	Days			0	
	Wrap	1	Days			0	0
2506	Grips & Electricians						0
2508	G&E Package – school						0
2512	G&E Rentals		Allow		200	200	200
2514	Expendables		Allow		100	100	100
2516	Loss & Damage		Allow		100	100	100
						Total 2500	**400**

Again, the gaffer and key grip will be students, but I have broken them down according prep, shoot and wrap to demonstrate how they would be budgeted if they were professionals. When you bring on professionals, you typically hire them for a day during prep to participate in tech scouts. You might also hire them for another day to supervise and participate in checking out gear, and then keep them on for a day after shooting to supervise returns.

If you do intend to hire professionals, be aware that they typically expect their full rate for prep and wrap days, even though prep and wrap days are usually much shorter than twelve hours. But when you hire a professional, you are asking them not to take another job, so you pay them for the day. Again, more on all of this in the next chapter.

As to Loss & Damage, I am allowing more for this than I did in Art because G&E gear is expensive. A single lost sandbag would cost at least $30 to replace.

Total funds assigned to production so far: **$4201**

Account 2700 – Camera

Now we come to the all-important question of what camera and lenses to use. As stated above, I am of the opinion that we often give too much credit to the camera. It's true that in the era of digital filmmaking even student shorts are expected to exhibit a slick look that was not so easily achievable back when students were still shooting 16mm film, and I understand that many schools do not own the most current professional cameras, but that doesn't mean that the cameras your school does own can't get the job done.[8]

The same is true of lenses. Having to shoot, for example, with a zoom lens instead of primes because a zoom lens is all your department can provide, is not going to make or break your film. The very shallow focus that can be achieved with many prime lenses is, I admit, a nice option to have, but shallow focus is also something of a fad. Back when video cameras could not easily provide shallow depth of field, the "film look," as it was called then, became synonymous with shallow focus. And that association has stuck.

I'm not saying to never rent a camera package. Having gear that makes you feel confident can contribute a great deal to your success. But really, when you think about it, what will make your film work is a compelling story with good performances. If you have those, then with the exception of bad sound, which is truly hard to ignore, most shortcomings your film might have will be forgiven (some digital cameras, for example, don't render color as well as other cameras, but if your audience is focused on that, and not your story, then you've already failed).

For this reason, as I will discuss in more detail when we get to the next account, I would prefer that we put funds toward hiring a professional sound mixer, someone who will record excellent production sound for us.

But that is just my preference. We should still figure out what it might cost to rent a camera and lenses and then decide if we can afford it. I'm not going to get into the relative merits of different cameras and lenses. That is beyond the scope of this book. Moreover, I have no desire to be a booster for some products and a critic of others. And, in any case, camera technologies are in constant flux. If you are interested in renting a camera for your production, then do your own research and consult with your cinematography professor and DP. What I will do is use as an example the camera and lens rentals on my most recent short.

On that film we rented an Alexa Mini, a professional camera favored by many of my students. It was a six-day shoot and the DP negotiated a flat, discounted rate of $3200 from a rental house she often does business with. *Orbiting* is only a four-day shoot, but we shouldn't assume that means we can get a lower rate for the same camera. Once we add in our pickup day and drop-off day, the camera will be out for six days, basically a week, during which time it can't be rented to anyone else. So, really, the difference in two days is minimal.

That said, let's assume, for the sake of argument, that our producer is a clever, personable and persuasive person who can indeed negotiate a prorated rental. Since $3200 for six days breaks down to $533/day, that same rate for a four-day shoot is $2132. And because I'm an optimist, I'll also assume an additional 10% student discount, making the total rental cost, for all intents and purposes, $1920.

Now we need lenses. On my film we rented a prime lens package for a flat rate of $800. Again, if prorated, that comes to $532, which I'll round down to $500, again assuming a student discount. In total, that's $2420, which is almost a quarter (roughly 23%) of our total production funds. However, we're going to go with it for now and see how the budget pans out.

Next up is crew. Again, we're not going to pay anyone. This assumes, though, that we have classmates who are familiar with the camera. Still, anything any-body needs to know about most any camera can be found online. Moreover, when the camera crew checks out the camera from the rental house, they can further review all of its features and functionalities with the staff.

Now we need to consider any other gear we might want to rent. My camera came with a standard follow focus and a wireless follow focus, so let's assume that our rental does too. And we can almost certainly get a monitor from school.

But do we want, for example, to rent a Dana Dolly or a doorway dolly or a shoulder rig? Technically, dollies are grip items, but I prefer to include them in the camera budget. In any case, it's likely we can get a doorway dolly from school, but to be safe I'll budget for one and also for a shoulder rig, which could be useful for covering Trevor when he is walking around the store and out on the streets. We need exact quotes and I was able to find a shoulder rig and a doorway dolly both for $20/day.

The last items we need to account for are hard drives and expendables (tape, dry markers, Sharpies, etc.). I'll allow $50 for expendables. As to drives, we'll need two, a primary drive and a backup drive, and two 8TB drives, which will give us more than enough storage space, even if we shoot 4K, shouldn't cost more than $200 each, tax included.

Here, then, are our projected camera costs:

Acct	Description	Amount	Units	X	Rate	Subtotal	Total
2700	**CAMERA**						
2702	Dir. of Photog.						0
2704	1st Assistant Camera						0
2706	2nd AC						0
2708	DIT						0
2710	Alexa Mini	4	Days		480	1920	1920
2712	Lenses		Flat		500	500	500
2714	Shoulder Rig	4	Days		20	80	80
2716	Doorway Dolly	4	Days		20	80	80
2718	Shoot Drives	2	8TB		200	400	400
2720	Expendables		Allow		50	50	50
2722	Loss & Damage		Allow		250	250	250
						Total 2700	**3280**

As to Loss & Damage, it is somewhat standard to allow 5% of rental costs. But my camera and lens rentals totaled $4000 and 5% of that is $200. But in our case, it comes to $121, even though it is the identical gear. So, I'm keeping that at $200 and adding another $50 to cover our other rentals and the gear we check out from school (monitor, sticks, etc.)

Total funds assigned to production so far: **$7481**

Account 2800 – Production Sound

Students in my program receive a great deal of training in how to record production sound and they are required to do so for each other on their first-year films. Our philosophy is that every directing student must acquire a basic level of competence in every major crew position in G&E, Camera and Sound, and that they must as also serve, at least twice, as assistant director. This way, they not only gain an understanding of the challenges specific to those key crew positions, which helps them develop realistic expectations about what is possible during production, but it also enables them to crew for each other during the length of their time in the program. After all, if every student is only a director, then who is the crew?

However, students can gain only so much competence in any crew position, especially during their first year. And this can be a problem when it comes to recording quality sound because the responsibility for doing that is not widely dispersed. A DP, for example, has numerous collaborators, not just in Camera and G&E, but also in Art and Wardrobe, such that no single person is solely responsible for creating quality images. It is a group activity with all the requisite benefits that entails. But in the sound department the onus falls almost exclusively on one person's shoulders, those of the sound mixer, who in many cases will also be their own boom operator, and that is a lot to ask of someone still learning the ropes.

For this reason, many of my students hire a sound mixer on their advanced and thesis films. They consider the money they spend on this to be well worth it and having suffered myself through bad sound on more than one film, I have to agree with them. This is why I suggested above that we should hire a sound mixer. *Orbiting* has a lot of dialogue and if it's not properly recorded it's going to hurt the film. Due to advances in digital sound technologies, a lot can be done these days in post to fix dialogue tracks, but that usually takes time and more time usually means more money and, in the end, only so much can be done to fix flawed production sound.

I'm not suggesting that students are incapable of recording production sound. Some of my students excel at it and continue to serve as sound mixers after their first year. But they can't record sound on every production. If in your program there are students who specialize in sound, both production and post, then you would be smart to work with them (and you may be required to). But let's assume that we don't have access to such students since that is often the case.

Never hire a sound mixer without references. In most cases, this means reaching out to classmates who have already worked with the person you are considering hiring. However, don't talk to classmates who have only just shot; they won't know. Reach out to students with finished films. This is because it can be difficult to say how good or bad your production tracks are until the dialogue edit and final mix are complete. If you're considering hiring a mixer who has not worked with anyone you know, then find out who has had to edit dialogue they've recorded and reach out to those people in confidence. Dialogue editors are in the best position to assess the work of production sound mixers because they have to clean up the tracks they record.

Currently, in Los Angeles, my students can hire a competent sound mixer with their own gear who will also operate the boom for $250/day, though they sometimes pay up to $350/day. I'll split the difference, which looks like this:

Acct	Description	Amount	Units	X	Rate	Subtotal	Total
2800	**PRODUCTION SOUND**						
2802	Sound Mixer w/Gear	4	Days		300	1200	1200
2804	Boom Op						0
2806	Batteries & Expendables		Allow		50	50	50
2802	Loss & Damage		Allow		100	100	100
						Total 2800	**1350**

The number of batteries that sound gear devours during production never ceases to amaze me, plus there are various expendables involved, which include gauze tape and foam covers for the lavaliers, or body mics. So, as with the makeup artist, we are going to replenish the sound mixer's supplies. And since on my last film one of the actors accidentally broke a hinge on the transmitter for their wireless mic, which I had to pay for, I'm including $100 for Loss & Damage.

Total funds assigned to production so far: **$8831**

Account 2900 – Transportation

I remember sitting in a production class not long after I started teaching when a student said to her classmates, "Look, I know I own a truck, but that doesn't mean I bought it to haul all of your gear around. It's getting wrecked." My advice, therefore, is to never ask your classmates to use their own vehicles to transport equipment for your film. Depending on the size of your production, rent a van or truck.

Whatever vehicle we rent for *Orbiting* has to be large enough to accommodate both Art and G&E, though not at the same time. The Art department can have a prep day to pick up at the prop shop and load into the house, and then G&E can have their own pickup day. As to the camera and lenses, since these are expensive, and must be jealously guarded, it is sometimes the case that the DP and 1st AC distribute them between their own vehicles.

But even then, caution is required. Some years ago, one of my students took a set of lenses home between shoot days. She did for this for safety, but rather than bring them into her house she left them in her car overnight. She lived in a gated community with her family, and so felt this would be fine, except in the morning the lenses were gone. And here is the key point: *equipment is not insured against theft while it is in an unattended vehicle.* In the end, the insurance company agreed to cover a portion of the loss, but the difference was extracted from the student and was of such an amount that it took her several years to pay it off in monthly installments.

Never leave gear unattended. Even when you take a lunch break, somebody must stay on set. But this still leaves the problem of where gear will go between shoot days. If on your own film you are going to be at the same location for more than one day, you might be able to lock it in there, but oftentimes G&E gear stays on the truck. On *Orbiting*, the only day we might fully load in is at the store. There will be nowhere to load into when we shoot the street scenes, and the less gear we drag into the house, the less likely we are to damage walls, furniture etc.

However, as I just said, gear left in an unattended vehicle is not insured. One solution to this problem is to pay to park the truck overnight in a lot with round-the-clock security. Such lots exist in Los Angeles and productions use them all the time. As an alternative, my students sometimes back their trucks into the equipment loading zone at school overnight, with the rear door of the container pressed right up against the wall of the building. This way, even if somebody did manage to break the lock, there would be no way for them to get anything out.

Without solving all of these issues right now, let's assume that we are going to use our truck to store and stage equipment. This means that someone, usually a PA, will have to stand fire watch during shooting, which is to say guard the gear. It also means that the truck must be large enough to function as a staging area. If it is packed to the gills, then whenever someone needs to retrieve a piece of equipment, they will struggle to do so. There must be enough room to organize everything for easy access. Since we won't have a ton of gear, a 15-foot truck should do the trick and also be big enough for Art.

Currently, a truck this size can be rented for $29.99/day in Los Angeles. This has been true for a long time. But this rate is subject to sales tax (presently 9.5%), so I'm going to bump it up to $33/day. As to insurance, based on an online search I did, a full damage waiver with no deductible will cost $14/day. Production insurance comes with vehicle coverage, but the deductible is usually high ($700 on my last film), so $14 is a bargain. I also received a quote of .99/mile, but since that is also subject to sales tax, I'll bump it up to $1.10/mile. And because LA is a big place, I'll allow for 200 miles and $50 for gas.

Here, then, are our projected transportation costs:

Acct	Description	Amount	Units	X	Rate	Subtotal	Total
2900	**TRANSPORTATION**						
2902	15' Container Truck						
	Prep	2	Days		33	66	
	Shoot	4	Days		33	132	
	Wrap	2	Days		33	66	264
2904	Damage Waiver	8	Days		14	112	112
2906	Mileage	200	Miles		1.10	220	220
2908	Gas		Allow		50	50	50
						Total 2900	646

As mentioned, allowing two days each for prep and wrap takes care of both Art and G&E, and keeping the truck for the length of the shoot will allow us to make our location changes and to also use it as staging area for gear during shooting. If we were only shooting at one location and planned to load in all of the props and gear for the length of the shoot, we could return the truck during production to save money, but that is not our situation. In terms of your own film, though, that is something to think about.

Total funds assigned to production so far: **$9477**

Account 3000 – Locations & Catering

We're almost out of production funds. We allocated $10,500 to shoot the film, meaning we have about $1000 left. So, we're about to cross our line in the sand. But that's okay. We're going to press ahead. There is no point in making revisions before we have a full picture of the budget, including post costs. But once we have that picture, we're going to have to rethink some of our decisions. This is typical: you begin with your dream version of how you hope to produce a project, then you revise your expectations to achieve what is actually possible.

Locations. I will have more to say about how to find locations in Chapter 8. For now, I will only reiterate that your goal is to write free locations into your script. We have succeeded in doing that for *Orbiting*. We have no location rental fees for the house, the streets or the store. This means we only have location expenses.

Our first location expense is permits. In Los Angeles a permit is required even to shoot in your own home, unless what you are filming is "personal use," which does not cover student filmmaking. Therefore, we need to permit our street locations and the house (the store does not need to be externally permitted since it is managed by the university). We may be able to pull a single permit for both street locations, but since I don't know that yet, I am going to allow for three permits: one for the boulevard, one for the residential street and one for the house. At the current rate, these permits will cost us $26 each.

As to the store, while there is no rental fee, someone will have to monitor the shoot. The store's manager can't simply hand us the keys and walk away. This means we'll have to hire a campus safety officer. But these are students, not police officers, so the rate isn't that high. It will cost us $25/hr. for the first eight hours then time and a half after that. There is likely also a processing fee for this payment, but it will be small so I'm not going to worry about it. I'll cover it by allowing payment for 12 hours even though the safety officer will be off the clock during the lunch break.

Our next location expense is parking. Let's consider the store first. College campuses are notoriously difficult places to park and there is usually a parking fee. When my students shoot on campus, they don't cover each other's parking. They only cover it when they shoot off-campus and paid parking is all that is available. That said, we have at least six extras coming to campus who are not students, plus the production designer, art director, makeup artist, sound mixer and four actors, for a total of 14 people. We will need to either pay for their parking or have PAs drive them to set. Assuming some combination of these two scenarios, I'll allow for 10 parking passes. Currently, these are $12 each for a total of $120.

As to the house, residential permit parking is common in Los Angeles, in which case we would have to buy guest passes for everyone. But for this exercise, let's assume we've already researched this and know that street parking is free. But even if we had to buy passes, we could significantly reduce those costs by having the producer coordinate carpools. In terms of the street locations, as discussed in Chapter 3, these will be near the house, which means we have no parking costs here either.

Next, we need to consider location supplies. If we set up catering and craft services, or crafty, in the backyard at the house, then we may need to rent tables, chairs, canopies (so people can get out of the sun or rain) and coolers (for water, sodas, etc.). We could maybe set up inside the house, but, again, the less we do in there the better. And we will likely need these same supplies at the store since they probably won't allow us to set up lunch inside.

On my last production we spent about $400 on these supplies. Since these types of rentals are typically by the week, it doesn't matter that we have a four-day schedule for *Orbiting*. But I'll assume a student discount and allow $350. Another location supply is walkie talkies. When we are shooting the street scenes, crew and cast will be dispersed between the house and the actual locations, and when we are shooting in the house, crew will be both inside and outside. We may have a similar situation at the store. So, unless we want to waste a lot of time having people run back and forth to communicate information, we need walkies. Currently, the standard rate for a walkie is $10/week and I'm going to suggest we get 15, for a total of $150.

Catering. The minimum compensation you owe anyone who works on your set is meals and a credit. Food is also a great motivator. Feed people well and they will work hard for you. That's why buying a bunch of pizzas or sub sandwiches or fast-food meals won't cut it. You have to do better than that. From time to time one of my students will have a family member cook for their production, and I hear it's usually pretty great. They also sometimes make deals with local restaurants. But most of them hire a professional film caterer and we are going to do the same.

One of the advantages of working with a caterer is that they can provide more than one type of meal each day, and so can accommodate all the various dietary restrictions and requirements of cast and crew. Caterers also just arrive and set up the food. When it's time to eat, everything is ready to go. No wasting time handing out takeout menus on set, or emailing them in advance only to have half of the cast and crew not respond, and nobody has to go pick up the food. Everybody, in other words, stays focused on shooting the film.

Currently, if we hire a caterer, we can expect lunch to cost about $10 per person. In addition to lunch, we also owe our cast and crew breakfast. On professional productions, a cooked breakfast is almost always be available, but we can provide bagels, cereal, Danishes, things like that, and coffee. Experience tells me to allow $3/person for breakfast.

Now we have to count how many meals we need to provide, and we're going to be very precise about it. Let's begin with the cast. We've got eight speaking roles. Trevor works all four days and the father and the store manager both work two days. Everyone else works one day. We know this because we did a script breakdown. That's 14 breakfasts and 14 lunches (based on our shooting schedule, we should be able to wrap the store manager long before lunch on the day we shoot the street scenes, but since I can't count on that, I'm not adjusting for it). Add to that our 12 extras, who only work one day, and we're up to a total of 26. But let's assume that four extras will be crew and set the number at 22. In terms of crew, we can count on the following:

Crew	Days on set
Director	4
Producer	4
Assistant Director	4
Cinematographer	4
Production Designer	4
Art Director	4
Costume PA	4
Gaffer	4
Key Grip	4
Extra G&E (house)	2
1st AC	4
2nd AC/DIT	4
Sound Mixer/Boom Op	4
Script Supervisor	4
Key Set PA	4
Set PA	4
Total	**62**

If we add this to our cast and extras, we get a total of 84 meals, both breakfast and lunch, which I'll just round up to 85. That is all the information we need to budget our food costs and to allow our producer to give the caterer an accurate head count for each shoot day.

However, I'm also going to assign funds for a second meal. Strictly speaking, a second meal is provided when a production goes into overtime. A production must feed its cast and a crew every six hours. Thus, if shooting exceeds 12 hours, a second meal is provided. But overtime is not an option on student films, or it should not be. That said, it is always a nice gesture on the last day of a production to bring in food after final wrap. And that is what I am calling a second meal. Sometimes this is pizza, but since we'll be wrapping out the store in the early morning, breakfast sandwiches and coffee would be better. I'll allow $100 for this.

Finally, we have to deal with crafty. This is comprised of snacks – fruit, chips, nutrition bars, water, sodas etc. – that cast and crew can rely on to keep them going during a shoot day. Between breakfast and lunch is six hours, and from the end of lunch to the end of wrap is typically five hours, so providing snacks to give people energy is essential. Experience tells me to assign between $50 and $75 a day for this. I'll roughly split the difference and assign $65/day.

Here then is our location and catering budget:

Acct	Description	Amount	Units	X	Rate	Subtotal	Total
3000	**LOCATIONS & CATERING**						
3002	Site Rentals						
	Trevor's House					0	
	Streets					0	
	Store - UCLA					0	0
3004	Safety Officer						
	Regular	8	Hours		25	200	
	Over-Time	4	Hours		37.50	150	350
3006	Parking – Store	10	Passes		12	120	120
3008	Shooting Permits	3	Permits		26	78	78
3010	Police (traffic control)						0
3012	Gas – location scouting		Allow		25	25	25
3014	Location Supplies						
	Tables, Chairs, etc.		Allow		350	350	
	Walkies	15	Walkies		10	150	500
3016	Catering						
	Breakfast	85	Meals		3	255	
	Lunch	85	Meals		10	850	
	Second Meals		Allow		100	100	1,205
3018	Craft Service Supplies	4	Days		65	260	260
3020	Loss & Damage		Allow		200	200	200
						Total 3000	**2,738**

Since our goal is not to cause damage at the house or the store, which is why we are not loading in all the gear at the house and will be eating outside at both locations, I'm only allowing $200 for Loss & Damage. Even that may seem excessive to you, but if we were to, say, gouge a wall at the house, it would cost at least that much to repair. Production insurance covers damage at locations but, again, the deductible is high. As to gas costs for location scouting, we don't have much scouting to do, but assigning funds for this is standard, so I'm allowing $25.

Finally, I included a line item for police supervision just to remind you that this can sometimes be necessary when shooting exteriors. When we shoot the street scenes, we'll need to keep the camera on the sidewalk. To put a camera off the curb in Los Angeles requires hiring sheriffs or police officers or traffic officers to control traffic and also paying a rental fee for the official vehicles they use. But we're not doing that, thus we have none of those expenses.

Total funds assigned to production so far: **$12,215**

Account 3500 – General Production Expenses

These are orphan expenses not so easily included in other accounts. Sometimes line producers put general expenses at the top of their below-the-line budgets. I like to put them at the end. This is the storyteller in me: a way to provide closure by wrapping up all the loose ends.

Our first general expense is production insurance. Your department should provide this, but almost certainly not for free (though I'm sure there are exceptions). The cost of insurance is directly related to what is being covered. These are called tiers. For example, in my program, tier 1 insurance covers losses up to $250,000 and tier 2 covers losses up to $750,000. Choosing one or the other tier typically depends on what gear you are using and also on how much liability each location owner expects you to carry. For *Orbiting*, tier 1 will suffice and it is currently available to students in my department for a flat rate of $380.

A second form of insurance that can be required is workers' compensation, which covers injuries sustained on a job. If your production is SAG signatory, you must provide workers' compensation coverage for the actors, as any production company or employer must do. For many years my students had to purchase a separate policy for this, but now it is included in both tiers offered by the department, and it covers everyone on the crew as well. The situation may be different at your school, so be certain about what your department's insurance actually covers.

Other general expenses include copying, printing and office supplies. We'll largely go paperless, though we'll print "sides," which are the scenes actors read at auditions. But that is a minimal expense and, in any case, my students are able to print them at school for free. So, we won't include any printing costs. But as a director, I still use a binder on set for my script, shot lists, floor plans, storyboards and script analysis. Also, the producer and AD often need binders for location agreements, permits, SAG paperwork, etc. We can recycle binders from previous productions but I like to archive the binders from my films. I'll therefor allow $30 for office supplies. It's a small amount, but it's still part of the cost of making the film.

Next, we need to consider meal costs during preproduction that we haven't already accounted for. Again, I'm going to cover tech scouts in Chapter 10, but when we tech scout all of our locations with the producer, DP, AD etc., our goal will be to do this together as a group on a single day. If we go out to the house first, then visit the street locations, then head over to the store, that's four or five hours at least, so we may buy everyone a meal. These kinds of stray food costs add up. If, for example, you meet at a café with an actor to discuss their character, and if you buy them a cup of coffee, that's money you are spending on your movie. So, I'm going to allow an additional $100 for meals during prep.

There may also be stray parking costs during preproduction. As will be discussed in Chapter 9 on casting, you might cover an actor's parking if you call them back for a second audition. And if you have to tech scout a location that only has paid parking, then you need to account for that. This might seem like nitpicking, but if you ignore all the small costs, they add up anyway, and then you find yourself over budget. For this reason, I'm going to include $25 for pre-production parking costs just to be safe.

Next up is first aid supplies for the set. These are an absolute requirement and it must be a well-stocked kit with various meds, from pain relievers to allergy pills, as well as burn gel, bandages, splints etc. I'll assign $50 for this. We should also assign funds for crew perks and adjustments, just as we did for the cast, since some of the same issues may arise. I'll allow $100 for that.

Finally, let's account for casting costs. These are a below-the-line expenses because casting directors are below-the-line personnel. This is why I did not include them in our Cast account. At minimum, we will have bottled water available for all the actors who come in to read for us. And since our producer will be at all of our casting sessions, as well as another classmate to read with all the actors (more on this in Chapter 9), we might provide some crafty for them as well. I'll assign $50 for all of this, which is more than enough.

This leaves the question of whether or not we will hire a casting director. I will leave off discussion of that until Chapter 9, and only say here that a casting director in Los Angeles can easily cost $1000, which we don't have available and will never have available, no matter how much we tweak the budget. So, it's off the table.

Our projected general expenses, then, are as follows:

Acct	Description	Amount	Units	X	Rate	Subtotal	Total
3500	**GENERAL EXPENSES**						
3502	Insurance		Flat		380	380	380
3504	Copying/Printing						0
3506	Office Supplies		Allow		30	30	30
3508	Parking – Prep		Allow		25	25	25
3510	Meals – Prep		Allow		100	100	100

Acct	Description	Amount	Units	X	Rate	Subtotal	Total
3500	**GENERAL EXPENSES Cont'd**						
3512	First Aid Supplies		Allow		50	50	50
3514	Perks & Adjustments		Allow		100	100	100
3516	Casting						
	Casting Director					0	
	Water, crafty etc.		Allow		50	50	50
						Total 3500	**735**

This wraps up the production portion of our budget.

Total funds assigned to production: **$12,950**

We are $2450 over budget. But as I've said, we're going to finish before we start revising.

II Postproduction Costs

Account 5000 – Editorial

Again, to save money in post, enroll in the relevant courses and do as much of the work yourself as possible. Thus, we're not going to bring on an editor. As to what software we will edit with, we should have access to it for free. My school has licensing agreements for multiple platforms, so we have no costs here either.[9]

The only things that might cost money, then, are titles and an additional hard drive. We likely won't need an additional drive, but drives do sometimes get dropped or even stolen, so I'm going to allow $200 for a replacement, just to be safe. As to titles, I paid for these on a recent film I made, but then on my next film I taught myself how to make them in Photoshop. You can certainly do the same on your film. We therefore have no costs here either.

Our projected editorial costs, therefore, are minimal:

Acct	Description	Amount	Units	X	Rate	Subtotal	Total
5000	**EDITORIAL**						
5002	Editor						0
5004	Additional Drive		Allow		200	200	200
5006	Titles						0
5008	Editorial Meals						0
						Total 5000	**200**

I included a line item for meals just to point out that if someone were editing for us for free, we might sometimes feed them. The way you work with an editor is by getting into the editing room with them and cutting the film. You don't just hand over the footage. So, if we were on campus several days a week cutting with someone, and if they were not getting paid, and if they were also not receiving course credit, we might occasionally buy them lunch.

Total funds assigned to postproduction so far: **$200**

Account 5100 – Score and Music Rights

Score. Unless you intend to compose your own score, which some filmmakers do, don't expect to get it for free, even if you team up with a student composer from your school's music department. Composers always have expenses, for example hiring and recording musicians, which may also require hiring a sound engineer, and possibly even renting a recording studio (though your school may have one). But even when a composer creates a digital score (as would likely be the case on *Orbiting*), they may need to purchase samples they don't already have in their library.

My advice is to negotiate a flat rate with a composer that covers their time and expenses. For my students, this is typically around $1000, and I'm going to budget that amount. This may seem like a lot but, as I will discuss below, we're going to ask our composer for more than just score. Moreover, as I will discuss in the Afterword, scores are often reworked several times or more, which means that composers typically put in a great deal of time and effort, even on short films. It is not the case that a film score is simply composed, recorded and delivered.

Music Rights. While you are editing your film, you can put any music in it you want to. People add score from other movies, pop songs, classical music, etc. But when it comes to the finished film, you can't do that anymore. Let's say you want to use a popular song by a popular artist in your finished film. You can't do that without paying for the right to do so. And you can't get around this by having a musician friend rerecord the song. It's true that this would save you the cost of paying to use the original artist's recording, but you would still have to pay for the publishing rights.

You have probably heard of what are called festival rights. These allow filmmakers to include songs in their films for festival screenings (and other public screenings that don't generate revenue). But for a song with only minimal recognition, such rights could easily cost $1500 and the price only goes up from there. In short, even festival rights are often beyond the means of most student filmmakers. Festival rights, which are a down payment on purchasing full rights, exist so that feature filmmakers who are going to festivals in search of a distribution deal can screen their movie with songs in it. But if the film gets distribution, the remainder of those rights fees must be paid.

Luckily, there is no place in *Orbiting* where playing a song seems appropriate, but we will almost certainly want music playing on the loudspeakers in the store. However, our composer can come up with a generic bit of muzak for that. They could compose something ironic and fun that contributes to the absurdity of Trevor's situation.

Something else we can have our composer create is sci-fi music. The script says that Trevor is watching an *X-Files* rerun on TV. We can try to get the rights to use some footage from that show, but I'm not hopeful. What would be easier is to never show the TV but with music and sound effects suggest that Trevor is watching a sci-fi program. If we add a flickering blue light on his face while he's looking towards the TV, that should do the trick.

Here then are our music costs:

Acct	Description	Amount	Units	X	Rate	Subtotal	Total
5100	**SCORE & MUSIC RIGHTS**						
5102	Composer		Flat		1,000	1,000	1,000
5104	Music Rights						0
						Total 5100	**1000**

Total funds assigned to postproduction so far: **$1200**

Account 5200 – Postproduction Sound

This account covers dialogue editing, ADR (automated dialogue replacement), foley, sound effects, or SFX editing, music editing and the final mix. Hopefully your school has the software, facilities and classes to allow you to handle these tasks on your own. That said, my students sometimes hire people to help them with post sound. By the time they've locked picture and are ready to complete sound, they often just want to finish. So, they bring on help.

On my last short I negotiated a deal with a post sound house to handle everything for $4000. But we can't afford that. What my students usually do is hire other students, or recently graduated students, who want to earn extra money and/or hone their skills. Let's anticipate doing the same. Since I once cut all the sound on a low-budget feature, I know what's involved. My estimate is that someone reasonably adept at dialogue editing and ADR could complete that work in about 30 hours. *Orbiting* is only a seven-page script, and while some scenes have a lot of dialogue, other scenes have little to no dialogue.

As to SFX editing and foley, there is probably more work to be done on these since every scene will ultimately include one or both of these elements. Thus, I will allow 40 hours for this. The person we hire will require the help of a foley artist, which is someone who creates sound effects in real time as they watch a film on a monitor in a foley stage, but since we used to do all our own foley when I was in school, I'm confident that one of us can fill that position for free.

We'll allow $20/hr. for both the dialogue editor and the SFX editor. I think that's the minimum we can get away with. But the advantage of hiring two people is that they can hopefully work simultaneously and in collaboration with each other.

As to the final sound mix, my department covers this for students. This was true when I was in school too. I'm therefore going to assume that it's true in most departments, especially those that have a mixer on staff or where students can specialize in sound and may mix films for course credit. Thus, I'm not going to assign any funds for the mix

Here, then, are our projected post sound costs:

Acct	Description	Amount	Units	X	Rate	Subtotal	Total
5200	**POSTPRODUCTION SOUND**						
5202	Dialogue & ADR	30	Hours		20	600	600
5204	Foley & SFX	40	Hours		20	800	800
5206	Foley artist						0
5208	Mix – school						0
						Total 5200	**1400**

If we do record ADR, which is when actors rerecord lines that were badly recorded on set, or record new or revised lines of dialogue that can be played off-screen, we shouldn't have to pay them, even if our production is SAG signatory, because the student agreement allows for a certain amount of ADR, again with deferred salaries.

Total funds assigned to postproduction so far: **$2600**

Account 5400 – Color and DCP

Color. In the age of digital filmmaking, colorists have become incredibly important. Sometimes as important as the DP. This is because the ways that they can manipulate images greatly exceeds what was possible in analog filmmaking when color timers, as they were called, could basically only alter exposure and the relative intensities of three colors: red, green and blue.

This means that you should not underestimate the advantages of working with an experienced colorist. I did so on my last short, which has a 14-minute runtime, and it cost me $1200. I might have been able to do it for less, but I wanted to mimic the look of Kodachrome to give the film a vintage feel and initially, at least, this required some experimentation. But even assuming I could have colored that film for less money, say $1000, that is still more than we can afford on *Orbiting* since we're already over budget.

However, cinematography students in my program are required to learn the basics of color grading and they often handle final color on the films they shoot. Probably there are students in your program with similar skills. So, we need not work with a professional. If our DP can grade the film, they will. And presumably they will do so for free because footage from it will eventually appear on their reel. Because of this, making the film look good is as much to their advantage as ours.

Still, it would be a mistake not to include some funding for color. Our DP may not be available when we are finishing the film, in which case we would have to work with another student who, since they didn't shoot the film, might expect compensation. As a rule, I generally do not consider it appropriate for students to charge each other for work, but in this instance, as with sound editing, we would be receiving a service we probably couldn't repay with reciprocal labor. So, I'll assign $500 for color.

DCP. A digital cinema package, or DCP, contains all the final image and audio files for your film in a format that can, among other things, be read by digital projection systems. With your student short, you only need a DCP if it is going to screen in a festival that requires one. Some festivals even dictate which companies can create a DCP for the films they screen. Currently, these cost about $100, which I am going to budget for, but with the understanding that we may not need one. But it is always best to assign funds for this, just in case.

Here are our projected finishing costs:

Acct	Description	Amount	Units	X	Rate	Subtotal	Total
5400	**COLOR & DCP**						
5402	Color		Allow		500	500	500
5404	DCP		Allow		100	100	100
						Total 5400	**600**

This completes our postproduction budget.

Total funds assigned to postproduction: **$3200**

This amount is about 21% of our total funding, which means it is right on target. As I said, we should expect to assign 20–25% of our funds to postproduction. So, it is our production costs that need to be tweaked. Before we do that, though, here is where we stand:

Total Production and Postproduction	**16,150**
Contingency (10%)	**1615**
Grand Total	**17,765**

We are $2765 over budget. Note that our overages in production are driving up our contingency as well. A contingency, again, is 10% of total production and postproduction costs, so every overage equals the amount of that overage plus 10%.

We could lower our contingency, but that is bad practice. On a professional production, we would not be permitted to lower it. This is because 10% is the bare minimum that bond companies require. A completion bond is a form of insurance. If a production goes hopelessly over budget, the bond company, also known as a completion guarantor, steps in to ensure that the film gets finished. In our case, since we have no guarantor, our contingency is our only insurance against disaster.

Moreover, we may decide during editing that we need to shoot pickups and part or all of our contingency might be used for that. We are therefore leaving our contingency alone. And we're leaving our postproduction expenses alone too. We began with percentages so that we would have broad criteria for making decisions and our projected post costs are already at the low end. Even if we did cut expenses in post, say the salaries for our dialogue and sound effects editors, we would still keep those funds in post. We could use them to work with a professional colorist, or give them to the composer to hire musicians, or use them to apply to film festivals. It is in our production budget where we must look for cuts.

III Revisiting Production Costs

Given that we are $2765 over budget, we need to revisit big-ticket items. Going back and nickel and diming every account in production won't be to our advantage. In the first place, doing that probably wouldn't get us to our goal. In the second place, it would likely create a situation where we have no wiggle room in a number of accounts. As I've said, if you only assign the bare minimum of funds to every account, you're going to come up short when you start spending money.

The question, then, is which big-ticket items should we revisit? The most obvious place to start is with our camera and lens rentals. We could also reconsider hiring a production sound mixer, but as I tried to explain, I think that is a worthwhile expense and, in any case, cutting the sound mixer's salary won't get us to our target. It's only $1200. Still, if we did that, it would bring our grand total down to **$16,445**, and for the sake of keeping our camera and lens rentals we could agree to that amount. It likely wouldn't be impossible to find the extra funds.

The problem, though, is that once you intentionally go over budget on one item, you are likely to keep doing it. The production designer or costumer or DP proposes one more thing that they absolutely need and you say yes. And you always say yes for the same reason: out of fear that your film won't be as good as it could be if you don't give them what they want. Besides, what's another $50 here, $100 there and $200 somewhere else when you're already over budget?

But that is a vicious circle. Ideally, yes, your collaborators should have everything they want and more, but you can give them the moon and that by itself won't make your movie great. Plus, focusing only on making a great movie misses the point. You want to make the best film you can, but the primary reason you are making a film is to learn how to be a filmmaker. If you get too wrapped up in demonstrating what a great director you are, then every misstep becomes crushing and rather than learning from those mistakes, you only beat yourself up about them.

It's simply not the case that we need to rent a camera and lenses to make a good film. So, let's put the funds for a sound mixer back into the budget and look at what it would mean to cut our camera and lens rentals instead. If we cut those, we save $2420. We also reduce our contingency by $242, for a total reduction of $2662. Here is what that looks like:

Total Production and Postproduction	13,730
Contingency (10%)	1373
Grand Total	15,103

Essentially, this brings us in on budget, especially since I'd now be willing to reduce Loss & Damage in Camera by $50, which gives us a grand total of **$15,048**. This means that cutting the camera and lens rentals is the right thing to do. Now, if you find even this final amount scary, then go back and reread the first three chapters about how to keep your production simple and inexpensive.

You can find the final budget for *Orbiting* in Appendix III. It is also available as a spreadsheet in the online resources for this book. But as I hope this chapter has made clear, a budget is a blueprint, a step-by-step guide to making a film. It is comprised of dozens of creative choices that in every case are linked to the intelligent distribution of funds. Again, the practical and the creative are one and the same thing.

Good luck budgeting your own film!

Notes

1 Big budget studio features are often an exception to this rule, but even then, there are limits on how far over budget a studio will go on a project.
2 "In the can" refers to raw, or unexposed, film stock, which is shipped in cannisters or cans. Once a roll of film is exposed it is returned to a can for delivery to a lab for processing. Hence the idea that shooting your film once meant (and in some cases still means) getting it in the can.
3 Typically, a contingency is 10% of the combined production and postproduction costs, in this case $13,500. If we calculate 10% of that it comes to $1350, not $1500. If our funding were significantly higher, my math would have to be more precise, but in this case the difference is minimal and my simpler method works well enough.
4 A film has to bring in revenue before deferred salaries are paid. For this reason, they are almost never paid on student films because there is a limited (almost non-existent) market for them. The goal is to go to film festivals. Not because festivals are career changing – in most cases they are not – but because it is fun to show your movie to audiences beyond your classmates, instructors, friends and family. A full explanation of the student agreement can be found on SAG's website. You may also be able to use the micro-budget short agreement, which is simpler.

5 Trevor's upfront salary is not taxable. But any salary totaling $600 or more, whether it is paid to a cast member or crew member, is taxable and we would need to issue that person a form 1099-MISC. The IRS provides directions for how to do this on its website.

6 In California, a studio teacher is required for minors even if those minors and the entire cast are nonunion actors. It is a state law, not simply a union rule, and a parent or guardian cannot stand in for a licensed studio teacher, except on weekends, and, even then, only if the minor is at least 16 years old. Please be aware of the laws in your state and/or city and follow them to the letter. It is illegal not to do so.

7 Distant locations present certain problems in terms of travel time for cast and crew during production, and we had to shorten our shoot day in Palmdale to accommodate this. Travel time is discussed in Chapter 8.

8 You can also research camera grants. For example, both Panavision and Arris currently offer these, but the selection process for both is highly competitive.

9 If you don't have access to free editing software, there are discounted subscription plans for students.

7   Find Crew

Once preproduction commences in earnest – typically five to six weeks before you go into production – it is time to start recruiting crew if you haven't begun that process already. Even if your crew is assigned as part of a class, you will almost certainly need additional crew members, as discussed below.

In the case of key collaborators, you should pursue them well in advance of prep. My students often lock in their producer and DP months before they go into production. If they don't, they risk losing them to other productions. Given the amount of prep time required of producers and DPs, they can only work on so many projects (again, the role of the producer is elaborated on in Chapters 8 through 10 while the role of the DP is covered in Chapters 10 and 12.

At the same time, if you are sharing your producer and/or DP with other directing students, work with those students to ensure that everyone gets equal attention from them. The best way to guarantee that, assuming shoot dates are not assigned, is to spread out your production dates so that ample prep time – at least three weeks – is provided between each shoot.

Key Collaborators

For our purposes, these are the producer, DP, PD and costumer though, as discussed in the previous chapter, if your film has complex VFX, you may need a VFX Supervisor and if your film has special makeup requirements, you may need prep time with the makeup artist.

Producer. To reiterate, this should be someone who is adept at planning and organizing, has a fondness for haggling, and is creatively attuned to your project. You want someone who can not only pull permits and schedule catering, but also weigh in on script revisions and casting. The best producers, therefore, are oftentimes advanced students who have already written and directed their own film(s) because they know exactly what it takes, both logistically and creatively, to get a film shot. My directing students often produce for each other.

At the same time, you probably have classmates who are primarily interested in producing and not directing – there may even be a producing track in your department – and, if so, you should consider those people as well. My one

DOI: 10.4324/9781003169864-7

caveat is that a student producer must have some production experience or they won't really be able to help you. They may even make expensive mistakes. This happened to me once as a student when my producer, a neophyte, pulled the wrong permit and our production got shut down. Mistakes, of course, are how we learn, but if someone is green, then no matter how eager they are to produce for you, my advice is to bring them on as a second producer to work under someone with more experience.

Director of Photography. If you have not been assigned a DP, then you will need to find one, unless you have already chosen somebody, either because you've worked with them before or because you know their work well and want to collaborate with them. If you need to find a DP, the best approach is to hold interviews, though I might call these meet and greets and not interviews, since you are almost certainly not paying a salary (I am always a bit dismayed when I hear a film student talk about hiring or, worse, firing someone whom they don't and never will have an employer–employee relationship with: a film school is a community and you are all in it together).

In terms of finding potential DPs to meet with, whether or not your department has a cinematography track, you almost certainly have classmates who are focused on shooting films, who take all the cinematography and lighting classes, and who are dedicated to learning the craft. These are the students to focus on.

When you meet with a potential DP, they should provide you with a link to their reel in advance. Even if someone hasn't shot any films yet, they should still have a reel comprised of creative exercises completed in their cinematography classes, and those can actually tell you a lot about someone's aesthetic and abilities. Undergraduates in my department often opt to work with first-time DPs because they want to collaborate with someone they know well and have been friends with since entering the major. This is important. One of your goals in film school should be to build lasting creative and personal relationships with people who will be your collaborators, and you theirs, for years to come.

Something else you might consider is organizing a showcase, as we do in my department, at which all the cinematography students screen their reels. We schedule this near the start of every school year and most of the directing students attend. It is a very productive and worthwhile event because once all the reels have screened, the directing students get to mingle and chat with the cinematography students whose work they found most interesting. Still, formal meetings usually follow these informal discussions.

The goal when you meet with a potential DP is to gauge what they could creatively contribute to your project. For this reason, you must let them read your script in advance. That way, they can arrive to the meeting with specific ideas about how they see your project. However, this is a two-way street and you must be ready to share your own ideas as well. No one is going to want to shoot for a director who has no vision for their project. Therefore, I advise you to complete your look book before you start these meetings. You don't have to show it to anyone yet, but you should be prepared to have informed creative discussions about your project.

Finally, as discussed above, avoid picking a DP who has several or more projects on their plate unless you are certain that they will be able to give you ample prep time, and that they will be able to do so in a productive and even safe way. On a film I made, the DP was slated to shoot another film soon after we wrapped. Since our final week was night shoots, the other film began bringing him in during the day for production meetings, creative meetings, tech scouts, etc. We weren't initially aware of this, but when the DP began taking naps during lighting, and when the producer of the other project began showing up on our set to talk with him, we figured it out and got him a driver because it simply wasn't safe for him to be behind the wheel of a car. It was all very stupid and I implore you not to create a similar situation on your own project.

Production Designer and Costumer. In my experience, these roles are rarely assigned, but if your school has design and costume programs, perhaps in the Theater Department, as is the case where I teach, then hopefully collaborations are not only being encouraged, but actively facilitated. Again, organizing a get together is an efficient way to begin. Select a time and place, then all the design and costume students can show up with their portfolios and all the directing students can show up with their look books and pitch their scripts.

If, on the other hand, there aren't design and costume programs at your school, it still shouldn't be difficult to find PDs and costumers to meet with. Certainly, students who have already shot films can make recommendations. In my program, as I've mentioned, the advanced graduate students compile contact lists of reliable and talented costumers, production designers, makeup artists, etc. Hopefully something like that is done at your school. And, again, there are online resources for finding crew.

Meeting with potential PDs and costumers is similar to meeting with potential DPs: you want to find out how they would creatively approach your project which means, once again, that you have to let them read your script in advance. I mentioned in Chapter 5 that PDs and costumers might even arrive to these meetings with a mood board or pitch deck that illustrates how they see your story and its characters. If anyone does that, and if you like what they've come up with, then move them to the top of the list. At minimum, though, each candidate should walk you through their portfolio. Even student PDs and costumers with no film experience should be able to do that because, like student DPs, they will have completed creative projects in their classes. This is, again, a two-way street and you must share your own ideas as well.

In sum, think of all these meetings – with potential DPs, PDs and costumers – as creative discussions and not as an opportunity for you to grill candidates about their qualifications. The other benefit of handling meetings in this way, is that once you choose people for these roles, you've already had a first creative meeting with them.

Budget. As mentioned in Chapter 2, and expanded upon in the previous chapter, you need to discuss budget with potential key collaborators. Don't bring anyone on to your project who can't work within your means. At the same time, don't have unrealistic expectations about what others can pull off on a tight budget. Still, most people you meet with will likely have at least a few money-saving ideas of their own.

Crewing-Up

I talked a great deal about crew in the previous chapter and will have more to say on the subject in Chapters 10 and 12. The issue now is recruiting crew. Again, a film school should function as an exchange economy: your classmates provide labor on your production – as grips, electricians, camera assistants, etc. – in exchange for your labor on their productions. This not only makes production possible; it also, as I've said, builds community.

The Ask. You, your producer and your DP, who may want specific people for their camera and G&E crews because they have well-established and productive working relationships with them, must formally reach out to other students.[1] You should do this in person when possible, though email is fine too. Keep in mind, however, that this can be difficult if you don't yet know your shoot dates. When shoot dates are assigned, there is no problem, but when they are not, don't drag your feet on picking dates, or other productions may gobble up most of the available crew. This is true even if the production dates you ultimately choose don't conflict with anyone else's. Students can only crew on so many films, so don't expect people to be available even if no one is crewing on another production at the same time as yours.

Also, don't forget that even when crews are assigned (usually along with production dates), you will likely still need to recruit additional people: PAs, extra grips and electricians, a script supervisor, etc. So, no matter what the situation is, it is always best to begin crewing up as soon as possible to avoid coming up short or having to hire outside crew, which has happened to some of my students because too many of them chose production dates that overlapped.

Crew Positions. In the previous chapter, I laid out the basic crew positions for a student film. Here they are again:

Assistant Director
1st Assistant Camera
2nd Assistant Camera
DIT
Gaffer
Key Grip
Additional Grips and Electricians
Production Sound Mixer

Boom Operator
Script Supervisor
Makeup Artist
Production Assistants or PAs

With the exception of makeup, my assumption, once again, is that you and your classmates are receiving basic instruction in all of these positions as part of craft classes dedicated to camera, lighting, coverage, sound, etc. I also assume that you and your classmates are crewing on the projects of more advanced students in order to hone the skills you are developing in those classes. Ideally, your department requires an introductory production course in which small, low-stakes projects are made with everyone rotating through all the primary crew positions. Crewing is mostly learned through hands-on experience.

In terms of the AD, if you have not been assigned one, there is really no need to meet with people. I've found that certain students simply gain a reputation for being good ADs, and those are the students to reach out to. A good AD is someone who is organized, has leadership skills since they will be running the set, respects safety and will enforce it, and understands the structure of production. If you have been assigned an AD and they will be learning as they go, as you will be learning as you go, then refer to Chapters 10 and 12. The former covers the AD's role during prep and the latter covers their role during production.[2]

As to camera and G&E, my assumption, again, is that unless your crew is assigned, then your DP is handpicking people. If they are not, my advice, at least in terms of the 1st AC, gaffer and key grip, is to reach out to advanced students who have more experience. Presumably, some of them owe you because you have already crewed for them. You can also, as I said in the previous chapter, hire professionals, but my hope is that your project is not so big and complex as to require that. Student film crews should, as much as possible, be comprised of students so that everyone has opportunities to learn and develop skills.

Still, if you truly do have difficult shoot days with many camera and lighting setups, then professionals, most of whom are marvels of efficiency and possess skill sets well beyond those of students, would likely get you through them. But professionals are expensive. For this reason, you might first try reaching out to alums, some of whom may be willing to negotiate their rate. Alternatively, if you can find professionals who are between jobs and who are also seeking to move up the ranks, then there may as well be room to negotiate. If someone has, for example, been working steadily as a grip or electrician, and if they feel they are ready to make the transition to key grip or gaffer, then offering them that role and credit may have value for them. In that case, you might be able to hire someone at half their usual rate. At the same time, there is always the risk when you low ball a professional that they may bail at the last minute if they get offered a job at their regular rate, so be careful.

Concerning additional grips and electricians, these can often be treated as hybrid positions and anyone who has received hands-on classroom training in lighting is qualified. In most cases, you will only need one or two people to fill these roles and, in the case of day exteriors, the gaffer and key grip may not even require extra help. As this implies, you won't always need to recruit additional grips and electricians for the length of your shoot. You may only need them on certain days. In the previous chapter, I suggested that for *Orbiting* we might only bring on an extra person in G&E for the two days at the house due to all the lighting. And even when you do need additional grips and electricians each day, it is not the case that these have to be the same people day-in, day-out. This kind of flexibility makes it easier to fill these positions.

In terms of DIT, or digital imaging technician, who is responsible for, among other things, properly offloading camera cards and backing up all the relevant data, that position can be combined with 2nd AC, though that is not optimal because it may force the person to periodically abandon one set of duties for the other. However, my students do sometimes combine these roles because of how difficult it can be sometimes to get crew. On my last short, I had two producers and during production one of them served as DIT because she was quite experienced in that position. If someone is going to be editing your film, you can ask them to serve as DIT during production. They can even make dailies, synch sound and start editing while you are still shooting, which can be incredibly helpful if they realize that you need to pick up another shot.

As all this suggests, combining positions when you can makes recruiting crew easier. The sound mixer, for instance, can be their own boom operator, especially if they are an experienced professional. And in the case of the script supervisor, if you don't have one, many of their typical duties can be disbursed among various other crew members, which I discuss in Chapter 12. Still, I encourage you to have a script supervisor. Since the rules of continuity should be part of your basic training at school, almost any classmate can fill this role. However, I advise some research, especially if your department does not provide formal training in this position. There are a number of excellent books on the subject, including *Script Supervising and Film Continuity* by Pat P. Miller (Focal Press, 1999).[3]

As to PAs, these can, as previously mentioned, be friends and family, but they can also be students who have less experience. In my department, undergraduates, especially freshman and sophomores, work as PAs on the productions of graduate students and seniors in order to gain set experience (by the time they are juniors they are usually ready to work on camera and G&E crews). Having one or two PAs each day during production to run errands, pickup crafty, drive people to set, help set up food etc., is a must, but it can also be helpful to have a PA during the final few weeks of prep to assist the producer. You may also need PAs in Art and Wardrobe.

Crew Size

Don't recruit more crew than you need. In the first place, since you have to feed everybody, that can get expensive. In the second place, every person you bring on potentially means one more production you now have to crew on. If your DP is recruiting specific people for camera and G&E, then, ideally, they owe those people, but in the end, it is your film they will be crewing on and so you will likely have to repay at least some of that labor if you haven't already crewed for those people in the past. Third, when you recruit too many people, you make it difficult for your classmates to find crew. Finally, when a crew is too big, it's often the case that people don't have enough to do, which can lead to a certain amount of chaos. When people are idle, that's when they start chatting, getting on their phones and laptops and disappearing at exactly the moment when the AD or DP finally does need them to do something.

In sum, keep your crew as lean as possible. In fact, if you have truly designed your production to be small and contained, you can likely get by with very few people. I crewed on a low-budget feature in graduate school and not counting the three actors, who rarely all had scenes together, there were never more than five crew members on set: DP, AC, gaffer/grip, sound mixer/boom op and, of course, the director, who served as their own AD, which was possible because there were not too many moving parts. Lighting was simple, coverage was kept to a bare minimum for aesthetic reasons, the story required little production design and the actors provided their own wardrobe. This was many years ago, and we were shooting film which is, in fact, simpler than shooting digital, but a contemporary director who built their career making small narrative films with small crews is Chloé Zhao. You might take some time to research how she did this.

Locking Crew

Be sure to get firm commitments. Your producer should communicate your production dates in writing in an email, including any prep and wrap days, and they should politely insist that people acknowledge those dates in a written response. Also, the goal is to lock in people who can and will work full shoot days. Even though some crew won't work every day, when people do crew, they should be there from call through wrap. Having, say, one gaffer in the morning and a different gaffer in the afternoon is inefficient because shooting time may be lost while the second gaffer gets up to speed. The one exception to this is PAs. They often come and go because of other obligations: class, work, etc. That's fine; the producer simply needs to ensure that there will always be one or two PAs on set at any given time.

Crew Structure

This will become clearer once you read Chapter 12 on set procedures, but a film crew is a hierarchy, with the director at the top. However, it is really the AD and DP who run the set. The former is in charge of how work is organized and the latter is in charge of every camera and lighting setup. Everybody else, including the producer, works in support of the AD and DP's efforts, which are in support of the director's efforts. Keep this in mind as you recruit crew. You are in every case looking for people who are good team players. There is little room for egos (including your own as director) on a film set. It is all about working together to get a film shot. But everyone must be willing and able to defer to the authority of the director–AD–DP triad.

Notes

1 The PD will likely also assemble their own crew, the costumer too (if they need help), but be prepared to recruit PAs for them as well.
2 Sometimes my students bring on a 2nd AD, but unless you have a large cast or many extras to wrangle, then the AD can rely on a PA to assist them when needed. It is not necessary for student productions to exactly mimic professional productions because when they do that, certain problem can arise, as I discuss in the section on crew size.
3 What you primarily lose when you don't have a script supervisor are the detailed notes they provide on each take and the marked-up script they create which graphically shows what action and/or dialogue each shot taken on set covers. While this information is indispensable to feature editors, it is less important on short films because the number of scenes, shots and takes you shoot will be but a tiny fraction of what a feature editor has to deal with. Of course, there are people who will disagree with me on this, so talk to your instructor.

8 Find Places to Shoot

As discussed in the first chapter, you should try to include locations in your story that you know you have access to for free or that you can reasonably expect to rent and/or permit for not much money. This does not mean that you need to write for specific locations – your apartment, your parent's house, your friend's art studio – though doing that would obviously be to your advantage. But you do need to keep in mind that certain types of locations are more easily and inexpensively secured than others.

If, for example, you include an office scene in your script, chances are you can find an office to shoot in for free somewhere on your campus. I have a number of times allowed students to shoot in my office. But if you include a bar scene in your script, that will be harder to find and may cost a lot of money, unless, of course, you know someone who owns a bar and who would be willing to let you use it for free. This assumes, of course, that their bar is appropriate to your story. If you need a dive bar and what they own is a sports bar, it may not be good choice, unless your PD has a number of not too expensive ideas about how to make it work.

But as pointed out in the chapter on budgeting, even when someone is willing to allow you to use their business for free, there may still be costs. I once wrote a short script to take place in a particular restaurant, and since I knew the owner, I was able to secure it without a rental fee, but I did have to pay $300 to one of the waiters to come in and unlock the restaurant in the morning and then remain on the premises to monitor production.

Free is almost never free, especially when it comes to businesses.

Film shoots inconvenience property owners. For this reason, the only incentive most private individuals and businesses have for letting you shoot on their property is if you pay them a rental fee. This becomes less true the further away you get from big cities because film production still seems to have a novel appeal in smaller towns, but it is true in many cases.

Location Scouting

In the case of practical locations, which are locations that already exist and don't need to be constructed – a store, a bowling alley, a house, a park, etc. – you have

DOI: 10.4324/9781003169864-8

to find them (unless, as just discussed, you have written for specific locations you already have access to). This is called location scouting.

My students sometimes designate a location manager, someone who will scout potential locations for their project, photograph those locations, bring everyone out to see them, negotiate with owners and then manage those locations during production. The latter primarily means ensuring that property is not damaged, though there are other considerations, as will be discussed in Chapter 12. Still, my student directors mostly scout their own locations in collaboration with their producer, then the producer negotiates rental fees and in concert with the AD manages those locations during production.

Shooting Schedule. Before you begin location scouting, schedule your production so that you don't waste time looking for locations you might cut because they require unwarranted company moves. I used the example in Chapter 2 of moving a scene in one of my films from a bar to the location where the protagonist worked so as to avoid a company move and to save a rental fee. Again, a location that is only good for one scene almost guarantees that you will have to make a company move, unless that scene is going to take an entire day to shoot.

In terms of finding locations, there are any number of ways to do this.

Get the Word Out. The first thing you should do is tell everybody you know what you are looking for. It is very likely that people will have suggestions. Also, pay attention to locations in your classmates' films. On my last short, I shot in a house that one of my students used for their film. They were friends with the owner, who often rented it out to productions – this is a cottage industry in Los Angeles – and after they introduced me to the owner, my producer and I took it from there.

Location Websites. There are also websites for finding locations, for example Giggster, which has listings in a number of cities. Some locations on these sites are expensive to rent, but not all of them, and owners are often willing to give discounts to students. Many Airbnb hosts will also rent their properties to film productions, though usually at an above-market rate since a movie shoot is likely to wreak more havoc than the typical guest might. Still, both these avenues are worth exploring since my students do find locations this way.

Go Look. Most every location I've ever shot in was found by driving around and looking for places to shoot, then asking the owners. Some of this legwork can be handled using map software that provides layered views, especially for exterior locations, and you should take advantage of that to lower your production's carbon footprint, but at some point, you are just going to have to go out and look.

This requires, of course, that you have some idea of where to look. I previously mentioned that for one film I made I needed a house location for a night exterior scene and a newspaper loading dock for another scene. In the case of the loading dock, I knew it was unlikely that a large newspaper would allow me to shoot at their facility and, even if they did, in addition to any rental fee, they would almost certainly require us to hire a monitor. My solution was to search online for small local newspapers just outside of Los Angeles. I found two, which I then scouted and, in fact, my producer secured one of them for free.

In the case of the house, I limited myself to neighborhoods where I knew homeowners would be more likely to rent their house to a production, which is to say places not populated by the rich and famous. There are neighborhoods in the Los Angeles area where production is common (it is a way for homeowners to make extra income), and everybody knows which neighborhoods those are, mostly because you see how often productions are in process there, and I focused on those. Since it was an exterior scene, I simply snaked my way from one street to the next stopping to photograph and pin each house that caught my eye.

Another option is rental properties that are vacant because they are between tenants. For my first feature we needed an apartment location for two scenes, an interior and an exterior, but it is a big deal to displace a renter for a film production. You may even have to put them up somewhere. So, the location manager drove around looking for "For Rent" signs. He then called the numbers on those signs and offered one month's rent (a lot less in those days) for allowing us to shoot half a day inside the vacant apartment and half a day in front of the building. He got a lot of bites and I was able to choose from a number of possibilities.[1]

The same is true of sidewalk locations, parks, beaches, whatever. Just look for them.

Location Shooting. This refers to out-of-town production. In Los Angeles, there is something known as the studio zone, or 30-mile zone, which is measured from the intersection of La Cienega and Beverly Boulevards. Any location outside of this zone is not considered local, and cast and crew must be compensated according to each union's rules. At my school, we measure the 30-mile zone from campus, and if a location is beyond it, but still close enough that cast and crew can commute, then travel time, up to an hour, is subtracted from each shoot day. When commuting is not possible, then the director must find somewhere to house cast and crew, and feed them three meals a day.

If you are planning to shoot out of town, one way to reduce costs is to include a location in your script, for example a house, where at least some of the action can take place and where cast and crew can also reside. Vacation rental properties often fit the bill, and this can even be integrated into the story, as several students of mine have done over the years: they simply sent their characters on vacation. That is a nice conceit because it means characters are stuck with each other, often in a remote locale, which offers numerous opportunities for conflict and tension.

Some of my students also write stories that take place where they grew up, usually as a way to grapple with past experiences, but the primary logistical advantage is that they can often count on their extended family to provide places for cast and crew to stay. They also typically know local business and property owners who will support them with free locations (which actually really are often free).

Creative Considerations

Any location you choose should include visual elements that will enhance the look of your film.

The reason I wanted to use the same house that one of my students used is because it had many windows, doorways and archways which, as I've said, all add depth to shots. In the case of the newspaper loading dock, I chose the one I did not simply because it was free, but because the conveyor belts were constructed of bright red steel and the walls were lined with enormous orange-colored shelving. Those colors really pop on screen. As to the house I needed on that same movie, I chose one with a long, columned front porch so that we could track past those columns as we followed the protagonist to the front door. And for the apartment on my first feature, we picked an old Spanish-style building with arched windows and doors. The apartment also had textured plaster walls, hardwood floors and a fireplace. All of those elements photograph better than carpeted floors and cottage cheese ceilings.

Character and story matter as well. For another film I made, I wanted one of the characters to live in what looked like a haunted house. We eventually found an old two-story craftsman badly in need of a paint job and with an attic turret where, in a Gothic novel, someone would almost certainly be held captive at some point. In addition to those elements, the house's interior, also rundown, included large wooden columns, paneled walls, unfinished wood floors and a winding staircase with a curved banister. All of those elements added a great deal to the look of the film, but they also contributed to engendering doubts about the character's intentions and motives.[2]

In sum, a location is not simply a place to shoot; it should add to the look of your film or reveal character or support the story. Hopefully all three.

This is true of exterior locations as well. As mentioned in Chapter 4 on shot-listing, I once shot under a pier. The weather-worn pilings which sliced through the frame in every shot, along with the waves lapping at those pilings in the wider shots, added a lot to the look of the scene. But having the two characters alone beneath a pier also added to the intimacy of the scene.

Practical Considerations

Once you find any location you like, there are a number of factors to consider.

Space. Is the location large enough to stage the action and shoot it? If it can't hold the actors, the camera, the dolly (if you plan to use one), lights, grip gear, the boom op, etc., then it's not much of a location. Be imaginative, though.

I once shot in a very cramped bathroom, but by putting the camera outside the bathroom door for the master, and then by putting the camera in the shower and also outside a window for some of the coverage shots, we were able to make it work (the doorway, shower opening and window frame were not visible in any of the shots, we simply poked the lens through each).

Power. Are enough outlets available? How many amps are available on each circuit? You want, at minimum, 15- or 20-amp circuits. Also, if you trip a circuit, will you have access to the breaker box? Is the breaker box grounded? If you can't visually identify a metal spike that has been hammered into the ground and which is attached to the box via a conduit, then assume the box is not grounded and either rent a generator or find another location (some breaker boxes are grounded to a metal pipe, which would also be visible, and some commercial properties use different grounding systems, in which case ask the owner or their representative about this). If you plan to use a generator, where will it live? Can you place it far enough away so that it doesn't interfere with sound recording?

Lighting: Where is the DP going to place lights? Will lights be hung from a ceiling? Is the ceiling high enough to do this and if so, what kind of grip equipment, for example wall spreaders, will be needed? Will everyone involved in G&E know how to safely use this gear or will they need training? Will lights be placed outside windows? Will this be done in a secure area, say a backyard, or will someone need to sit fire watch? Will these exterior lights be tented for night scenes shot during the day? Will extra crew be needed for that? Will windows be blacked out, netted or covered with ND? If so, how many windows are involved? Would it just be easier to shoot at night or dress the windows and let them burn out?

The Sun. Where will the sun be at the time of day you plan to shoot? Knowing this is a must for exterior scenes, but most interior locations have windows, so knowing where the sun is going to be can be just as important when shooting in, say, an office as it is when you are shooting in a park. If, based on your schedule, the sun is going to turn that office window into a white-hot mess, then either reconsider when you will shoot that scene or find an office with a northern exposure. If the location is exterior, will you be able to stage the action so that the sun remains behind or to the side of the actors and not in their faces? Keeping the sun behind actors is typically considered desirable because it provides even exposure which requires less fill. Will you need silks, reflectors and possibly even lights?

Sound. How noisy is the location? Is it close to a schoolyard, a freeway, a train station or a major boulevard? Does it sit under an airport flight path? What other ambient noises are present? Refrigerators? AC vents? Buzzing fluorescent lights? Can these noises be controlled, muffled, shut off? You don't want to shoot at locations with sound problems if dialogue is involved.

Bathrooms. You may remember from Chapter 3 that one of the main reasons we decided the exterior locations for *Orbiting* needed to be near the house was so cast and crew would have access to a bathroom. If no bathroom is available at a location, you must provide one, either a porta potty or an RV with a toilet. An RV can be useful at some exterior locations because the costume and makeup departments can set up inside it. But I cannot stress enough how important it is to have at least one clean, working bathroom at a location. Over the years several of my students have tried to get around this by having a PA drive cast and crew to a public bathroom – in every case because they were shooting at a remote location – but this puts an undue burden on people and every one of those shoots ended in conflict and strife.

Makeup and Wardrobe. Where will these departments set up? There should be some private space where they can work with the actors. It is also benefi-cial to have a place where actors can go to rest, to focus and to keep out of the way of the crew as they are lighting and setting up gear. When a location is an apartment or a house, there are usually rooms available for these purposes. But when you shoot exteriors and at certain commercial properties, say a grocery store, you may need to provide such spaces. I just mentioned that an RV can serve this purpose, but you can also rent popup tents along with other location supplies.

Staging Area. Is there a staging area for equipment? Another for props and set dressing? How secure are they? If you intend to stage anything on a truck, is it possible to get the truck close to set? Is there a driveway or loading dock where it can be parked or will you need to permit or at least commandeer a spot for it on a street adjacent to the location?

Crafty and Catering. Where will crafty live and where will the cast and crew eat lunch? Is there an interior space where lunch can be set up or will food be served outside? If the latter, will this require canopies, tables and chairs, etc.? In many instances, catering will take place outside unless weather (biting cold, for example) won't allow for this. But as I've pointed out, the less you do inside a location, the fewer opportunities you have to cause damage.

Parking. Are there safe and secure places for cast and crew to park? Will parking have to be purchased? If so, is the location excellent enough to warrant that extra expense, even if people carpool? As I've said, my students typically don't cover parking when they shoot on campus, but when they shoot off-campus and only paid parking is available, they do cover it. If people will be parking on the street, are there any parking restrictions that will make this difficult? In LA, the most common restrictions concern street cleaning and residential permit parking.

Contact. Who is in charge of the location? Will they give you keys to get in and out, or will you be relying on them to let you in? If so, how will you contact them?

Permit. Does the location require a permit? Again, to shoot anywhere in Los Angeles, a permit is required, but some locations can be more expensive to permit than others. In some incorporated cities in LA County, for example Malibu, permits can in some instances cost hundreds of dollars. If permits are required where you are shooting, research costs before you lock any location.

As all of this suggests, the ideal practical location has unrestricted parking, consistent sunlight that will remain behind or to the side of the actors (if exterior), numerous 15- to 20-amp circuits and high ceilings (if interior), at least one clean bathroom, secure staging areas, private spaces for makeup and wardrobe and sheltered areas for crafty and catering. The ideal practical location also does not require an expensive permit or additional insurance. The example I used in the first chapter was shooting at an airport, which could require that a rider be attached to your insurance policy to cover additional liability for damage, and that always costs more money.

Photographs. Finally, when you scout any location, always take numerous pictures of it from every possible angle. This will allow you to create a 360-degree collage of every space. This not only provides a record of the physical features of each location, which will help you when you make final decisions, but you and your collaborators can later use these pictures to make decisions about shots, lighting and set dressing.

Negotiating for Locations

In the case of private property, this obviously means negotiating with owners. In the case of public property – sidewalks, streets, parks, beaches, etc. – this means dealing with whatever entity sanctions film production at those places, for example the city or the Parks Department. If you are shooting in Los Angeles, FilmLA will tell you whose permission you need before they can issue a permit. If permits are required where you are shooting, the local permit office should be able to tell you the same.

Be Clear. Always be up front with location owners. Tell them how many people are coming, how many cars and trucks, how much equipment will be used, and how much of the overall location you will be commandeering. While you may only be shooting in the living room at a house, you may want to use the kitchen for crafty, the backyard for catering, a bedroom and/or den for makeup and wardrobe, and the garage for staging gear. If you are not up front about all this, the owner may become upset on the day you arrive. People tend to imagine student shoots as being small, and often they are, but sometimes they are not, and you don't want to get into a situation where an owner suddenly asks for more money, or shuts down your production, because they feel they are unexpectedly being taken over by an occupying force.

This happened to me on the night exterior shoot discussed above. The owner of the house hadn't really considered how inconvenient our shoot would be. But neither had we exactly explained that to them. So, they threatened to toss us if I didn't give them an extra $1000. The AD and producer talked them down to $500, but it was still a big hit financially. Our mistake, though, was that we never walked them through everything we planned to do, in particular the number and size of lights we needed to set up and the number of crew we needed to do that.

Location Agreement. The way you guard against these kinds of surprises is by having owners sign a location agreement. This is a contact that lays out all the terms for using a location, including which areas you have access to and the agreed upon rental fee. A standard location agreement is included in the online resources for this book and you should have the owner of every location you shoot at sign it. But even with a signed release, a location owner could still raise the rental fee at the last minute if they wanted to. After all, what recourse would you have in the moment since you need to shoot your film? So, again, always be up front with location owners about everything you plan to do, including any tech scouts you intend to conduct prior to production (again, these are discussed in Chapter 10).

Moreover, always be sure to negotiate with the actual owner. Someone can give you permission to shoot in, say, their apartment, but you also need permission from the person or business that owns or manages the building. If you don't get that permission, you can get shut down. This might seem like a long shot if the owner doesn't also live in the building, but it's never smart to take those kinds of risks, nor is it ethical to do so. Besides, if someone who lives in the building calls the owner or the management company, perhaps because you are making a lot of noise or tying up an elevator as you load in equipment, then the owner or someone else with authority will show up, and they may even call the police.

Something like this happened to me. On my first feature, we rented a house to shoot several scenes in. The two people living in the house represented themselves as the owners but on the day of the shoot the person who actually owned the house, and was renting it to these people, came by because a neighbor called them. While we avoided disaster, we only did so by way of dumb luck: a person on our crew just happened to be from the same East European country as the owner and used this as a way to connect with them and smooth things over. As I remember it, they even exchanged a recipe. Still, we lost well over an hour of shooting time.

This example represents a rare instance of fraud, so don't worry about it too much; the real point is this: always deal directly with the owner. And if there is more than one owner, you must be sure that all of them are on board. One of the issues on the night shoot where we almost got shut down, was that we had only dealt with one of the owners. He co-owned the house with his brother via an inheritance and it was his brother who became upset about the size of our production. So, in addition to our failure to fully explain our plans, we also failed to speak to both people who had a stake in the property.

Rental Fees. When you negotiate rental fees, always play up that you are a student. In fact, get a letter from your department on letterhead indicating this. It will often get you a discount and it may even get you a location or two for free (keeping in mind that free is almost never free). But even with a student discount, some locations can still be quite expensive to rent. A student of mine once shot on a standing spaceship set, one that rented for $6000/day, but because he was a student, he got it for $3000/day. It's not possible to argue with a 50% discount, but that is still a lot of money.

So, my advice, once again, is not to write for expensive locations. If you can afford them, so be it. My student was clearly confident that he had the funds to rent this spaceship set. But if money is tight, as it usually is on student films, then follow all my advice about locations in Chapter 1.

Locking Locations

Proof of Insurance. No one is going to let you shoot on any property, whether public or private, unless you have liability insurance. The person who handles production insurance in your department should provide you with a certificate of insurance, or at least a letter, that can be presented to all interested parties.

Permit. If a permit is required, you also need that. The permit office will also ask for proof of insurance. Be aware that in Los Angeles, securing a permit may, in some instances, require that you notify local residents and businesses of your plan to shoot in their neighborhood. Oftentimes it is enough to post flyers, but in the case of night shoots, street closures and when parking spots on a street will be permitted, a filming survey may have to be hand delivered to property owners within a certain radius of the location. This survey is not a request for permission to film, but it is the case in some instances that a certain percentage of area residents will have to sign off on your production (it depends on the neighborhood). Be sure to follow all the rules that govern permits where you are shooting.

Much, if not all of this, can be handled by the producer and PAs, but once you have insurance, a signed agreement and a permit for a location, you can consider that location locked.

Before you lock any location, though, be certain it meets all of your needs, and not just those described above under creative and practical considerations. For instance, whenever a great deal of lighting and/or set dressing is required at a location, including any set construction (on a film I made the production designer built a bathroom inside a laundry room so that I could block the action more effectively), then don't lock in that location until the DP and/ or PD have seen it, signed off on it and given you an estimate for how much everything they need to do will cost.

Building Sets

If your school has a sound stage, then building a set may be an option. As to why you would want to build a set, the usual reasons are cost and/or access. The first set I ever helped any one build, back when I was in school, was a prison cell. Gaining access to an actual cell seemed out of the question, so my classmate chose to construct one. The toughest parts were the bars and the lock on the cell door, and I don't think we pulled those off, but had we had more experience, we probably would have.

As this suggests, don't overreach. It is one thing to build an art gallery or a motel room or a bathroom or even a prison cell, and another thing entirely to construct a drug store or a restaurant or, even more implausibly, a space station. In my experience, complex sets like those, at least on low budget films, which most student films are, almost always have major imperfections that reveal themselves onscreen and require that you endlessly cut around them while editing. But if you are realistic about what you can pull off, then building a set can be fun and doing so gives you a number of advantages. Most significantly, it gives you a great deal of control over lighting, sound recording and camera angles.

As to lighting, sets typically don't have ceilings, which makes it easy to light from above, either from a catwalk or by securing lights to the tops of flats (these are discussed below). Moreover, sound stages are, by design, quiet, which almost guarantees good-quality sound. And since on a soundstage you can, within reason, determine how big a set will be, and need often only build two or three sides of it, and can even include wild or flyaway walls that can be removed and replaced during shooting, you gain many more options in terms of camera placement. When you shoot in, say, an apartment, there are not only limits on where you can place the camera, but you are also often restricted in your lens choices because getting the camera far enough away for long lenses may not always be possible.

Another advantage to building sets is that you don't need to pay rental fees, permit them or negotiate with owners. You also have everything you need at your disposal: sufficient power, bathrooms, safe and secure areas for staging equipment, etc.

But there are a number of factors you need to take into account if you plan to build a set. First, even if your school has flats available – these are sections of wall that can be recycled for use on multiple sets – they may not have as many flats as you need and/or they may not have certain types of flats you need, say ones with doors and windows, and in that case, those will have to be constructed.

Your production designer should know how to do this, and have the requisite tools. If they don't, then they may not be the right person for the project. Still, basic flats are only 4x10 sheets of lauan screwed or nailed to frames constructed of 1x4 lumber, which means they are not that difficult to make, and online tutorials are available. It is also not very difficult to position flats side by side, to plaster and sand all the seams and screw or nail holes, and then to paint or even texture them (say to give the impression of concrete).

Where artistry comes into play is with the addition of architectural details: moldings, soffits, arches, flooring, latticed windows, etc. If you just build a square room with no architectural details, or with few windows or doors, then it's going to look like a set. Someone needs to know what they are doing, including how to draw up plans for the set, and have a good eye for details.

There are also safety issues, but adding braces to flats, screwing them into the floor and sandbagging them is something anyone can learn how to do. Every production design program I am aware of teaches set construction, so, again, it's simply a matter of bringing on the right production designer because if you have to hire a construction manager, it may cost you.

The other issue when you build sets, is that you have to fully dress them, and if your school doesn't have a prop shop, then you may have to rent props, which at a certain point can become expensive. It depends on the size of the set and what you are trying to pull off. You can bring items from home, but making a set that's been constructed look believable usually requires a great deal of set dressing.

This is, of course, not true in every case. One of my students constructed a cave, and in that instance, the texture and irregular shape of the walls was what mattered most (the walls were, in fact, prefabricated since it was a rented cave set that could be assembled on site). Another of my students used diffusion material for the walls of his set which he pumped light through to create a futuristic hospital room with only a bed, some medical machinery and a few metal chairs for the people visiting the patient. He wanted the room to be antiseptic with few human touches. And in the case of, say, an art gallery, which is a type of set a number of my students have built over the years, a certain minimalism is actually required (though you do have the problem, not insurmountable, of getting art on the walls that would believably be displayed at a gallery).

But in the majority of cases, don't underestimate what it takes to make a set that's been built not look like a set that's been built. Be reasonable about what you can pull off. Talk to other students who have already built sets, discuss with them what they gained from doing so, but also the obstacles they faced, and whether or not they feel they overcame all those obstacles. Finally, be sure to watch their films to see what did and didn't work. But my students often successfully build sets, and you can too.

Notes

1 We, of course, had to fully dress the vacant apartment we rented, but that allowed us to create the exact environment we wanted.
2 Never shoot in an unsafe location. This "haunted" house was old and a bit rundown, but it was not rickety. It was, in fact, regularly rented out to productions.

9 Find Actors

As mentioned in previous chapters, finding actors appropriate to your roles can be a long and difficult process. At the same time, hearing your script read aloud at auditions is exhilarating. It gets you excited all over again about your project and reenergizes your preproduction efforts.

The basic casting process is this:

1. Post a breakdown on casting sites
2. Review submissions
3. Schedule and hold auditions
4. Schedule and hold callbacks
5. Offer roles to actors

I'll explain each of these steps in turn. But a word of advice at the outset: to get talented actors for your project, you have to first instill confidence in them about your project, which requires that you execute each phase of the process in an *organized and professional way*, especially once you begin inviting actors to audition and meeting with them in person.

Work closely with your producer on casting. They should organize and schedule all auditions and callbacks. They should also attend every casting session so that you have someone you can talk to in the moment about every actor that reads. But it is up to you to know what you want and to communicate that in your casting breakdown, which includes a synopsis of your story and a description of each role you are reading for.

You can also reach out to actors who have been in classmates' projects. In that case, you've seen their work, you know what they can do, and that's a big plus. But even when you are familiar with someone's work, you should still audition them to be sure that they are right for the role and that you work well with them. You can also search for actors on IMDB Pro, but this requires a subscription and you would likely have to go through the agent or manager of any actor you found. But untold numbers of smaller projects are archived on that site, along with the actors who are in them, and you can limit your search criteria to that range.

DOI: 10.4324/9781003169864-9

When to Cast

Don't start the casting process too soon. Reading actors months before you are scheduled to shoot can be counterproductive. Actors are always hustling for work, so they typically won't commit to a student film months before it goes into production, or if they do commit, and then get a job, say on a commercial or a feature or a TV show, and if that job conflicts with your production dates, then they will almost certainly choose the job.

My advice is to begin casting about four weeks prior to your production. The process will take at least two weeks, maybe a bit longer, such that when you do finally offer roles, actors should be confident about whether they are available or not. But this means that once you do start casting, you must cast hard, which is to say move quickly and hold as many casting sessions as possible in as short a period of time as possible bringing in as many actors to read as you can.

Also, never stop casting until you find actors you want. On my second feature I was still casting some of the smaller roles after production commenced. I had to give up my days off to do this, but it was worth it. Never throw your hands up and say, "I can't find anyone right for the part." Keep searching. As I often tell my students, if casting doesn't feel like one of the most time-consuming activities you are engaged in during prep, then maybe you're not putting enough effort into it. This isn't always true, it depends on how many roles you have and how specific the requirements are for those roles, but do plan to dedicate significant time to the process.

Post a Breakdown

There are various casting sites you can use. Popular ones include Casting Networks, Backstage and Breakdown Express. You can also find casting groups on Facebook. And if your school has a Theatre Department, there should be a formalized way to reach out to actors there. You and your classmates can also organize a mixer and invite all the acting students.

When you post on casting sites, there is specific information you have to provide.

Title. While it's okay to list your project as "Untitled Student Film," it's better if you don't. I once got a well-known actor to read a script simply because he liked the title, and it worked out, he ended up being in the movie. While some actors seem to submit blindly to projects, most don't, and if you want to grab the attention of those actors, then having a good title doesn't hurt.

Synopsis. While I'm sure your script is interesting, or dramatic, or quirky, or funny, or relevant and meaningful (perhaps all of those things), actors scrolling through posts on casting sites won't be able to read your script. They will have to rely on your synopsis. It should be clear and concise and engender specific rather than generic expectations. A synopsis that ends with a phrase like "and her life is changed forever" sounds like a million other stories.

Let's take *Orbiting* as an example. It could be described like this:

> When Trevor agrees to go to the store to buy his mother a feminine hygiene product, he gets more than he bargained for.

But that is not a synopsis, it is a logline, and not a very good one. Moreover, it misrepresents the story: Trevor agrees to nothing; he has no choice but to go to the store. Worse, it is vague and engenders few expectations. It reveals little about what makes the story fun and interesting. Yet I often see synopses like this one on casting sites. A synopsis is not a teaser, but a spoiler. It should include both events and character motivations and capture the story's tone:

> Trevor, an aspiring but not very talented sci-fi novelist who has moved back home with his parents in order to pursue his passion, is justly humiliated when his father interrupts his writing and sends him to the store to buy his mother a feminine hygiene product. But after he loses the coupon his mother gives him, his increasingly ridiculous attempts to buy two douches for the price of one, which he must do or risk getting kicked out of the nest for good, reveal to him the truth of his situation: he is utterly unprepared for adult life. The only question is, will he grow up?

That synopsis covers the story, but without getting bogged down in too many details. It attempts, at least, to be intriguing, rather than cryptic and vague. It also reveals that the story comprises a series of well-motivated events that build to a moment of self-realization and choice for the protagonist. That moment is important to include because it makes the role attractive to actors, who typically don't want to play flat characters. Finally, it attempts to capture both the tone of the story and its attitude towards Trevor, which is lightly mocking but sympathetic.

You're going to have to sell your project again and again: to actors, to costumers, to production designers, to classmates and professors, and maybe even to people who might give you money, so developing a good synopsis is important. Don't write a lazy logline. Write a synopsis that sells your story. Lastly, pay attention to grammar and syntax. Some synopses on casting sites are painful to read. They seem thrown together and sloppy. Again, you have to instill confidence in actors about your project, not uncertainty, concern or dismay.

Characters. List each character by name. If you have unnamed characters, make up names for them. Roles called Angry Onlooker 1 or Cashier 2 will not entice anyone to submit. Be specific about anything that matters, whether age, gender, race, sexuality, ability, whatever. If to play a character an actor needs to speak Spanish, or play tennis well, then include that information. Your story dictates the requirements of each role.

Also, don't be afraid to include information about physical appearance. The reason actors have headshots is so casting directors know what they look like. If a character needs to be thin or heavy or short or tall for the story to work, then say so. A student of mine made a film about a young woman with an eating disorder, and it took her a long time to find someone who could believably portray the physical attributes of the character.

But there are many ways physical appearance can matter. For a film I made, the casting director brought in a number of incredibly handsome actors to read for a role. But I said, "That's no good because the audience will know right away that his character is a heartbreaker, we need to find somebody quirky." It's true that some degree of subjectivity is involved in that distinction, but it is probably also true, for example, that Bradley Cooper and Michael Cera are not receiving offers for the same roles.

Finally, say something about each character's personality, but do so in a way that will attract actors. A character may, for example, be "spaced out and directionless" but actors will almost certainly be more interested in playing someone who is "searching for their purpose in life."

Production Dates. There is no point in reading actors who are not available when you are shooting. So, don't post before you know your shoot dates. Perhaps you can say, "Shoots in April," but specificity is better. This way you avoid pursuing actors who can't be in your film.

Union Status. Your production is either union or nonunion. It's up to you. But SAG actors cannot work on nonunion projects. My advice therefore, is to make your production SAG signatory. This is not to say that you can't find talented nonunion actors, you can, but if you can also audition SAG actors, you gain more options.

Besides, it doesn't cost anything to become SAG signatory unless workers' compensation is not included in the production insurance your department provides. In that case, yes, you need to decide about the extra costs, but even then, you don't need to decide right away. You can start the SAG paperwork, which you should do early because the process takes some time, then hold your auditions, and once you find the actors you want, if none of them are SAG, then don't follow through on signing the agreement because you don't need to. But if you do find one or more SAG actors you really want, then with the paperwork already started, you can easily and quickly complete the agreement.

Compensation. The minimum you owe actors is "meals, credit, copy," which is to say breakfast and lunch every day on set, screen credit, and a copy of the finished film. After that it is up to you whether or not you offer salaries. You can typically indicate in a casting post that you will pay actors without having to commit to an amount. That said, actors looking to do student films for the experience and to build up their reels are probably scrolling through both paid and unpaid projects. At the same time, if you list your project as unpaid and don't get many submissions, try relisting it as paid to see if that makes a difference.

Whenever you don't get a lot of submissions try reposting the project. Improve the synopsis and character descriptions and try again. But as I said in the first chapter, if a role requires a middle-aged actor, you simply may not receive many submissions and there may not be much you can do about that. The issue again, is this: actors in that age range are typically established and working and don't want or need to do student films.

Review Submissions

Headshots. Go through all the headshots you receive. Again, what actors look like matters. In the first place, consider whether they look the right age for the part. They don't need to be the right age; they just need to be able to play that age. High-school comedies, for example, are full of 20-something actors because those actors, being adults, can work full days.

But every role, as discussed above, has physical requirements, and headshots provide information about that. You often hear people say about an actor that they looked the part or they didn't look the part, or that they were right for the part or were not right for the part. Makeup, hair and wardrobe play a significant role here, so use your imagination, but you still need to ask yourself as you look at each headshot, "Can I see this person in the role?" This entails very subjective judgments, but it's your movie, so your subjective judgments are valid.[1]

At the same time, even when you can't see an actor playing the role they submitted for, can you see them in another role? This often happens. An actor submits for one role (usually the lead) but seems perfect for a supporting role they did not submit for. Bring them in for the supporting role.

Resumé. Next, reviewing submissions means going through each actor's resumé. It includes all of their credits as well as where they studied acting and/or where they are studying now. Don't get too wrapped up in this. If an actor has few credits and/or if they haven't studied acting, that doesn't mean they aren't good. It likely means they only recently caught the acting bug. If based on an actor's headshot you can see them in a particular role, then bring them in to audition for that role and *don't make any judgments* until after they have read for you.

At the same time, credits and training matter. If an actor has, for example, been in a number of student films, that means other student directors saw something in them, and it also means they know the score: low to no pay on a student production with few amenities. And if they also have any professional credits, not as a background extra, but in a speaking role, or at least in featured extra roles, then you should be impressed and interested. It is always easier to work with actors who have some experience. They make you a better director. And since actors with experience have already been on a number of sets, they know the drill and can help speed up the shooting process. This is, again, why I'm suggesting you make your production SAG signatory: you will receive submissions from more experienced actors.

In any case, once you've reviewed all submissions, select the actors you want to audition. Select as many as possible, or else you are limiting your options.

Choose Where and When to Hold Auditions

Book a Space. Audition actors at school. You should be able to book audition spaces and/or classrooms for this purpose. Somebody in your department is tasked with managing physical spaces, so there must be some process for signing out rooms for casting and rehearsals. This means that the availability of rooms will determine the exact times you hold casting sessions. Under no circumstances should you cast at home. Inviting actors to audition in your apartment or house is unprofessional and if I were an actor, I would refuse to do it. Again, you must instill confidence in actors if you want them to be in your movie.

Devise a Schedule. Try to book spaces in two- to three-hour blocks. This is more efficient. Casting for a half hour here and an hour there makes it difficult to get people to help you. You need someone to read with actors (this can be a classmate; it does not need to be another actor) and, as I said, you want your producer at all your casting sessions. So, schedule fewer but longer blocks of time to cast, but still schedule as many sessions as you can.

Also, schedule some sessions during the day and some sessions in the evening. Most actors have jobs. But some work during the day while others work at night. We're all familiar with the movie trope of the aspiring actor who waits tables at night so that that they can go to auditions during the day, but that is a real phenomenon. So, keep it in mind.[2]

Book Actors

Send a Message. To schedule actors, direct message them through the casting site or send an email. The only time you may need to get on the phone is if an agent or manager has submitted on behalf of an actor. They may want to talk to you before agreeing to send the actor in for an audition.

Keep It Short. Book auditions in 15-minute slots. As discussed below, an audition should not take longer than that. An audition is a first look at an actor. If you like an actor, you will have them return for what is called a callback. And callbacks are longer. This is also discussed below.

Overbook. Double or even triple book each 15-minute slot because many actors who agree to audition for your project won't actually make it. Why this is I cannot say, and perhaps it is only a phenomenon in Los Angeles where I teach, so check with more advanced students in your program to find out about their experiences if you are not in LA. But if you only book one person for each slot, you might end up sitting around a lot with no one to audition.

Sides. Be sure to send each actor the scene they will be reading. As mentioned in the chapter on budgeting, these are called sides. By sending sides in advance, you give actors the opportunity to become familiar with the scene. You gain nothing by having actors perform what is called a cold reading, plus it's bad form to do so.

   If you are auditioning for a role with no lines, then write a scene with lines for auditions. I had a character in a film once who never spoke. Her purpose was to silently judge others. It was not a minor part; she was the sidekick to a major supporting character. But when we held auditions, we wrote a dialogue scene in which her character shuts down a guy who is flirting with her. The scene had nothing to do with the movie, but everything to do with her character. So, write something that is in character for the role.

Improvisation. If you are considering doing improvisations during auditions, please think this through. First, you will need longer than 15-minute slots. Second, are you sure you know how improvisation works? It is a craft and people study how to do it. Perhaps the actors coming in will be adept at it, but you still need to know how to direct it. Lastly, one of the primary things you want to learn from an audition is whether or not an actor can perform your written lines, which improv cannot tell you. So, unless your project specifically requires actors to improvise as part of their roles, then it is probably more appropriate to save improv for callbacks or rehearsals, and even then, it is not required.

   Speaking for myself, improv is most useful during rehearsals. It can help you figure out what a scene is really about. Moreover, if a written scene is not working, improv can help you find a new structure for it and even discover new lines of dialogue that are more effective than the lines you've written. For example, I was once rehearsing a scene in which one character points out to another character all the mistakes they have been making in their life. As we were running it, though, it just felt wrong and the actors and I suddenly realized that the first character should instead be encouraging the other character and building up their confidence. So, we started improvising that version of the scene and it became the scene we shot.

   I must point out, though, that we did not shoot an improv; we wrote a new scene to shoot based on the improv. One reason you shoot written scenes is so you have the same basic material in every take of every shot, otherwise good luck cutting it together. If actors are improvising new material in every take, the continuity problems this creates may overwhelm you in the editing room.

Maps, Parking and Contact Info

In addition to sides, send actors a map of your campus with your building and the recommended parking areas clearly marked. Do this even if major navigation apps provide the same information. When it comes to getting people to places on time, redundancy is never a bad thing. Also, include your phone number, or the producer's phone number, so that actors have someone to text if they get lost.

If only paid parking is available, make that clear, including how much it will cost. This doesn't mean you reimburse actors for parking, you can't afford that, but don't leave them to be surprised about it. If you decide to have an actor return for a callback, then in that case you might pay for their parking, but otherwise, it's up to them. However, if there are times when parking is free, perhaps on weekends, then schedule as many auditions as you can during those times. Doing so will almost certainly encourage more actors to show up.

Signs and Sign-in Sheets

Post Signs. My students post signs directing actors to their auditions beginning at the parking structure and ending at the door to the room where they are holding auditions. You should leave a trail of breadcrumbs as well. College campuses are often a confusing maze of buildings and walkways. Include the following on your signs: the title of your project, the word "Auditions," the name of the building and the room number, along with a big arrow pointing actors in the right direction.

Sign-in Sheet. Place a sign-in sheet, along with some chairs, outside the audition room. This sheet should ask actors to provide their name, email and phone number. Many actors don't include their phone number on their head shots, and if you get it now, that makes it easier to contact them down the line if you decide to have them return for a callback or want to offer them a role.

The other reason you provide chairs and a sign-in sheet is so that actors know you are there. If you are inside the room with the door closed holding an audition when another actor arrives, they may think no one is at home. But if they see chairs and a sign-in sheet, then they know to sit down and wait. Also, have hard copies of the sides in the waiting area. Organize them by role if you are reading for multiple parts. Most actors will bring their sides, often with notes on them, but sometimes we all forget things. Finally, as a courtesy, have bottled water in the waiting area.

What You Need in the Audition Room

Reader. When you are directing, never read with actors at your auditions; it prevents you from focusing on their performances. This means you need someone who can read the other parts in each scene. It can be anybody. They don't need to be an actor. In fact, in my opinion, they should perform as little as possible. Their job is to feed lines to the actor who is auditioning. I'm not saying they should read like a robot, but a flat reading is better than a bad, hammy reading.

Producer. Again, you need your producer in the room. They will help clarify your thoughts about each actor who reads, though only after those actors have left the room. In the first place, they may see things you don't. When directing, we can sometimes be hypercritcal during auditions. This is because no actor is going to exactly fit the ideal version of a character we have built up in our minds. But a producer can ground you in reality by drawing your attention to what each actor who reads *could* potentially bring to a role. Additionally, if you are on the fence about an actor, your producer can help you resolve that uncertainty.

This is why you don't have your producer read with actors either. That is not their role. They are there to advise. It is always good to have a creative confidant on a film, someone whose opinion you trust, and who you can bounce ideas off of. Keep this in mind when choosing a producer. Otherwise, as I've said, you will diminish their role, relegating them to pulling permits and scheduling catering without, at the same time, giving them a creative stake in the project. And in the long run that may cause tension and disappointment.

Table and Chairs. There should also be a table in the room to put all your stuff on: notepads, pens, sides, laptops, etc. Moreover, it always feels more professional and organized when filmmakers sit on one side of a table and actors sit on the other side. That's exactly how it is done at industry auditions.

Camera. Finally, you need a camera on a tripod. Record every audition because you won't always remember later what you liked about an actor's perform-ance, or what you had concerns about. You must still write up notes on every actor who reads, and discuss every actor with your producer, but video always provides a more perfect record.

The Audition

Auditions typically have a five-part structure.

Introductions

Invite the actor in. Thank them for coming. If you have kept them waiting, apologize. Introduce yourself and also the producer and the person who will be reading with them. Chat them up a bit to put them at ease. But honestly, most actors, in my experience, are fearless and tend to enter a room like they own the place and immediately command everyone's attention. I consider that a good thing. Don't have misgivings about shy actors, but actors who are always performing tend to have a strong presence on screen. They're just doing what they do.

Give the actor the opportunity to ask any questions they might have about the character or the story. Don't get into a long-winded discussion, but when an actor seeks clarity, that's a good sign as well. It is also a good sign if they share with you, unbidden, what they like about the scene they are being asked to read. When an actor likes how something is written, that means they've connected with the material. You can choose to believe they are just flattering you, but they wouldn't flatter you if they weren't interested in the role.

Finally, try to get a sense of what it would be like to work with an actor if you did cast them. If an actor comes in with an attitude, even if you kept them waiting, take note of that. Actors have as much of an obligation to play nice as everybody else on your film does. So, be wary of including people on your production who may cause tension and strife (this includes you too, by the way; don't be a difficult director.)

Also, be wary of actors who try to take charge of an audition. If somebody thinks that working on a student film is an opportunity for them to teach you "how it's really done," then maybe they are not the right person to have on a student film. We always want to learn from people with more experience, but when somebody uses their experience (if they really have experience) as a way to show off, then they are not trying to help you.

These kinds of personality problems are rare, but that said, you are not just looking for the best actors to play your roles, you are also looking for actors you feel confident you can work with. You have that right; it's your movie.

First Read

Actors sit during auditions. That is standard practice. There is no reason for them to be up on their feet performing. That is for callbacks. Again, an audition is a first look at an actor. Besides, your camera is going to be locked down, so if actors are moving around, you won't be able to record them.

Place a chair across from the camera. The frame should be a loose medium shot that will work for every actor who sits in that chair with only minor adjustments. The person reading with them should be next to the camera. That way you get the actor's eyeline close to the lens, which will give you a better view of their face when you review their footage later.

Now, almost every actor who comes in is going to ask if there is a particular way you want them to play the scene. Tell them, "No, let's just see what happens." The goal with a first read is to find out what each actor's take is on the character and the scene (based, of course, on their limited knowledge since they won't have read the full script yet). This is not a test but an opportunity for the actor to share their interpretation of the scene. It's also an opportunity for you to be surprised. More than once I have been forced to reconsider how I understand a scene based on unexpected readings at auditions.

At the same time, don't expect actors to have done a lot of preparation. They almost certainly won't be off book yet, which is to say they won't know all their lines and will have to refer to the script during the audition. That's okay. So long as they have worked out what they think the basic intentions are of the character in the scene, then they have done enough. And if they haven't done that, take note.

In any case, once the camera is recording (the person reading with actors can handle this), have the actor say their name and identify which character they are reading for. Then, once they feel ready, they can start the scene. There is no reason for anyone to read stage directions. The actor and the person reading with them simply run the scene.

When the scene is over, thank them and say something positive and encouraging.

Adjustment and Second Read

Now that the actor has read the scene once, give them a performance adjustment and have them read the scene again. Do this whether you loved their first reading of the scene or were disappointed by it. Giving an actor an adjustment and allowing them to read the scene again is part of the etiquette of auditions. It is, at minimum, a courtesy you owe them.

I will talk more about performance adjustments in Chapter 11 on rehearsals, and you are advised to read that chapter before holding auditions, but the idea is to get the actor to play the scene in a different way. Typically, this means changing their character's intention. For example, I was auditioning for a role once using a scene in which the character goes over to a friend's apartment to check on her because she has been through a bad breakup and isn't answering her phone. When she gets to the apartment, she discovers it is a mess and that her friend is crying in her pajamas. So, she encourages her friend to get dressed and suggests they go out for the night.

There are multiple ways to play that scene, but two obvious ways are:

1. Comfort a friend who is in distress
2. Tease or kid a friend out of their depression

Those are different intentions and they are determined by how seriously the character takes her friend's plight. If she identifies with her friend's pain, she will provide comfort. If she thinks her friend is being dramatic and self-indulgent, then she won't comfort her.

My preference was for the second version – kidding the friend out of it – but whichever intention an actress chose for their first read, I gave them the other intention for their second read. That was the adjustment I provided. I either said "You are worried about your friend and believe they may do something rash," or I said, "Your friend does this all the time, she's a very dramatic person."

There are two important things you can learn from giving an actor an adjustment and letting them read a scene again. First, if the adjustment you give is clear and concise and the actor still plays the scene the same way again, or if they take it in a direction that has little or nothing to do with the adjustment you provided, then it may be that they are not good at taking direction. Actors who are not good at taking direction will slow you down on set and, in the end, you may never get the performance you want, no matter how hard you try.

Second, if you didn't like an actor's first performance, but they nail it the second time around using the adjustment you gave them, then that actor can not only take direction, they may also be a stronger candidate for the role than you first thought. And you wouldn't have learned that if you hadn't given them a another chance.

But all of this assumes that you are giving clear and concise adjustments. Taking direction is a skill, but so is giving direction. Don't blame actors if you can't make yourself understood. If you look at my adjustments above, they are quite simple. All I am doing is defining for the actor what their character *believes* to be true about the situation. And that belief determines their character's intention. You don't need to do more than that, but you need to do it well.

In any case, now that the actor has read the scene a second time, the audition is over.

Wrap Up

Thank the actor. Reiterate your shoot dates. Ask about their availability for those dates. And give them a timeframe for when you expect to make decisions about callbacks or, in the case of smaller roles, when you expect to make offers (if you were casting *Orbiting* for example, you wouldn't hold callbacks for Scott and Amber, the power couple Trevor bumps into).

If you really like an actor, you can also ask about their availability for rehearsals if they were offered the role, but don't mislead anyone into thinking you're giving them a part when you still have other actors to read and haven't even held callbacks yet.

Notes and Discussion

The first four steps – introductions, first read, second read and wrap up – should not take longer than ten minutes. You want to see as many actors as you can in the shortest possible amount of time. Auditions, again, are a first look. This leaves five minutes for notes, discussion and refocusing. If you will be casting for several hours, even short one-minute breaks are helpful.

As to notes, don't write them while an actor is auditioning because that is distracting. Wait until they leave. Include in your notes your thoughts about each actor's strengths and weaknesses for a role as well as what they told you about their availability for your shoot dates. If an actor is uncertain about their availability, then note that. And if you have any misgivings about working with an actor, indicate that as well and spell out why. Don't be overly judgmental, though. They did, after all, come out to read for your movie.

Review Auditions

Watch the Video. This is why you shoot every audition and take notes. Don't review every actor who auditioned, just the ones you are interested in. Take some time to do this, and get input from others if you feel you need it. Again, this is where your producer comes in but sometimes my students send me audition footage to review, though often this is footage from callbacks.

Callbacks

A callback means that you call back certain actors for a second audition. This time, though, actors read with other actors. And if the scene calls for it, they can be up on their feet as they perform. Since you should also record callbacks, you may need your DP present to handhold the camera. Finally, when you bring any actor in for a callback, let them read the entire script in advance. There is no reason to have actors read the script before this.

Signs, Sides and Water. Again, post signs for your callbacks (you may be in a different room this time) and again provide water and sides.

Pair Actors. There are various ways to hold callbacks, but my advice is to bring back two to three actors for each major role and have them perform scenes with each other (characters that don't interact should not be called back at the same time). This way you can see how different actors gel or don't gel with each other. This may mean that you need actors to stay for an hour or two as you try out different combinations, with some actors waiting outside the room while others are inside performing. But if you are upfront about this, there is no problem. Actors, after all, know they are competing for roles. But this is why, in my opinion, you should call actors for callbacks and not email or message them: it avoids misunderstandings.

You also want to figure out during callbacks which actors you work best with as well as which actors are most enthusiastic about the project. But if you spend time working with each actor, you will figure that out.

Improvisation Revisited. If you are keen on doing improvs during callbacks, just be sure you understand the parameters. You can improvise anything, from how a character wakes up in the morning and what their routine is at the start of the day to how they open a door or put on their shoes. For the most part, though, when we talk about improvisation, we mean that each actor in an improvised scene has a clear objective to play.

Let's say you wanted to improvise a version of the scene I described above in which a character checks on a friend who has been through a bad breakup. The first character, as I said, wants to comfort a friend or kid them out of their depression (or any number of other possibilities). But what does the second character want? What is their objective in the scene? It can't simply be to refuse to be comforted or kidded out of their bad mood. That won't give them anything to do. The first character says, "Cheer up," and the second character says, "No." The first character says, "Let's go out," and the second character says, "No."

But if the first character says, "Cheer up," and the second character says, "Please don't patronize me," now you're getting somewhere because now the second character has an objective as well, which is perhaps to be listened to, or to be taken seriously. In other words, each character now wants the other character *to do something*. Without objectives like that, an improv has nowhere to go. Each character must be focused on changing the behavior of the other character. As will be discussed in Chapter 11 on rehearsals, this is true of most scenes, written or improvised. So, you are, once again, encouraged to read that chapter before beginning auditions and callbacks.

At the same time, all acting is a form of improvisation. One actor plays an action and another actor responds to that action *in the moment*. If we return to *Orbiting*, when Trevor gets to the second register and says to the cashier, "Hey, Linda, I know you, right," there are a number of ways to deliver that line. The actor could flirt, he could flatter (he has fond memories of Linda), or he could apologize (he wishes he didn't have to take advantage of his "friendship" with Linda, but he's in a bind and needs help).

Those are all *actions*. And whatever action the actor chooses, the actor playing Linda must respond to it. In the script it says that she raises her eyebrows, but does she do that to manifest surprise, to ridicule him or to offer a warning ("Don't try to get over on me, buddy.")? Since there are multiple possible actions that can be played, and since whichever action is played must be an effective response to the action just played by the other actor, then the choice of an action, which must be made in the moment, is a kind of improvisation.

Because of this, doing improvs at callbacks won't necessarily tell you anything you can't learn by just running the written scenes. But it's up to you. Keep in mind, though, that if you call back several actors for each major role, doing improvs with them might take many hours.

Review Callbacks

Watch the Video. As with auditions, take some time to review what happened at callbacks. Ask yourself what each actor brings to the role and to the project, consider the chemistry between different actors and consider what it would be like to work with each actor. But your goal is to decide on a first choice and a second choice for each role.

Offer Roles to Actors

First Choices. Call the actors who are your first choice for each part and offer them the role. And while you have them on the phone, confirm their availability again for your production dates and determine their availability for rehearsals.

Second Choices. In the case of your second choices, you should call them as well to break the bad news, you owe them that, but don't do this until you have firmly locked in your first choices. For obvious reasons, it's difficult to go back to an actor after you have already told them no.

Casting Directors

My students sometimes hire a casting director. There are many in Los Angeles. But even if you aren't in a city where commercial production is common, you may be able to find regional casting directors, people who work with production companies that are based elsewhere.

If you are going to hire a casting director they should be able to provide two specific services: access to talented actors they know because they have read them for other projects and, in addition to that, the ability to reach out to agents and managers who will take or return their phone calls. In short, you are paying for their connections.

If a casting director is only going to post breakdowns on casting sites and pre-read actors, while that will simplify the process for you, it is not a service that is worth much money. As mentioned in the chapter on budgeting, hiring a casting director, at least in Los Angeles, will cost $1000 or more, which is only worth it if it buys you some access to actors who might not typically submit for student films.

Such a casting director may also post breakdowns on casting sites, but if they can't also go to bat for you to convince somewhat more experienced actors, or the people who represent them, to consider your project, then they are not offering enough.

Another possibility is to find an assistant to a casting director who has experience pre-reading actors, and so knows many actors, and who might be willing to cast your project in return for a casting director credit and maybe also a small fee. This provides a way for them to build their resumé as they work towards becoming a professional casting director.

But whether you work with a casting director or handle the process with your producer, which is a perfectly productive and viable way to manage it, do put some time and effort into casting your roles. Your film deserves that.

Notes

1 Focusing on the physical appearance of actors is sometimes disparaged as casting to type, or typecasting, but every director has to find shorthand ways to impart story information, including information about characters, and who we cast in roles provides one way to do that. Still, casting against type can be interesting, so be flexible and imaginative as you go through headshots.
2 When scheduling child actors to audition, keep in mind that they have school and also that the parent or guardian who will accompany them to the audition may have to negotiate their work schedule.

10 Collaborate and Communicate

Once you are about four weeks away from production, it is time to start meeting with your collaborators. Depending on your personality, you will either relish these meetings or be anxious about them because everyone will expect you to know what you want and to be able to articulate that clearly. But trust me when I tell you that if you have followed the steps laid out in the previous chapters, and if you follow the steps below and in the remaining chapters, you will quickly settle into your leadership role.

In terms of key creative collaborators – director of photography, production designer and costumer – don't expect to meet with them over and over again. Three solid creative meetings with your DP should be enough and as to the PD and costumer, unless elaborate world building is involved, you may find that only two creative meetings are required because once you have settled on a plan, the idea is to let them do their work and any questions they might have along the way can usually be answered via email or by way of a short phone call. The costumer will at some point need you to approve all their wardrobe choices, but the production designer is not going to run every piece of set dressing by you, and even in cases when they require your approval, this need not necessitate a meeting.

For example, I once needed an old pickup truck for a film and this was being handled by Art. I had a generalized image of the truck in mind – I wanted it to not only be dinged up but also two-toned because that to me has a certain vintage feel – so the production designer periodically emailed me pictures of candidate vehicles until we settled on one that we both liked. But as to dressing the sets on that film, once the PD and I settled on the general look, feel and color palette for each location, which took a single meeting, I left everything to him and his crew. In short, avoid being a micromanager and making unnecessary demands on people's time.

One reason for this is that in addition to creative meetings, people will also have to give you time for production meetings, especially the DP, who will help the producer recruit crew and secure gear and will also meet with you and the AD to finalize the shot lists and shooting schedule. The DP and/or PD may also participate in some location scouts if there are, for example, questions about the viability of certain locations and, in addition to that, there will be tech scouts.

DOI: 10.4324/9781003169864-10

The person you will spend most of your time with during preproduction is the producer. I have discussed their role in detail throughout many of the previous chapters and, as I have hopefully made plain, the two of you are a team and must function as such.

In any case, what follows is not, strictly speaking, a chronology but something closer to a hierarchy of tasks. It is not the case that you have to complete one stage of preproduction before you can begin another, though this is true in some instances. You can't, for example, pull a permit for a location until you've secured that location, but it is certainly possible, indeed necessary, to jump back and forth between casting, creative meetings, location scouting, finalizing shot lists, rehearsals, etc.[1] How this all works will become clearer as we go along, but communication is key, as is collaboration.

Creative Meetings

Director of Photography. In addition to sharing your look book with your DP, you should also recommend movies and/or or TV episodes they can watch that are relevant to the look and feel of your film. They should also make similar recommendations to you. Looking together at the work of photographers and painters might also be useful. But, as discussed in Chapter 5, establishing a visual template for a film is important, keeping in mind, of course, that different scenes will likely require different approaches to lighting, lens choices, camera movement etc. This is why I typically don't recommend entire movies or TV episodes for the DP to watch. Instead, I identify specific scenes that relate to scenes in the script we are shooting. This, to me, is more productive. After all, deciding how to shoot a film is a matter of settling on specific, not general, approaches, ones that will lead to particular, desired effects.

For example, I once had to shoot a driving sequence during which it transitions from day to night. This is always tricky, especially since I did not want to use dissolves because those can seem, for better or worse, old fashioned. But I found an excellent example of what I wanted to achieve in *Cop Car* (2015). It demonstrated that by alternating interior and exterior shots of the vehicle along with carefully placed insert shots, a smooth transition from day to night can unfold using only cuts. We didn't borrow any specific shots from that sequence, only the structure. However, for the concluding shot of our driving sequence, when the previously mentioned pickup truck arrives at its destination, the DP and I did steal a shot directly from the TV show *Rectify* (2013) in which they put the camera in the bed of a truck and let it bounce and shake as the truck crept down a rough road. I just thought that was a neat effect.

As this suggests, you and your DP will also create shot lists together. You will have your preliminary shot lists but, again, don't present these as a *fait accompli* because that would shut the DP out of the creative process. One solution to this, which my students sometimes do, is to ask the DP to create their own preliminary shot lists, after which you can come together and compare your approaches. However, in my experience, most DPs prefer to brainstorm shots with the director, using the director's preliminary shot lists as a starting point. I like that approach too because I think it leads to a fruitful give and take. And, as just suggested, some shots can even be borrowed from reference sources. But it is up to you and your DP to decide how you want to shot-list together.

It can, of course, be difficult to shot-list certain scenes if you don't have a location yet, but it is never impossible. You can agree on a basic approach and then make that approach more specific once a location is secured. And, as mentioned in Chapter 4, once you have your locations, visiting them with the DP to shot-list can also be productive. Moreover, if you have the luxury of rehearsing with actors on location prior to production, then having the DP on hand, not the entire time but near the end of these rehearsals, can be a real boon in terms of picking shots and finalizing blocking. The DP can use their phone's camera to try out different angles.

Finally, as you and your DP work out a visual approach to each scene, including lighting, this is when you will also begin to develop an equipment list, both camera and G&E, which includes everything that needs to be rented or specially requested from your department's equipment office because it is not part of the standard equipment package that they supply. This list is discussed in more detail below, but my advice is not to ignore your budget as it is being developed. If a shooting strategy, no matter how attractive, is going to require rentals you can't afford, then come up with a different shooting strategy. And if a particular location is going to require many extra expenses, say for lighting, then find another location.

Production Designer and Costumer. Meet with each of these department heads individually to discuss your script – its characters, story and themes – as well as any specific ideas you have about design and wardrobe. For example, I have always been very interested in color motifs, like the one I identified in *Beale Street* (Chapter 5), and I often work closely with my PD and costumer to build such motifs into my own films.

For this reason, after holding individual meetings, get together once with both the PD and costumer to discuss how the two departments might collaborate. Think of my example from *Chinatown* (Chapter 5) in which design and costume elements work in concert with each other to create the color scheme of a drought. But there are many ways costumes and production design can creatively work together, so do think about possibilities. There are also practical considerations. If, for example, your PD plans to paint a location a particular color, that may place certain constraints on the costumer in terms of colors they can use so that characters don't simply blend into the background or clash with it for no good reason.

Moreover, encourage your DP to coordinate with both departments, especially Art. I once had to shoot a number of scenes in a rather cavernous night club and the DP and PD worked together during prep to figure out ways to fill all the empty space, including hanging a number very interesting practical lamps from the ceiling, which made what was essentially a huge black box look like a more intentionally designed club space.

Production Meetings

While you and the producer will likely be in contact every day, it is a good idea to hold a weekly production meeting during which you go over issues related to crew, equipment reservations and rentals, locations, scheduling auditions, the cost report, etc. These meetings should commence about six weeks before production and when you are two weeks away the DP and AD should join so that tasks can be assigned, updates shared, and problems discussed and resolved.

It is also a good idea, right before shooting starts, to hold a final production meeting with key department heads during which you read through the script and discuss every scene so as to ensure that a plan is in place to complete each one of them. This meeting is discussed below.

Equipment List

As mentioned, when you and your DP hold creative meetings, you will begin to decide on any special gear you want. What I mean by special gear, again, is anything that is not included in the equipment package your department provides. Perhaps at your school there are not standard equipment packages, but where I teach there are basic packages for each level of production. Every student receives the package appropriate to their production, which keeps things fair. At the same time, students at each level can also petition for additional gear, for example a doorway dolly (we have a limited number) or a Dana Dolly (we only have one) or even just additional C-stands, flags and sandbags.

This petition process serves to ensure that additional gear is to some degree equitably distributed, but only if petitions are submitted in a timely manner. Because of this, each DP must submit a comprehensive equipment list to the producer as soon as possible. If there is competition for gear at your school, keep that in mind. Of course, competition is only an issue when multiple productions are scheduled to happen simultaneously. This can be the case even when shoot dates are assigned. In the undergraduate program in my department, for example, there are typically two sections of the senior-year production course, which means that up to four shoots can be scheduled each week, all on the same days.

At the same time, in our graduate program, shoot dates are not assigned, at least for advanced productions, and in that case, to better ensure access to gear, we bring all the students together as a group to negotiate their production dates. This helps minimize the number of productions that overlap. If shoot dates are not assigned in your department, you and your classmates are advised do the same, assuming a similar practice is not already in place.

In any case, when the DP submits their equipment list, they must understand, given everything I said about budgeting in Chapter 6, that they may not get everything they want to rent, unless they are willing to chip in funds to get specific footage they would like to have on their reel. And the producer must keep in mind that if each location has not yet been tech scouted, then the DP may yet add items to the list. Until the DP has seen every location, they won't know everything they might need to light those locations. But for all the reasons just cited, it is better for the DP to submit a partial list, rather than no list, as soon as they can.

Equipment from School. Be aware of your department's reservation policies. In mine, once a student has purchased production insurance, they can reserve an equipment package as well as petition for additional gear. Whatever the policy is at your school, it is almost certainly the case that submitting your equipment reservation sooner rather than later is best.

Equipment Rentals. If the DP has a relationship with a specific rental house, whether camera or G&E, then probably they should deal with that rental house. If not, it is up to the producer. Keep in mind, though, that most rental houses offer significant student discounts, so there is really not a lot of room to negotiate. This is not to say, though, that no one should ever try to politely haggle. However, don't push too hard or be demanding because that reflects badly on all students and can affect how other student productions are treated down the line.

Expendables. Finally, the DP must provide a list of all expendables they will need: tape, gels, bounce boards etc. As mentioned in the chapter on budgeting, you can chip in with your classmates to buy a basic cache of expendables for all your shoots. But even then, it is likely that each DP will have to submit a list of additional items. If your film has, say, a party scene, and the DP requires colored gels for this, then those are not items everyone should chip in on.

Camera Tests and Workflow

Your DP may choose to shoot camera tests. They may want, for example, to test certain lenses or filters to see how these affect the image, or they may want to try out different frame rates or other camera settings, for example shutter speeds. There are many possibilities.

But whether such tests are done or not, you are advised to establish and test the workflow you will follow. This primarily has to do with how footage is captured and then how that footage progresses through all stages of postproduction, from dailies to final output.

In the days of analog filmmaking there was basically a single workflow, at least for student films: shoot negative, process it, strike a one-lite workprint, edit that, conform the negative to the locked workprint, strike timed answer prints, then add an optical soundtrack. If those steps give you a headache, then you're in for a treat with digital workflows, which are not only more complicated and require that you master even denser terminology and concepts, they also vary depending on what camera is being used, on how that camera is configured (codec, resolution, bit depth, frame rate, log vs. linear, etc.), on what editing software will be used, which in turn determines how media must be structured on your hard drives, what software will be used to create dailies and whether or not proxy files need to be created, etc.

You must also establish a workflow for sound. Will you be recording double system or will you be feeding sound directly into the camera (this is only likely on very small projects)? If you are shooting double system, how will you synch sound to picture? Will smart slates be used or will you be relying on an audio scratch track from the camera, or will you simply match slate to audio? Sometimes, all three methods are brought to bear. Establishing a workflow for sound is easier than establishing one for picture, but you shouldn't just wing it.

So, unless you are shooting with a DSLR using single-system sound and cutting in a consumer editing program from which you will make your final output, please be sure that the image and audio tracks you capture, and how you organize and manage them, will be compatible with every phase of postproduction.

It's not possible to cover workflow in detail here. It is up to your department to teach these processes, but a workflow worksheet is included in the online resources for this book. After you and your DP (and editor if you have one) answer all of the questions on it, talk it through with your instructor or with the staff who manage postproduction at your school. And once you've done that, test it because decisions made at each step, and these include errors, have consequences down the line, some of which can make it difficult and time consuming to finish a project. Even if a workflow has been established by your department or instructor, you are advised to test it before you go into production.[2]

Tech Scouts

On professional productions, tech scouts may take place before locations are locked. This way the line producer can be certain that any location they do lock works for everyone, not just the director, but also the DP, gaffer, sound mixer, production designer, etc. But that means a lot of tech scouts, which is usually not feasible on a student film since most crewmembers won't be able to commit that much time to a project in prep. The DP and PD may, as I've said, participate in some location scouts if there are questions about the viability of any potential locations, but more than that you can't expect. For this reason, on student films, tech scouts typically take place after locations have been secured.

This means that as you and the producer are location scouting, you must keep in mind everything I covered in Chapter 8 about power, sound, bathrooms, parking etc. This way, when you hold tech scouts, you are primarily, though not exclusively, taking key crew members on a tour of each location so that they can become familiar with them. Additional details about production will also be worked out during tech scouts, for example whether or not additional G&E gear is required, but if key crew members don't get to at least tour a location before shooting commences, then a lot of time will be wasted when everyone arrives at that location to shoot. People won't know where to park the truck, where gear should be staged, where power outlets are, where makeup and wardrobe should be situated, etc.

Ideally, you will set aside a single day to tech scout all of your locations. This won't always work out – there are many schedules to juggle, including those of each location owner – but it is the most efficient approach. The producer can handle all the scheduling, organize a carpool, and then in half a day or less the process can be complete. Try to finish tech scouts at least a week before production commences, if not sooner. This won't always be possible, but do everything you can to try to make that happen.

Participants. At minimum, tech scouts include, in addition to you, the producer, AD and DP. The gaffer, PD and sound mixer should also attend, especially for interior scouts. However, if the sound mixer is a professional and not a classmate, you would have to pay them, a luxury you likely can't afford, in which case you and the AD will stand in for them, as discussed below. Finally, if the key grip is available, they should participate too. If you are hiring people in G&E, though, you will run up against the problem of salaries again, which is one more reason I think that department should be populated with students.

Power. The DP and gaffer need to know where all the power outlets are as well as how many amps on each circuit and which circuits control which outlets, appliances and lighting fixtures. This means inspecting the breaker box which, again, must be grounded (see the section on power in Chapter 8). At newer residences and commercial properties, the circuits should already be labeled but at some older locations they may not be. In that case, the gaffer will have to label each circuit using paper tape and a Sharpie. Since this will require turning breakers off and on to determine what they control, do not do it without the owner's express permission.

But whether circuits need to be labeled or not, each circuit should be numbered and then those same numbers should be affixed to each outlet along with the available amps, otherwise crew won't know when they will trip a breaker if they plug in another light (this becomes less critical when LED units are being used, but labeling outlets is a good habit to get into, especially if you will be receiving a mixture of older and newer lighting units from your department).

Finally, if a generator is going to be used, it must be decided where it will be situated. Sound is always an issue with generators, even with so-called movie-quiet generators (which should be avoided because they are huge, expensive to rent and must be towed to the location), so the goal is always to place a generator as far away from set as possible. Even then, the key grip should be prepared to rig some sound baffles around it using sheets of plywood (you can find online tutorials for this).

Lighting & Grip. In the case of exterior locations, the DP and director determine how the action could be staged to keep the sun behind or to the side of actors and then, along with the gaffer and key grip, determine what gear will be required: silks, reflectors, bounce boards, etc. In the case of interiors, the DP, gaffer and key grip must consider the placement of lights and what, if anything, they will need for this in addition to light stands (wall spreaders, wall plates, risers, etc.). The DP also determines how many windows they have to deal with, and where the sun will be when shooting takes place, which might require ND and/or rigging grip nets outside windows (assuming those windows are on the first floor).

The DP also considers whether they will be blacking out any windows or tenting them. Some of this can be discussed in advance by showing the DP location photos, but nothing will likely be finalized until everyone actually sees each location. As to window dressing, which is handled by Art, the DP and gaffer must tell the PD in advance which windows they expect them to dress.

Since any or all of this can cost money, it must be run by the producer, who may insist that less expensive solutions be devised. Covering many windows with ND, for example, or tenting them, may be luxuries your production can't afford.

Finally, as all these issues are worked out, the DP and gaffer provide the AD with estimates for how long each of these activities will take during production and they let the producer know if they will need additional crew to pull anything off.

Camera. Is there enough room to block the action as well as set up the camera and other necessary gear for each shot? If a location is cramped, then you and the DP should mock up the action using other people on the tech scout as stand-ins for the actors. This is especially important if you plan to use a dolly or a second camera.

Sound. As I have said, when dialogue is involved, don't pick locations that are near freeways, busy boulevards, schoolyards or that sit under airport flight paths, etc. No sound mixer, even if they attend tech scouts, can fix such problems. But as I've also said, unless you are shooting on a sound stage, most locations will still have sound problems: buzzing fluorescent lights, humming refrigerators, AC vents etc. If the sound mixer will not be part of tech scouts, it is up to you and the AD to identify and consider solutions to these issues (typically shutting off the offending devices), so that the AD can communicate this information to the sound mixer. If at all possible, bring sound gear on tech scouts, including wireless mics, to listen to each location, which makes it easier to identify problems.

Art. The production designer will take their own photographs of each location and measure the dimensions of each space. This will allow them to create floorplans, which they can share with the gaffer and DP, who may, if they wish to, use them to draw up lighting plans. But in terms of Art, if you think back to my discussion of Trevor's bedroom in Chapter 5, any furniture and props a PD pulled for that set would have to fit in the room. The PD should also discuss camera placement with you and the DP to determine what actually needs to be dressed (there is no point in dressing what won't be seen) and the three of you should discuss how best to exploit the most visual aspects of any location, including, but not limited to doorways, archways, hallways, alcoves, windows, etc.

Logistics. This is primarily the domain of the AD, who must determine where cast and crew will park, where the truck will be parked, where gear will be staged, where props and set dressing will be staged, where makeup and wardrobe will be situated, where actors will go when they are not working, where crafty and catering will be set up, what location supplies will be required for this and what bathrooms are available. Even if you and the producer have already worked all of this out, you must share this information with the AD. Treat this as a discussion, though, since the AD may have better ideas about how to handle some of these matters.

In terms of cast and crew parking, if this will not be in a parking lot or structure, then the AD devises a plan to spread it out over several streets near the location. Film LA, which issues shooting permits in Los Angeles, actually requires student productions to do this. But if you take up all the available parking on a street, someone who lives on that street or has a business on that street may complain. And if that happens, and cars have to be moved, then at least some people will have to turn their attention away from shooting the film. The simplest way to avoid this is to assign each department a street to park on, and then include that information on each day's call sheet (these are discussed below).

As to the truck, if there is no guaranteed parking spot for it at a location, then the AD should ask the producer to permit a space for it on the street directly adjacent to the location. With such a permit, a temporary no parking sign can be posted, one which is legally enforceable. If such permits aren't available where you are shooting, then you'll just have to snag a spot.

In terms of load-in – Art, Wardrobe, Camera and G&E – the AD also devises a plan for this. Typically, Art loads in first since sets need to be dressed in advance of shooting and this has to be scheduled with the location owner. Gear may also be loaded in the day before, but usually that happens on the day of production. If stairs are involved, or an elevator, then the AD accounts for the extra time this may add to each department's load-in.

Safety. This is everyone's responsibility, but the AD is in charge of safety on set and, as will be discussed in the last chapter, they hold a safety meeting at the start of every shoot day. In preparation for this meeting, the AD notes where all the exits are at a location, they pick a spot where everyone will gather for a head count if the set does have to be evacuated for an emergency, they determine where fire extinguishers should be placed for ready access and they identify any unique hazards that cast and crew need to be made aware of (a former classmate of mine, now an accomplished director, once fell into an empty pool while demonstrating to an actor how they wanted a particular bit of action to be played, which shut the production down for several days while they recuperated).

Finalize the Shot Lists

This is done in collaboration with the DP and AD since both are responsible for keeping your production on schedule. Let's take as an example the shot list from Chapter 4:

1. Establishing Shot: Martin's house – entire scene
2. Medium Shot: Martin in window waiting, reacts to truck arriving, exits frame
3. Reverse Wide: Truck arrives, driver retrieves box and meets Martin who exits back to the house as the driver returns to the truck and drives away
4. Closeup: Martin standing in window, reacts to truck arriving, exits frame
5. Medium Wide: Front door – Martin hurries outside / Martin goes back inside
6. Two Shot (profile): Martin meets deliverywoman, receives the box, both enter and exit frame

I called this a preliminary shot list, but to simplify matters let's recast it as one that was worked out with the DP. Finalizing it will require the following: putting the shots into shooting order and thus renumbering them; adding information about focal length; clarifying any camera moves (in this case there are none); adding production notes; and assigning a reasonable amount of time to complete each shot. As to this last requirement, let's also say that this will be the first scene up at the start of a shoot day at a new location, which means we'll have to account for setup time. With that in mind, the final shot list looks like this:

Scene 1: EXT. MARTIN'S HOUSE – DAY – Martin receives a box

Shot	Type	Lens	Movement	Action	Notes	Start	End
1	Master	Wide		Entire scene	Off load gear, set up, blocking, makeup etc.	8:00	9:30
2	MS Martin	Normal		Martin waiting, reacts to truck, exits frame		9:30	9:50
3	CU Martin	Long		Martin waiting, reacts to truck, exits frame		9:50	10:10
4	MW Martin	Normal		Martin exits house / goes back inside		10:10	10:40
5	Rev. Master	Wide		Truck arrives, driver retrieves box and meets Martin who exits back to the house as the driver returns to the truck	Turning around	10:40	11:20
6	Two Shot	Normal		Martin meets deliverywoman, receives the box, both enter and exit frame		11:20	11:50

Shooting Order. The easiest way to determine shooting order is to create an aerial view of the scene, or floorplan. Here is a floorplan for the scene we are considering now:

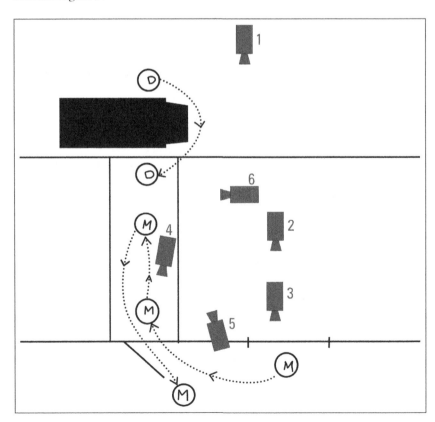

Note that the physical positions and movements of each actor throughout the length of the scene are clearly indicated (M = Martin; D = deliverywoman). Likewise, each camera position is also clearly indicated (in the case of shot 3, the camera won't actually be moved closer, or much closer; instead, as specified in the shot list, a longer lens will be used, but it's simply easier to show the change in shot size this way).

Note as well that the number assigned to each shot matches the number assigned to it in the final shot list. Those same numbers would now also be assigned to the corresponding frames in the storyboards. This way, all three documents communicate the same information, though in different forms.

Finally, note that continuity is maintained. In each shot Martin is always moving screen-right as he exits the house to the meet the driver, then he is always moving in the opposite direction, which is to say screen-left, as he heads back inside. Likewise, the driver, at least once they reach the curbside of the truck, is always moving screen-left as they walk towards Martin, then they are always moving screen-right as they head back to the truck. Essentially, the action line, or 180-degree line, runs from the front door to the truck, and since every camera position is on the same side of that line, screen direction is maintained. Because of this, even when Martin exits the window, the direction of his movement is consistent.

I'm sure your instructors have instilled in you a healthy respect for screen direction, and I discuss it more in Chapter 12, so I won't say more here, except to add that floorplans provide an easy way to ensure that you don't violate it. Still, if this isn't clear, go back and look at the storyboards in Chapter 4 which use arrows to indicate screen direction (storyboards also help establish continuity).[3]

In any case, the reason this is correct shooting order is because shots 1, 2, 3 and 4 can all be taken without any crew or gear, except for the camera, having to be significantly repositioned. With shot 5, though, the camera is now looking in the opposite direction. This means that everything which was previously behind camera – both crew and gear – may now be on camera and, if so, will have to be relocated.

This is called turning around (or sometimes, more colorfully, flipping worlds). It is typically time consuming, so you always shoot out one side of a scene before you *turn around* to shoot out the other side of the scene. If you don't, you must repeatedly move crew and gear around as well as repeatedly alter lighting setups, at least in the case of interior scenes, though in the case of this scene there may be reflectors and/or large silks set up that would now have to be broken down and/or repositioned. This is why in the notes column of the shot list I indicated that shot 5 entails turning around. It is a reminder to begin preparing for that sooner rather than later.

As to shot 6, it is logical to shoot this last because when we turn around for shot 5, we can reposition crew and gear so that they will also already be off screen for this shot too. Moreover, shot 6 is our least important shot. Both the master and the reverse master cover the action of Martin receiving the box, so if we fall behind schedule, we can drop shot 6 and still know that we have all the material we need to cut the scene together. Prioritizing shots is important.

Focal Length. I chose not to designate specific focal lengths – 28mm, 35mm, 50mm, 85mm, 100mm, etc. – but you and your DP can certainly do that. I just find that on set you often discover that the lens you thought you were going to use is not the lens you use. You think, for example, that 35mm will be wide enough but then you discover you need to go wider, perhaps because the set is cramped. So, except in cases of special lenses, say a fisheye lens or an extremely long lens that will be rented, perhaps 1200mm, I typically don't designate specific focal lengths in shot lists. But there is nothing wrong with doing so. It's up to you and your DP.

Timing Shots. While a certain amount of guesswork goes into this, there are still logical assumptions involved. A few key ones are these:

1. When you start at a new location, more often than not you have to account for setup time: unloading gear, staging it, building the camera, etc. This means that the first shot at any location will typically take *significantly* longer to complete than subsequent shots.
2. Master shots almost always take longer to shoot than coverage shots. When you shoot a master, you are starting a new scene which means you must account for the time it will take to block the action and light it (unless all this has been done in advance). Even in the case of day exterior scenes you may, as suggested above, have to account for lighting if you are planning to set up silks, reflectors, etc. And when you light a master, it is always the case that you are lighting the entire scene. This will take more or less time depending on the size of the location and what the camera is seeing, on whether you are shooting interior or exterior, and on whether it is a day or night scene, but lighting a master is rarely something that can be done quickly.
3. While coverage shots almost always take less time to complete than master shots, not all coverage shots are equal. A closeup for an important dialogue scene is going to take much longer to shoot than a simple reaction shot, like the two reaction shots of Martin in the window. You must not only account for how long it will take the dialogue to unfold – is it a one-page or a three-page dialogue scene – but you must also consider the time it will take to give the actor adjustments and to shoot multiple takes, usually many more takes than you would shoot for a simple reaction shot.
4. Camera movement (discussed below) always adds time to shooting a shot. Take that as a given. And if the camera move is part of a oner, expect to spend a lot of time on that.

If we apply all these principles, my timings make sense:

   Shot 1: Master 8:00–9:30. As we should expect, this shot will take the longest to complete. In addition to setup, the entire scene will have to be blocked, the frame set and the entrance of the truck rehearsed so that it lands in that frame where we want it to. Moreover, Martin will need to be lit in the window and both actors will have to go through makeup and wardrobe. All of that will take an hour, probably longer, leaving us 20–30 minutes to get a usable take.

Shot 2: MS Martin 9:30–9:50. Since Martin will already be lit in the window, and since we should be able to reposition the camera quickly on sticks, and since there is not a lot of acting involved, meaning we may only shoot a couple of takes, 20 minutes seems adequate, even if Martin's lighting requires some small tweaks.

Shot 3: CU Martin 9:50–10:10. This shot mostly only involves swapping lenses, but I'm still allowing 20 minutes for it. Except in cases of simple insert shots, I don't like to assign less than 20 minutes to any shot because I think that encourages a point-and-shoot style of filmmaking that disregards craft. Always provide time do things right. In this case, that will entail, in the first place, setting the frame. The camera will almost certainly have to be slightly repositioned to do that. Second, since we'll be on a long lens, focus is going to be critical, so I want to allow some time for that, including rehearsing a possible focus pull for when Martin exits frame. Finally, we may shoot additional takes since Martin's performance matters a bit more in this shot than in the previous one.

Shot 4: MW Martin 10:10–10:40. I'm allowing a half hour for this shot because we're going to have to significantly reposition the camera, swap lenses again and do some lighting. When Martin opens the door, we will likely see into the house and whatever we see will have to be lit. We could frame the shot so as to avoid this, but I suspect the shot will look better – have more depth – if it provides at least an oblique view into the house. Also, we may key Martin or at least provide some fill when he comes outside using bounce boards or reflectors and/or we may position a silk. Moreover, since Martin will be moving, we'll have to rehearse that action, including two focus pulls: one for when he exits the house towards camera and one for when he re-enters the house, moving away from camera. We can shoot these actions separately or combine them in each take by having someone hand him the box off-screen before he turns around and goes back inside, but either way, this is not a shot we can simply hammer out.

Shot 5: Reverse Wide 10:40–11:20. I'm allowing 40 minutes for this because we are turning around. Moreover, this is a second master and we can't expect that all the blocking we did for the first master will carry over to this one since it is a completely new angle. There is a good chance we'll have to rehearse the entrance of the truck again, including giving it a revised mark for when it stops, and we may have to tweak some or all of the marks for Martin and the deliverywoman so as to achieve the best view of their actions from this angle (marks are discussed in the Chapter 12, but cheating them from one shot to the next is common).

Shot 6: Two Shot 11:20–11:50. I could allow 20 minutes for this shot, but we will have to significantly reposition the camera, swap lenses yet again and, since this shot will have a narrower field of view than both masters, we'll probably have to give both actors new marks so that they are in frame. We will then have to rehearse the action of Martin receiving the box so that it all takes place on screen (in wide shots, actors have a lot of freedom of movement, but when you get into tighter shots those same actions have to be more constrained). And, again, there may be lighting involved: we might key each actor, or provide each with some fill, or use a silk again.

Camera Movement. There are no camera moves in this scene, but let's say that while shot-listing the DP and I decided that a short push-in should be added to Martin's CU (shot 3). This could be done with a Dana Dolly and in the final shot list that would look like this:

Shot	Type	Lens	Movement	Action	Notes	Start	End
3	CU Martin	Long	Push-in	Martin waiting, reacts to truck, exits frame	Dana Dolly	9:50	10:30

Note that I am allotting an additional 20 minutes to complete the shot since we would have to set up the dolly, get the camera on the speed rails level it, determine the exact start and end points of the move, then rehearse that move along with the focus pull before we start shooting. What we could also do is use the Dana Dolly for both shots 2 and 3. In that case, we would set up the dolly, find our framing for shot 2, take that shot without any camera movement, then swap lenses and begin rehearsing the move for shot 3. That would look like this:

Shot	Type	Lens	Movement	Action	Notes	Start	End
2	MS Martin	Normal	Static	Martin waiting, reacts to truck, exits frame	Dana Dolly	9:30	10:00
3	CU Martin	Long	Push-in	Martin waiting, reacts to truck, exits frame	Dana Dolly	10:00	10:30

If we can seamlessly transition from shooting the medium shot to shooting the closeup, as would be the case if there were not a camera move, then that will be more efficient (the actor, for example, won't have time to wander off while we futz with the dolly). In any case, if we were to add a push-in to Martin's closeup, then the storyboard would also be revised, and it might look like this:

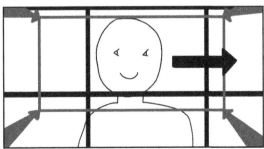

3. CU Push-in: Martin excited, exits frame

Storyboards should always indicate camera movements using arrows. In some cases, this may require that you draw more than one panel to show the start and end of a camera move. This would be the case if we were, for example, to revise the master and begin with it looking down the street towards the arriving truck before panning with the truck as it parks in front of Martin's house, revealing him in the window waiting:

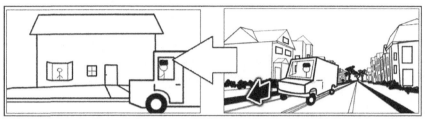

1. Master: delivery truck approaches, pan left with it to reveal Martin's house with him waiting in the window

These panels may read backwards to you, but the arrows clearly indicate the sequence of events.

Number of Shots Each Day. As I've hopefully made plain, there are only so many shots you can shoot each day. A shoot day is never longer than 12 hours, including setup time and wrap. You must also take a lunch break, which even if you schedule that for 45 minutes is going to take an hour (lunch begins when the last person in the catering line gets their food). And, if you make a company move during a shoot day, that also counts as time you are not shooting. Even the time you spend blocking and lighting counts as time you are not shooting.

There is no easy formula for what constitutes a reasonable number of shots. If we take the scene above, I am allowing about four hours for five camera setups and six shots (shots 2 and 3 are, once again, the same camera setup: Martin's MS and CU in the window). But that includes setup time. If we were to follow this scene with another scene in front of Martin's house, setup time would no longer be a factor and we might get off the same number of setups and shots in three hours or less. But if our next scene were inside the house, then we would have to factor in lighting, and in that case, it might again take us about four hours to get off the same number of setups and shots.

When you time shots, always consider the difference between camera setups and shots. When you move from shooting, say, an OTS of an actor to shooting a CU of that actor, you are getting two shots out of the same camera setup, thus the transition from shooting the first shot to shooting the second shot usually happens quickly.

But when you transition from shooting, say, a master to shooting an OTS, those are completely different camera setups, so the transition takes longer, especially if it is an interior scene with lighting. The DP may add highlights to coverage shots that were not used in the master. They may also add a bit more fill on the shadow side of an actor's face because it is sometimes the case that lighting ratios are a bit more contrasty in masters than in coverage shots. The DP might even subtly alter the direction of the key light in a coverage shot depending on whether the camera is providing a profile view or a more frontal view of the actor.

These are things you will learn through experience; my point for now is this: don't underestimate the time is takes to compose and light each shot. This all happens much more quickly for day exterior scenes, but even then, you can't expect to knock off a new shot every ten minutes. My advice, therefore, is to be realistic about what can actually be accomplished by using the principles laid out above to estimate how long it will take to shoot each shot you have planned.

Finalize the Shooting Schedule

If scenes have been deleted or new scenes have been added during script revisions, then the shooting schedule will obviously have to be revised. It is also possible that once all the shot lists are finalized, the shooting order of certain scenes will change. If, for example, you scheduled a scene at the end of a shoot day because you thought it would require only a few shots, but now realize it is going to take many more shots, then you may want to move it earlier in the day when the crew will still be fresh and ready to work quickly.

But whether or not scenes have been added or deleted, and whether or not the final shot lists require rethinking the shooting order of certain scenes, never go into production with a shooting schedule that has not been approved by both the DP and the AD. If they are not confident that each shoot day can be completed, then you are in trouble. So, always take some time during prep to talk through the shooting schedule with them. As you do this, keep in mind all that I have said about cutting and/or combining scenes to make a schedule work. It is never too late to improve a shooting schedule.

Final Wardrobe Approvals

Presumably, the costumer has been keeping you in the loop as they make decisions about costumes, in which case you may be approving wardrobe piecemeal. Alternatively, you may meet with them to approve everything all at once, in which case they should provide you with choices and anything you don't choose can be returned. If the costumer is planning a final wardrobe fitting with all or some of the actors, that is an ideal time for you to review their work. Since they will likely try to schedule all these fittings on the same day, you can simply attend and approve items in collaboration with each actor as they try various clothing on. If you will be renting any costumes, though, the costumer should at least send pictures before they check out anything from a costume shop so that money isn't wasted renting items that won't be used.

Crew Deal Memos and Cast Appearance Releases

Before shooting begins, the producer or AD gets signed releases from all actors, extras and crew members. When an actor signs an Appearance Release, they are, among other things, giving you the right to use their likeness in the film and in any promotional materials. It is very important that every actor and extra sign this release. A former classmate of mine did not get a release from an actor on a feature he made and when the actor later decided that they did not like how they came off in the film, he was forced to cut them out of it.

As to the Crew Deal Memo, this lays out the terms of service – what crew are expected to do and what they are prohibited from doing while on set, for example no drug or alcohol use – plus it establishes that all work is for hire, meaning that no one's labor on the project gives them any claim to even partial ownership of the film, which remains your intellectual property (though if your department is financing your project, then they are essentially functioning as a studio and may own the film outright).

A standard Crew Deal Memo and Appearance Release are included in the online resources for this book. It is always best to get these signed before the first day of production, but that won't always be possible due to people's schedules, in which case anyone who hasn't signed one can do so *before* they begin work when they arrive for their first day on set. Since everyone is required to check in with the AD when they arrive to set (see call sheets below), it is usually easiest if the AD handles this and then turns each document over to the producer.

Finally, if your production is SAG signatory, then the producer completes the agreement and downloads blank time sheets and related forms from SAG's website.

Final Production Meeting

As mentioned, it is a good idea to hold a final production meeting a few days before shooting begins. The AD runs this meeting and, in addition to you, the producer, DP, PD, gaffer and key grip should be in attendance, along with the sound mixer if they are a student.[4]

Find a room at school where everyone can sit around a table and then talk through each shoot day, from load in to wrap. It can be helpful to read the script aloud in *shooting order*, beginning with shoot day 1, stopping to discuss each scene before moving on to the next one. If there is dialogue, roles can be assigned and the AD can read stage directions. But if you don't read through each scene, some production issues may fall through the cracks.

The purpose of this meeting is not to talk through final shot lists, floorplans and storyboards. You've already discussed those at meetings with the DP and AD, though you will almost certainly be required to talk these through with your instructor at some point. Still, have copies of the final shot lists, floorplans and storyboards on hand because you will likely refer to them (especially if concerns arise about the number of shots that are planned). The main purpose of this meeting is to review the plan for completing each and every scene. If the scene above were to be discussed, we would certainly review the following:

- Picture Vehicle. Where is the delivery truck coming from – is it being rented or borrowed? How is it getting to set? Is the actor playing the deliverywoman insured to drive it and, if not, how will that be handled during shooting?
- Permits. Has the producer permitted several parking spots directly in front of the house so that the delivery truck has space to pull up? Who will be posting those signs and when (they have to go up a minimum of 24 hours in advance)?
- Props. Does Art that have an appropriate box for the scene, including backup boxes, and how will the box be weighted so that it is neither too light nor to heavy?
- Signage. Is signage being used on the truck and, if so, is it ready to go?
- Call Time. Since this is the first scene up at the start of the day, is an 8:00am call time best? As discussed in Chapter 3, when shooting day exteriors, it is best to be ready to shoot when there is sufficient light for a first take. If call time were to be pulled back, maybe to as early as 5:00am depending on the time of year, will work lights need to be set up at the start of the day, and if so, should the actors come a half hour later since we might not want to block with them in the dark?
- Setup Time. Have we allowed sufficient setup time based on where gear will be staged and what gear the gaffer and key grip intend to use, as determined during tech scouts?
- Breakfast. Finally, since this is the first scene of the day, where will breakfast be set up? Who will be in charge of this: the producer or will they delegate breakfast to a PA?

Holding a final production meeting is important, so carve out a couple of hours for it.

Schedule Catering

Catering can be scheduled weeks in advance of production, but once the final production meeting has been held, a revised lunch schedule may have to be submitted to the caterer. If, as in the example above, call time were pulled back three hours, then lunch would have to happen that much sooner. Again, cast and crew must be fed after six hours.

The producer must also work out a plan for crafty. In the budget for *Orbiting*, I allowed $65 a day for this, but that is an average cost over the length of the shoot. Always purchase as much crafty as possible prior to the first day of production and then supplement it along the way. If the producer delegates crafty to a PA, especially one without a lot of set experience, they should provide them with a shopping list to ensure that in addition to chips and pretzels and things like that, healthy options are also available.

Note: no one should go out of pocket on your production unless absolutely necessary. Give the producer petty cash for crafty and other supplies. In terms of props and gear, which are discussed next, most prop shops and rental houses, in my experience, will allow other people to pay with your credit card so long as you provide them with a copy of your driver's license and a letter authorizing them to do so. Alternatively, you can phone in with your credit card information or pay online.

Schedule and Organize Pickups

This must be handled as efficiently as possible. Think back to *Orbiting*. I budgeted two prep days for the truck to accommodate both Art and G&E. This was only feasible, though, because that project has just one interior location – the house – which requires significant set dressing. If on your film you have multiple interior locations that require significant set dressing, and if Art can't load into all of them on the same day, then you may need a second truck for props and set dressing. As to Wardrobe, people in that department typically use their own vehicles to transport costumes to each set.

Proper Equipment Checkout. When you accept any piece of equipment, you are agreeing that it is in good working order. This means that if you get to set and discover something isn't working, it will be assumed by your department's equipment office or by the rental house that it was damaged on your production. This makes you liable for repair or replacement costs, even if you feel absolutely certain that the item was already broken when you picked it up. Moreover, if you discover that an essential piece of gear is not working, say the camera or sound recorder, then you won't be able to shoot. For both these reasons, gear must be tested during checkout.

I'm not saying that every C-stand has to be set up, but every flag and net should be counted and inspected for tears, which are common and usually not a problem, but any flag or net that is badly torn should not be accepted. Every light stand and barn door should be inspected, every scrim counted and every light should be plugged in and turned on. And while it is not necessary to test every stinger, each one should still be inspected to ensure that there are no exposed wires or cracked plugs. I could go on and cover every potential G&E item, but I think you get the idea.

Likewise, every piece of camera and sound gear must be tested. The camera should be built on sticks, powered up, configured according to the project's workflow, and test footage shot. Every camera accessory should also be tested along with every lens in order to ensure that each one mounts properly and that its focus and diaphragm rings are in good working order. Similarly, the sound recorder should be powered up and audio recorded using each mic and input.

What all of this implies is that that key crewmembers must participate in checkout. Where my students always run into trouble is when only a few people participate in equipment pickups. It's more work than they can handle, so items fall through the cracks, and faulty equipment, if there is any, is only discovered on set when it is too late.

No one – not the staff in the equipment office at your school, or the staff at rental houses – wants to give out faulty gear, but it is still up to your team to ensure this doesn't happen. This is why, at minimum, the DP, 1st AC, gaffer, key grip and sound mixer (if they are a student) must participate in equipment pickups. And unless you are rehearsing or holding a last-minute casting session or location scout, you should help out too.

Call Sheets

Finally, the AD is in charge of call sheets. They distribute one for each day of production. For the first day, it should be emailed to cast and crew the afternoon before and include an encouraging message about how exciting it is to finally go into production. After that, each call sheet should be emailed once wrap for the current day is complete so that the AD can include a note of gratitude and a positive account of how work progressed that day. Even if work went badly, the AD can still thank everyone for their patience and goodwill. Here is a sample call sheet for the first day of *Orbiting* (the street exterior scenes):

UCLA Film/TV

Director	Karen Glienke	310-XXX-XXXX		Date	3/10/XX	Day 1 of 4
1st AD	Marla Student	323-XXX-XXXX	**Orbiting**	Breakfast	5:00 AM	Available at craft services - backyard
Producer	Armando Student	323-XXX-XXXX		Lunch	12:00 PM	Backyard at house

Location	456 Maple Street, Los Angeles 900XX		Nearest Hospital	
Sunrise	6:08 AM	**CALL TIME**	West Side Community Hospital	
Sunset	5:54 PM		123 Magnolia Avenue, Los Angeles 900XX	
Weather	Sunny 58 AM 72 NOON 64 PM	**6:00 AM**	310-XXX-XXXX	

SCENES	SET AND DESCRIPTION	CHARACTERS	D/N	PAGES	LOCATION/NOTES
8	EXT CITY STREET	1,6	D	2/8	8100 Block Western Boulevard
	Trevor runs from store manager				
9	EXT RESIDENTIAL STREET	1,7,8	D	1	456 Maple Street - east of house
	Trevor bumps into Scott and Amber				
3	EXT RESIDENTIAL STREET	1	D	1/8	456 Maple Street - west of house
	Trevor walks forlornly to the store				
2, 11	INT LIVING ROOM - PRE LIGHT ONLY				456 Maple Street
	Mom and dad send Trevor to the store / Trevor returns home				
	TOTAL PAGES	1 3/8			

TALENT	NAME	CHARACTER	STATUS	RPT	SET	H/MU	MINOR	SPECIAL INSTRUCTIONS
1	Jafar Actor	TREVOR	SW	5:30 AM	6:00 AM	6:30 AM	N	
6	Rodrigo Actor	STORE MANAGER	SW	5:30 AM	6:00 AM	6:45 AM	N	
7	Max Actor	SCOTT	SWF	8:00 AM	8:30 AM	8:45 AM	N	Appearance Release needed
8	Ada Actor	AMBER	SWF	8:00 AM	8:30 AM	9:00 AM	N	Appearance Release needed

PARKING		LOCATION NOTES	
SEE MAP: Actors park on Maple. Camera and G&E park on Oak, NE of house. Art and Wardrobe park on Oak, SE of house. Sound, Makeup and Scripty park on Rose, NW of house. Everyone else parks on Rose, SW of house.		Do not enter house upon arrival. Enter through side gate into backyard. Crafty and breakfast will be available there. Please be as quiet as possible. Bathroom is through back sliding door, off left side of kitchen.	

CREW	NAME	PHONE	RPT	CREW	NAME	PHONE	RPT
Director	Karen Glienke	310-XXX-XXXX	5:00 AM	Gaffer	Bryant Student	310-XXX-XXXX	5:30 AM
1st AD	Marla Student	323-XXX-XXXX	5:00 AM	Key Grip	Dehanza Student	310-XXX-XXXX	5:30 AM
Producer	Armando Student	310-XXX-XXXX	5:00 AM	Script Supervisor	Anthony Student	565-XXX-XXXX	5:30 AM
Director of Photography	Vittoria Student	213-XXX-XXXX	5:00 AM	Sound Mixer/Boom	Sarah Professional	213-XXX-XXXX	6:00 AM
1st AC	Ingrid Student	415-XXX-XXXX	5:30 AM	Makeup	Aerin Professional	323-XXX-XXXX	6:00 AM
DIT/2nd AC	Adam Student	626-XXX-XXXX	5:30 AM	Set PA	Victor Student	310-XXX-XXXX	5:30 AM

First, crew call, which is the time that work commences, is clearly indicated, as is the address of the location, which in this case is the house that is serving as a base camp. Additionally, every participant is assigned a time to report, typically a half hour before call, so that they have time to eat and to prepare for the day's work. Key personnel, though, are expected to arrive an hour early so that in addition to eating they also have time to review, yet again, the production plan for the day, and to deal with any last-minute problems, say someone calling in sick.

Next, information is provided about which scenes are to be shot, in what order, as well as which actors are in which scenes. Note that since the actors playing Scott and Amber are not in the first scene, they report later. Such staggered call times are common. The AD uses the timed shot lists to determine when to call actors. In the case of scene 8, which is the first scene up on this day, the shot list might look like this:

Scene 8: EXT. CITY STREET – DAY – Trevor runs from store manager

Shot	Type	Lens	Movement	Action	Notes	Start	End
1	Master - oner	Wide		Trevor, in the lead, runs from store manager. After Trevor exits behind camera, the store manager stops in a MS and delivers his line.	Off-load, setup, relocate to Blvd, blocking, shoot, return to house	6:00	8:30

In other words, assuming it is bright enough to start shooting by 7:15, and assuming that by then key crew have relocated from the house to the boulevard and also blocked the action, set up the camera and gotten the actors through makeup and wardrobe, then shooting can probably be finished by 8:00 since the scene is being covered in decidedly simple oner. That allows a half hour for everyone to get back to the house in time to start blocking scene 9 at 8:30.

Lastly, in terms of scenes, the call sheet also indicates, as discussed in Chapter 3, that once the street exteriors are complete, pre-lighting will begin for scenes 2 and 11 in the living room.

As to status, SW means that the actors playing Trevor and the store manager start work on this day. SWF means that the actors playing Scott and Amber start work and finish work on this day. On the next two call sheets, then, it would be indicated that the actor playing Trevor works (W), but on the final call sheet, the one for the shoot day at the store, it be would be indicated that he works and finishes (WF). The same would also be indicated for the store manager on the final call sheet. The reason to keep track of this information is because it must be submitted to SAG via a Day Out of Days or DOOD report (SAG supplies a template for this on their website), and it is simply standard practice to migrate this information to call sheets because that allows the AD to easily keep track of each actor's schedule.

Finally, note that information about the weather is also provided (so that people can plan ahead in terms of clothing) along with information about parking, about how to access the house, about where breakfast will be available and where the nearest emergency room is located in the event that someone gets injured on set.

In any case, once the call sheet for the first day of a production has been distributed to cast and crew, the final countdown begins. But before we turn to production, we need to consider rehearsals, which are the subject of the next chapter.

Notes

1   Since casting and location scouting have their own chapters, they are not discussed in this chapter, nor are rehearsals, which are covered in the next chapter.

2   For example, when you create proxy files, these obviously need to be at a lower resolution than the original camera files so that the editing software can handle them, but it also matters what computer you will be running that editing software on. Don't assume that proxy files that play back well on a high-end desktop system at school will do the same on your comparatively sluggish laptop if you intend to edit on both or only on your laptop. Discovering a discrepancy like that after all your proxies have been rendered will leave you feeling very unhappy, to say the least.

3   If you need more help understanding screen direction, there are dozens of online videos that cover the 180-degree line. I also talk more about screen direction in Chapter 12.

4   If there are special costume or makeup requirements in a number of scenes, then those department heads need to attend the final production meeting too. But if there are only special requirements in one or two scenes, as when I once shot someone walking into a river fully clothed, which required that a plan be in place to dry the actor off between takes and have dry clothes ready for each time the camera rolled, then those are things that can be discussed in advance of the final production meeting, perhaps over the phone, and then the AD can communicate what is planned to everyone at the meeting.

11 Rehearse It Before You Shoot It

It is not always possible to get together with actors to rehearse your script prior to production. They may not be available or they may not all be available at the same times. But as I said in Chapter 9 on casting, always ask actors about their availability for rehearsals when you offer them a role. Any actor willing to commit to a major part in your project should also be willing to at least try to work this out.

At the same time, rehearsing does not always require running scenes with actors. Talking through what happens in each scene is also a rehearsal. And that can be done individually with each actor, even via a video communication app. In other words, it is not necessary to get all your actors together at the same time or to even meet them in person in order to rehearse.

At some point you do need to run scenes with all the actors prior to shooting them, but any shaping of scenes you can do in advance of production will be helpful and save you time on set. And even when you do get actors together you will discover that talking about what happens in a scene and why those things happen is more productive than running a scene over and over again. Why this is the case, will become clearer as we go along.

What do I mean by shaping a scene? Directors, and actors, all work differently. But they don't work *that* differently. In most every case, the goal of rehearsals is to establish the intentions of characters in each scene and the means by which the actors playing those characters will attempt to realize those intentions.[1] This has to do with *objectives* and *actions*. What do the characters want? What do they do to try to get what they want? *Objectives* and *actions*.

This does not happen in a vacuum, though. When people talk about the performances of actors, they often invoke certain ideals: they say that performances should be truthful and naturalistic. The goal is to create the impression of real people in real situations. There is nothing wrong with that, but naturalism will only get you so far. You are, after all, trying to tell a story, and so performances must also serve to progress the story.

For this reason, naturalism is less important than *plausibility*. In fact, so long as a performance plausibly moves a story forward, then naturalism may not matter much at all. Think of a comedy you like. I will pick *Schitt's Creek*. Over time

DOI: 10.4324/9781003169864-11

the tone of that show became more sentimental, but when it began, many of the actors' performances ran a narrow gamut from the exaggerated to the grotesque. But their performances still plausibly moved the story forward in each episode.

Plausibility

Films are dramatized fictions. There is often no narrator to directly address the audience and tell the story in words, as is the case in prose fiction. Instead, we eavesdrop on characters as they interact with each other, and those interactions, called scenes, are how we glean most of the relevant story information. Even films that use title cards and voiceover will still typically have such scenes, and those scenes, as much as the title cards and voiceover, must move the story forward. The question is, how do scenes do that? In the first place, scenes lead to outcomes.

Here is a simple example. Let's say that at the start of a scene two characters – the protagonist and their adversary – are poised to do battle. But let's also say that the protagonist does not want to fight; instead, they try to persuade their adversary to join them in an alliance against a common enemy because that would be to their mutual benefit. And let's also say that the adversary, once they realize what the protagonist wants, works to convince them that they must each follow their own path alone, which is why they must fight.

As discussed in the chapter on casting, each character in a scene typically wants the other character(s) in the scene *to do something*. In this case, the protagonist wants their adversary to form an alliance and the adversary wants the protagonist to fight. Those are both objectives that can lead to an *outcome* and whichever outcome is achieved, that will move the story forward. If the protagonist prevails, then two enemies will become allies, and that means new story events are now possible that were not possible before they joined forces.

At the start of most any scene a set of story premises will be in place and by the end of that scene some of those premises will have been revised and new ones will have been introduced. And that moves the story forward. Most scenes, in other words, *set the stage for future story events*. Put differently, most scenes make the rest of the story possible.[2] This won't be true in every case, but even if a scene is just a shot of your protagonist staring sadly out a window, you are likely showing us that to justify something they will do in a later scene. And whatever that is, it will be something they would not do if they were not sad.

And this brings me to the crux of the matter: justifying future events. Sticking with the example above, if viewers do not believe that the protagonist has successfully gained their adversary's trust, that they have truly convinced them to change their mind and join forces rather than fight, then the outcome of that scene – their alliance – will likely seem contrived and unconvincing, in short, *implausible*. And in that case, the rest of the story will suffer. Future story events, or at least some of them, will not feel justified.

A certain amount of persuasion is always required in storytelling. You are selling your version of events to an audience, just as you do when you tell a story to a friend. And when you tell a story to a friend, maybe they believe your version of events, maybe they don't, and the same is true of audiences. Maybe they believe you, maybe they don't. And since you don't get to tell your story directly, but must largely use your actors as surrogates, then the plausibility you seek to achieve is mostly achievable through their performances.

Your script needs to work too, but that is not enough. In fact, your script can become a crutch. This happens when, as director, you rely on it too much to tell the story. You think that just because the actors are speaking the right lines of dialogue and following the script directions (they sit, they stand, they open a door), that somehow the story is unfolding. But then you get to the editing room and struggle to make the footage work. It all matches the script, but little of it actually tells the story.

Your script won't direct itself. It is up to you to ensure that each performance moves the story forward in a plausible, credible way. And this brings us back to *objectives* and *actions*. These are what most scenes are made up of. They are the raw materials that you shape during rehearsals. I will provide practical advice on how to do this, but first we need to look more closely at how objectives and actions lead to plausible outcomes.

Objectives, Actions and Outcomes

Let's take an example from my favorite movie, *The Apartment* (1960), written by Billy Wilder and Izzy Diamond and directed by Wilder. It tells the story of two lonely people, an accountant, C. C. Baxter (Jack Lemon), and the elevator operator, Fran Kubelik (Shirley MacLaine), he falls in love with. Near the beginning of their budding romance, it is revealed that Fran recently had an affair with Baxter's boss, Jeff Sheldrake (Fred MacMurray), a relationship she ended because Sheldrake did not follow through on his promise to divorce his wife and marry her. But right before Baxter and Fran are set to go on their first date, Fran meets Sheldrake for a drink.

When Fran arrives at the restaurant she says, "Good evening, Mr. Sheldrake." That formal greeting is intended to keep him at arm's-length, but as anyone who has ever been in love knows, she wouldn't be there unless she were interested in getting back together with him. The question, then, is what would motivate her to take him back? The answer is a commitment that he will, as promised, divorce his wife and marry her. That is her *scene objective*. To get that commitment.

What does Sheldrake want? He wants Fran back, but on his own terms, without having to make that commitment. So, he tries to convince her that neither of them can be happy so long as they remain apart. That is his *scene objective*. He seeks to take advantage of Fran's feelings for him in an attempt to reestablish the *status quo* of their relationship.

Again, each character in a scene typically wants the other character(s) in the scene *to do something*. Fran wants Sheldrake to make good on his promise and Sheldrake wants Fran to admit she can't live without him. Without objectives like that, a scene typically has nowhere to go, and if a scene isn't trying to get somewhere, it can't move the story forward. If you say, for example, that your character's objective in a scene is to be happy, then you're ignoring story to focus only on character. Besides, everyone wants to be happy. Fran wants to be happy. The question is what will make her happy. And we know the answer: a commitment from Sheldrake.

That is an objective that can be pursued. Fran can actively try to change Sheldrake's mind, and thus his behavior, which will lead to an outcome. So, it is essential, at least in dialogue scenes like this one, that each character be focused on changing the behavior of the other character(s).

As this implies, each character can potentially fail. If there is no chance of failure, then nothing is at stake. If Fran fails to get a commitment from Sheldrake, then she can't be with the man she loves. That is what is at stake for her character. What is at stake for Sheldrake is his ego, his belief that as a powerful and successful man he deserves whatever he wants.

It follows from this, that at least one character will succeed. This won't always be the case. Some scenes end in a stalemate, in which case the conflict will be picked up in a later scene. And some scenes are simply about a character trying to accomplish a task, one they may fail to complete, for example they fail to pick up their kid from school on time, in which case their failure will engender new story events. And some scenes, as I said, are just about a character staring sadly out a window, in which case their sadness will lead to new story events. But in the scene that we are focusing on now, either Fran will succeed and Sheldrake will fail or Sheldrake will succeed and Fran will fail.

And again, what is most important is that each character's success or failure seem plausible to the audience. If Fran takes Sheldrake back, which she does, we must *believe* that she would do that. The only reason the scene exists is to *earn* that outcome; otherwise, the filmmakers would just have them get back together. But they can't do that. What they must do is provide a scene that serves to convince us, the audience, that Fran would take a man back into her life who has repeatedly lied to her and strung her along.

That's a hard sell, which is to say, difficult to pull off. But such is the nature of storytelling. It requires that you get the audience to believe your story, the story you want to tell, which in this case is a story about a woman who takes back a dishonest, manipulative man.

Every scene is a little story, one that is either believable, or plausible, or not. For this reason, writing is key. How the scene is written, whether or not it contains the events that will make an outcome possible, is important. But equally important are *actions*.

Actions are the tactics actors use *moment to moment* to try to get what their characters want. To plead is an action. To scold is an action. To mock is an action. To apologize is an action. To flirt, flatter or seduce are all actions. Almost any verb you can imagine is an action that an actor can *direct at another actor* in a scene (or sometimes direct at themselves, as discussed below).

Again, and I apologize for belaboring the point, characters have objectives. They want other characters to do something. And each action an actor plays is typically aimed at another actor in the scene in an attempt to influence the behavior of that actor's character, including their beliefs, until a new narrative state of affairs is plausibly and convincingly achieved.

Let's briefly consider how this works in the scene with Fran and Sheldrake. As mentioned, Fran begins by saying, "Good evening, Mr. Sheldrake." There are any number of ways to deliver that line, which on its surface reads like a respectful greeting, but Shirley MacLaine, who plays Fran, uses it in an opposite way to challenge Sheldrake's authority, to even embarrass him. He is, after all, a married man and this is a clandestine meeting in a public place, so she is immediately not playing by his rules. She is taunting or provoking him. That is her *action*.

And her action is a success: Fred MacMurray, who plays Sheldrake, glances over his shoulder to make sure that no one heard her say his name. And this helps Fran in her quest to get what she wants: a commitment. She's letting Sheldrake know from the outset that she will not be manipulated by him anymore, that she's in charge now, that they are playing by her rules.

But Sheldrake only partially defers. He replies, "Please, Fran, not so loud." That line could be delivered as a command, or as a rebuke, or in any number of ways that would allow Sheldrake to reassert his authority, but Fred MacMurray delivers it as an appeal, as a request. That is his *action*. In later scenes he is quite forceful when Fran doesn't play by his rules or questions his motives: he dismisses her concerns, he chastises her, he accuses her of being unreasonable. But doing any of those things here would not help him get what he wants. So, with his line delivery, his action, he is asking her to please cut him some slack until she's heard what he has to say.

And some of what he has to say does get to her. For example, he tells Fran he misses her. His action is to reassure her or, more specifically, to assure her that his feelings for her are sincere, that their past relationship was important to him. And as he is doing that a waiter brings Fran a frozen daiquiri, her favorite drink, which Sheldrake ordered in advance of her arrival. This allows him to demonstrate that he is considerate, which is an action. And his two actions together cause Fran to become nostalgic, smile and say, though a bit sadly, "Like old times." In other words, she admits she misses him too and the times they spent together in this restaurant. But by admitting that, she is showing her cards, and she realizes that, so she catches herself, switches tactics and bitterly says, "Same booth, same song."

Now, that line is literally true. They are in fact in the same booth they always met in when they were having an affair, and the piano player is in fact playing the same song, their song (it's called "Jealous Lover" and he begins playing it as soon as he sees Fran come through the door), but Fran means something quite different. Shirley MacLaine delivers the line as an accusation, as if to say, "Here we go again, you're trying to manipulate me by ordering my favorite drink and giving me the same old song and dance about how much you love me." And in that way, she tries to get back on track in pursuit of her objective.

Her line reading demonstrates the difference between *text* and *subtext*. The words literally mean one thing but she infuses them with a different meaning. But the fact that Fran crumbles for a moment and admits she still has feelings for Sheldrake is significant. If we are going to accept at the end of the scene that she takes him back, then we need to know near the beginning of the scene that he can still affect her, that she is still vulnerable to his charms, that her tough stance is mostly a façade.

And we learn all of that primarily by way of Shirley MacLaine's performance. "Like old times" could also be delivered bitterly along with "Same booth, same song," but that wouldn't help tell the story. And perhaps the first time around MacLaine did deliver the line as an accusation, and if so, then Wilder gave her an adjustment. There is, of course, no way to know what happened on set, I am only trying to point out again that it is up to the director to ensure that each performance moves the story forward in a plausible, credible way that earns each scene's outcome.

In any case, now that Fran has shown her cards, the scene's outcome begins to seem inevitable. When Sheldrake flatters her by saying, "I'm so crazy about you, Fran," she replies, "Let's not start on that again, Jeff. Please. I'm just beginning to get over it." That line could as well be delivered as an accusation, or even as a demand, but Shirley MacLaine delivers it as a plea. She is begging him to please stop tormenting her. She's not giving up on her objective, but her tactics are becoming less effective. She is little by little giving Sheldrake more power. And again, we understand she is doing that mostly because of Shirley MacLaine's performance.

This is why Fred MacMurray, as Sheldrake, understands it too. The more he sees Shirley MacLaine, as Fran, break down – and she does eventually start crying – the more confident his character becomes. At the same time, Sheldrake is not stupid. He is a master manipulator. He knows what Fran wants, and so after he wears her down by playing on her emotions, he surprises her (that is an action) by saying, "I spoke to my lawyer this morning," and with that, he's got her. The scene concludes with Fran calling him, "Jeff, darling."

That's quite a reversal, from "Good evening, Mr. Sheldrake" to "Jeff, darling." But it is *earned* because Fran believes she has gotten what she wanted. She believes she has attained her objective. And that leads to an outcome: they get back together.

It is a complex outcome because we know it is actually Sheldrake who has succeeded. He has in fact not given Fran anything, he has only said he talked to his lawyer, which is vague and noncommittal, all the more so because he never mentions marrying Fran (as I said, writing is also key, it must provide the events needed to keep the story going). But Fran, blinded by her feelings for Sheldrake, feelings she can't hide, despite her best efforts – as revealed though MacLaine's performance – takes his statement to mean more, and that is all that matters.

In this way, the scene reaches a credible and convincing outcome. At the start of the scene, they are not a couple. Then little by little we are convinced that Fran will take Sheldrake back.

And once we have been convinced of that, the rest of the story can unfold. First, Fran stands up Baxter, which thwarts his romantic desire and puts their relationship on hold, then Sheldrake begins again the process of stringing Fran along until this time around she becomes so despairing that she attempts suicide. But until Fran attempts suicide Baxter cannot save her, and until he saves her and becomes her caregiver their mutual affection cannot grow, and until their mutual affection grows Fran cannot realize that it is Baxter who loves her and not Sheldrake, and until she realizes that she and Baxter cannot get together, which is the end of the movie.

Again, each scene typically serves to make the rest of the story possible.

And this process happens moment to moment, little by little one step at a time, with the performances of the actors doing much of the heavy lifting in terms of communicating the story that is unfolding and earning the outcomes of scenes.

The great Russian acting teacher Konstantin Stanislavski likened scenes to scores. A score is composed of musical notation which specifies not only what is to be played by each musician, but how, within certain limits, they are to play it. He encouraged his students to compose a score for each scene, one that comprised all the actions they would play in pursuit of their character's objectives (he actually did not use the word objective; we talk about objectives, but Stanislavski said that in each scene a character has a *problem* they must solve, but both terms convey that characters are trying to accomplish something).

The obvious takeaway from Stanislavski's analogy is that a scene, as it is performed by actors, is like a piece of music, as it is performed by musicians. Each action must unfold in the right order and in the right way. Just as every error made by a musician is not the score, so too is every missed or misplayed action by an actor not the story.

Actors have to play the story. If Shirley MacLaine did not reveal her character's true feelings by admitting that she misses Sheldrake (as opposed to accusing him of endlessly misleading her) and if she did not later beg him to stop tormenting her (as opposed to demanding that he stop playing games), then the outcome of the scene would not be earned. Until we and Sheldrake both know that Fran is susceptible to his manipulations, he can't plausibly close the deal.

For this reason, actions are more important than objectives. Without objectives there cannot be outcomes, but without actions those outcomes cannot be earned. Actions, which are performed, primarily tell the story. That is the whole point of my example from *The Apartment*: the moment-to-moment unfolding of actions earns the scene's outcome. Otherwise, as I said, the filmmakers would just have Fran and Sheldrake get back together. But they can't do that.

Rehearsals, then, are mostly about helping actors understand why they would play one action rather than another. Why they would, for example, scold and not flatter, or beg and not demand.

Picking Actions

For actors, picking actions is largely a matter of reacting moment to moment to what is happening in a scene as it is happening. Acting is reacting, as the saying goes. If an actor, for example, registers that their character has just been insulted by another character, then they must react to that. They may defend themselves. Or they may respond in kind and insult the other character. Or they may try to make that other character feel guilty for having insulted them.

And the measure by which many actors judge their moment-to-moment responses, is whether they are truthful or not. This is sometimes called *the truth of moment*. It means that in the moment an actor must respond truthfully to what has just happened to their character.[3]

But this is still difficult because it is almost never the case that there is only one truthful response to an action that another actor plays. All three responses I proposed above are truthful responses to being insulted. The dialogue, of course, can provide guidance. If the first character's line is "That dress you have on is hideous," and if the second character's line is "Well, I think your hair is a joke," then probably they are insulting each other.

However, if the scene is trying to reverse normal expectations, then it may be that the characters are playfully teasing each other. Never take dialogue too literally. Subtext, provided by actors, always means more. But for the sake of simplicity, let's assume that the first character, at least, is delivering an insult.

With that established, let's change the second character's dialogue. If after being told their dress is hideous the second character's line is "I like this dress," it is now less apparent what action is meant to be played. Are they defending themselves or are they trying to make the other character feel guilty? Or are they doing something else entirely, perhaps asserting that the other character's opinion of their dress choice is meaningless to them?

Again, dialogue is rarely on the nose. At one point in the scene with Fran and Sheldrake, for instance, she takes a bite of shrimp and says, "They don't make these shrimp like they used to." But, of course, they make the shrimp like they used to. The meaning behind that line, its subtext, is that once, for a while, the time that she and Sheldrake spent in this restaurant was filled with happiness and promise, but now everything is ruined and nothing is the same.

And we know this is what Fran means because Shirley MacLaine's voice cracks when she delivers the line. She is pitying herself. She may also be trying to make Sheldrake feel sorry for her, which potentially serves her objective (though he seems immune to such appeals), but self-pity is an action too. Characters mock themselves, pity themselves, blame themselves, reward themselves, psych themselves up, etc. all the time.

But Fran's moment of self-pity reveals something else. It demonstrates that solving the problem of what action an actor should play is a matter of determining or specifying what their character believes to be true about the situation. This will lead to an emotional response which will lead to an action.

Because Fran believes that her chance for happiness is gone, she feels miserable, and because she feels miserable, she indulges in self-pity.

Returning to my example above, if we want to know what action the actor should play when they are insulted, we need to know what their character believes about the insult and how that makes them feel. If the character believes their friend has broken trust, then they may get angry and demand an apology. But if they believe they need the other character's approval, then they may feel wounded and pout. If, on the other hand, they don't think much of the other character's fashion sense, then they may feel amused and mock or dismiss them.

All those actions can be played with the line "I like this dress." Try it out and you'll see.

What these examples reveal is that actors must always assess the actions directed at them by other actors in a scene; they must *appraise* them in light of *their character's concerns*. This is done in the moment. An actor can't anticipate another actor's action, they can't know, to stick with our current example, that their character has been insulted until the insult takes place. They must treat the insult as a *new* piece of information that now has to be dealt with.[4] And the first way they must deal with this new information is by appraising it in terms of their character's concerns. Doing that will lead to an emotional response which will lead to an action (more on why this is the case in a moment).

When Sheldrake tells Fran he is crazy about her, he is, as I said, flattering her. That is the action Fred MacMurray plays. And once Shirley MacLaine registers that Sheldrake is using flattery, she has to appraise that action. She can either accept it as an expression of his love or reject it as a ploy. She actually does both. Her initial response is to look surprised and moved. And those emotions almost lead to an action – it seems for a fleeting moment that she might declare her love for him – but then she catches herself again and switches tactics. She *reappraises* his action and rejects it as a ploy. We know this because she suddenly looks pained and begs him to stop tormenting her: "Let's not start on that again, Jeff. Please. I'm just beginning to get over it."

Fred MacMurray now has two new pieces of information to deal with: Fran's slip up, the way she almost tells him she loves him, and her plea that he please let her move on with her life because she is finally getting over him. His response is to smirk and say, "I don't believe you." In other words, he appraises her two actions to mean that she is not getting over it, that she is still in love with him. This leads to an emotional response – confidence bordering on cockiness – which motivates him to brazenly accuse Fran of lying to herself and to him. In this way, he tries to get her to own up the fact that she can't live without him, his objective in the scene.

What I hope you are noticing is that the process repeats again and again. Every action Fred MacMurray directs at Fran must be acknowledged, appraised and responded to by Shirley MacLaine, just as every action Fran directs at Sheldrake must be acknowledged, appraised and responded to by Fred MacMurray.

Once you understand this, and it took me awhile to figure it out when I first started directing, but once you understand this it will become clear to you, as it did to me, that picking actions, what are often called *beats*, is a matter of repeatedly asking and answering three questions:

1. What has the character just learned?
2. How does that make them feel?
3. What does their emotion compel them to do?

What I gained when I started breaking down beats with these questions was a shorthand method of giving actors adjustments. I mentioned earlier that perhaps Wilder had to give an adjustment to Shirley MacLaine for the beat when she says, "Like old times." Her first instinct, a truthful one, may have been to play it as an accusation. But, again, that doesn't help tell the story. So, if that did happen, and for the sake of making a point let's pretend it did, then Wilder had to fix it.

There are multiple ways he could have done that. The easiest way to give an adjustment is to just tell the actor what you want to see. So, Wilder might have simply said, "Smile and reminisce when you say that line." Another easy way to give an actor an adjustment is to act out the beat yourself. In this particular case, that would be called giving a line reading because it's all about how the line is to be delivered, and maybe Wilder did that. Both approaches work, so don't hesitate to use them in a pinch, but they are sometimes disparaged as results-oriented direction.

But an equally simple way to adjust a beat is to clarify for an actor what their character has just *learned* – both their recognition of the action just played by the other actor as well as their appraisal of what that action means for their character. Thus, I might have said something like this to Shirley MacLaine if I were tasked with adjusting her performance:

"Look, you came into the restaurant ready to do battle with Sheldrake, but rather than argue with you or defend himself he tells you he misses you and then you discover that he has also already ordered your favorite drink. It catches you off guard. So, I don't think your first thought is that he's manipulating you, I think your saying to yourself this is nice, this is how it used to be, maybe he really does care."

With that said – and I tend to speak to actors as if they *were* the characters, which you are not required to do – but with that said, I could trust that the rest of the beat – emotion and action – would logically or intuitively follow for her and not need to be mentioned. And the reason it would intuitively follow is because beats are based on how thoughts and feelings motivate our behavior in everyday life.

Let's say that one night you see a shadow move past your bedroom window. If you have no reason to believe that someone should be outside your bedroom then you will probably appraise that shadow as being dangerous, which will initiate a feeling of fear and that will motivate you to do something. You may check that all your windows and doors are locked, or you may call for help, or you may do both.

Emotions, which are responses to our concerns, motivate specific behaviors. We seek solace when we are sad, we lash out when we feel angry, we defend when we feel threatened, we seek protection when we are frightened, we offer help when we feel sorry for or concerned about others. There are other possible behaviors associated with these emotions, but they are limited. We might, for example, withdraw when we feel sad rather than seek solace, but it is unlikely that we will do a little dance. That is something we are more apt to do when we feel very happy.[5]

This isn't about realism *per se*. The beat we are considering now is not in the scene to capture the truth of how people experience lost love, though it may do that; its main job, again, is to help make the outcome of the scene plausible. And one of the ways it does that is by being itself plausible because it moves intuitively from *knowledge* (K) to *emotion* (E) to *action* (A):

K: This is nice, maybe he really does care
E: Comforted, touched
A: Let down my guard, reminisce, admit I miss him too ("Like old times.")

With that done, Fran can now catch herself and *reappraise* his actions in a negative light:

K: Wait a minute, he's doing it again, playing on my emotions
E: Frustrated, hurt
A: Accuse him of lying, of stringing me along again ("Same booth, same song.")

My adjustment above is an attempt to change Shirley MacLaine's appraisal of what just happened to her character in order to engender a different emotional response – Fran is heartened now, not hurt or angry – which leads to an approving and not a disapproving response: she smiles and reminisces, thus admitting she misses Sheldrake too.

Because of this, what you are always looking for when directing actors is an emotion expression followed by an action. If you don't get that, then an actor is simply going through the motions. As almost any professional editor will tell you, cutting into a shot after an actor's emotion, rather than cutting into it on their emotion, will almost invariably make a beat seem mechanical. Editors might not use the word emotion, they might say, "We want to see the character thinking about or processing what has just happened before we see their response," but *emotion expressions are how actors perform the act of thinking*.

This is actually quite commonplace. We all use emotion expressions to communicate our thoughts. A friend is telling you about something unusual they ate and, as you listen, you crinkle your nose and raise your upper lip, a look of disgust, and in that way, without saying anything, you communicate that you think what they ate sounds awful. Or you are telling a story about something frightening you experienced, but rather than say you were scared you make a facial expression or perhaps a sound, maybe a faux scream, to demonstrate how scared you were. Or a friend disappoints you and you simply frown wordlessly.

Actors just happen to be really good at this type of nonverbal communication. They artfully use gestures, facial expressions and vocal expressions, as when Shirley MacLaine's voice cracks as she says, "The don't make these shrimp like they used to," to communicate their character's thoughts – their appraisals – to the audience. Actors, after all, know that they are acting and they know who they are acting for: the audience.

This is important. I began this discussion of objectives and actions with the observation that films are dramatized fictions. There is often no narrator to tell the story in words, which in prose fiction can include going inside the minds of characters to tell us exactly what they are thinking. But this is not to say that we have no access to the thoughts of characters in films. We do, and one way we gain that access is by way of their emotions and the actions those emotions motivate.

Because Shirley MacLaine smiles at Sheldrake, which is the emotion expression she performs, we know that Fran believes, even if only for a moment, that Sheldrake cares, and this explains why she reminisces and admits she misses him too. Later, when Fred MacMurray smirks, which is the emotion expression he performs, we know Sheldrake is confident that Fran still loves him, and this explains why he accuses her of lying to herself and to him.

In other words, as each character receives new information, they appraise that information in light of their character's concerns, which leads to an emotion that in every case reveals what their character believes, which in turn explains what their character does next. If this were not the case, if we could not track the changing beliefs of characters, then we could not follow how Fran transitions from believing Sheldrake is a liar to believing he is sincere.

If the beliefs of characters don't change, and if the audience can't follow those changing beliefs, then a story can't move forward. So, again, what you are always looking for in a performance is an emotion expression followed an action.

Perhaps you've heard someone describe a performance as wooden. A wooden performance is one that lacks emotion. The actor is simply going through the motions. We may think that the only reason we don't like wooden performances is because they are unrealistic, which they are, but we also don't like them because they are unartistic. Part of the art of performance is to communicate to the audience the thoughts and motivations of characters and wooden performances, since they are opaque, give the impression that a character has no mind and is an automaton.

Practically speaking, an actor giving a wooden performance is not *in the moment*. Being in the moment, again, means paying attention to what is happening and responding to it truthfully. Acting is reacting, but reacting, at least in mainstream films, is always an appraisal that leads to an emotional response which leads to an action.

When actors don't pay attention to each other, when they don't register that their character has, for example, just been flattered, and if, in addition to that, they don't think through what that action means to their character (flattery, again, can be understood as a compliment or a ploy), then they won't know what emotion to portray, and that will lead them to just mechanically execute whatever the script says they are supposed to do next.

This is not to say that actors do not feel the emotions they perform, they do, that is also part of being in the moment, but to help an actor be in the moment the best direction you can sometimes give is to simply remind them to pay attention, to watch and listen and *learn*.

Script Analysis and Rehearsals

All of this brings us back to Stanislavski's notion of a written score, which is a form of script analysis. When you analyze a script, even your own, which you may not know as well as you think you do, what you are doing is determining what the characters want and what they might do to get what they want. I say what they *might* do because you really don't know what will and won't work in every case until actors play the scene.

All acting, as I said in Chapter 9, is a form of improvisation. One actor plays an action and another actor responds to it. And since there are almost always multiple possible responses, and since whichever action is chosen must be an effective response to the action just played by the other actor, then that choice, made in the moment, is a kind of improvisation.

The great acting coach Uta Hagen described it as a process of trial and error. In her book *Respect for Acting*, she says this: "Test the action to see if it really gets you where you want. Only dismiss it if it has no before and after. Then look for another one."

In other words, rehearsal is a process of discovery. But since every action must not only be truthful but also serve the story, which is to say have a "before and after," as Hagen puts it, you also need a plan.

Here is a very simple scene I often use with my undergraduates. It is about a young woman who pops by her boyfriend's house unannounced because she is concerned that things have changed between them. Her objective is to get him to come clean, to let her know if they're still a couple or not. Meanwhile, the boyfriend wants to convince her that she is overreacting, that there is nothing wrong. The issue is he's lying. His real goal is to avoid having to actually break up with her, but the way he can avoid that is by putting her at ease. That is his objective.

Again, each character wants the other character *to do something*. Moreover, both objectives can lead to an outcome: either the boyfriend will come clean or the girlfriend will be assured that there is nothing to worry about, in which case, her fears will be allayed. And each of those possible outcomes has the potential to generate new story events.

EXT. CHAD'S HOUSE - DAY

Claire arrives and knocks on the door. She is about
to knock again when the door is opened by Chad.

> CLAIRE
> Hey Stranger.

Chad steps outside, shutting the door behind him.

> CHAD
> Claire, I really can't come out
> to play right now, I'm preparing
> for this important audition.

> CLAIRE
> No, I wasn't, I mean, I was on my
> way home and I thought I'd just
> stop by to say hello. It was a
> bit strange the last time we saw
> each other.

> CHAD
> Last night? It wasn't weird last
> night.

> CLAIRE
> Okay, maybe it wasn't weird. But
> you haven't called and I thought
> maybe something was wrong.

> CHAD
> Claire, I just woke up an hour
> ago.

> CLAIRE
> Ugh. I know. I feel like such an
> asshole.

> CHAD
> You're not an asshole, sweet
> Claire.

> CLAIRE
> No, I know. Um. Well, I'll let
> you work on your audition...
> Maybe we'll do something tonight?

                    CHAD
        Yeah, but I... I think I just
        want to stay in tonight. I've got
        this throat thing.

                    CLAIRE
        Throat thing? Are you sick?

                    CHAD
        No, I'm fine... I just... I'm
        sorry, I just want to feel good
        for my audition.

                    CLAIRE
        No... It's all right. Maybe
        tomorrow night.

                    CHAD
        Yeah, tomorrow night would be
        okay.

Claire is quiet. A long silence follows.

                    CHAD
        Claire?

                    CLAIRE
        Yeah, so I'll call you tomorrow
        night.

                    CHAD
        Thursday night.

                    CLAIRE
        God, you're a genius, I could
        have just said Thursday night.

                    CHAD
        Goodbye, Claire.

                    CLAIRE
        Bye.

They kiss, almost like they have to. Claire walks
off. Chad goes back inside.[6]

I'm going to compose a score for the scene. As I do so, I will discuss how the score relates to rehearsals which, as I said at the start of this chapter, are largely about talking through what happens in each scene and why those things happen. This always has to do with the changing knowledge of characters. So, as I move through the scene, I'm going to keep asking and answering the three questions I proposed earlier:

1. What has the character just learned?
2. How does that make them feel?
3. What does their emotion compel them to do?

To be clear, this was not Stanislavski's approach. I developed these three questions to better understand how scenes work and to make my direction more precise and comprehensible to actors. For this reason, don't insist on the three questions when talking to actors. They won't be familiar with them. Simply focus on the changing knowledge of characters and let the rest follow. This has helped me and my students, so it should help you too.

The scene opens with Claire knocking on Chad's door. That's what the script indicates. But what does Claire know? What does she believe about the situation? In the first place, she knows it was weird last night. Whether it actually was weird or not doesn't matter. She believes it was (they ran out of things to talk about and Chad abruptly went home early, claiming he was tired). She also knows that Chad said he would call and that he hasn't called. The beat is this:

K: It was weird last night and now Chad is avoiding me
E: Worried, insecure
A: Force him to talk about it

But really, that beat precedes the scene. It's what brings Claire to his house. Now that she's there, is anything else going through her mind? The answer will depend on how the actor and I choose to portray her character (assuming I am directing). Is Claire self-aware or not? After all, popping by unannounced can be risky. The person may not be happy to see you.

The question, then, is does Claire know that what she's doing could backfire? I think the answer should be yes. The outcome of the scene, her realization that it is over between her and Chad, will be more effective if at the beginning of the scene she is worried that her own behavior could contribute to that outcome. So, Claire has additional beats at the start of the scene:

K: Maybe this is a bad idea
E: Anxious, doubtful, conflicted
A: Reconsider

K: But I really need to know what's going on
E: Determined but still anxious
A: Follow through

None of this is in the script, but that doesn't matter. As I've said, if you just mechanically shoot a script, you may not get the story. So, I don't want to simply open on Claire knocking on Chad's door. Her character is not so resolute as that. And this means the actor and I will have to talk through how to achieve these beats.

This will begin, as I've stressed, with the character's knowledge. If the actor and I agree that Claire is aware that popping by Chad's may be a bad idea, but that she also believes she needs to know the truth, then something like this might unfold: Claire walks towards Chad's door, then she hesitates, an uncertain look on her face, which perhaps leads to her to turn back, but then she puts on her game face, heads up to the door and knocks. Or maybe this all happens at the door: she's about to knock, stops herself, then knocks.

Mostly it would be up to the actor to realize the beats. So long as we agree on what Claire is thinking, then portraying the emotions and actions is a task she needs to accomplish. Always give your actors room to be inventive, to be in the moment, to follow their instincts. That way they can surprise you.

At the same time, don't hesitate to shape what unfolds. If I were actually directing this scene, my preference would be for some version of the first option – Claire's hesitant journey towards Chad's door – because that strikes me as more expressive. Claire would have to force herself to traverse the distance of his walkway. But I still wouldn't tell the actor exactly how to do that, at least not to begin with.

What I hope you are noticing, though, is that blocking, which is composed of actions, is also determined by the knowledge and emotions of characters. You can move actors around however you want, but looking for gestures and movements that underscore specific beats can be very effective. This is called *movement on a beat change*. If the actor playing Claire did turn to leave after she hesitates on her way to Chad's door, that would physically mark the first beat, her indecision, and if she then turned back towards Chad's door, that would physically mark the transition to the second beat, her resolve to follow through.

Actors and directors use movements on beat changes all the time. In the scene with Fran and Sheldrake the actors are sitting in a booth and so can't walk around, but that doesn't stop them from using movements on beat changes. For instance, when Fran says, "Like old times," she not only smiles, she also embraces herself, a physical expression of how cozy and comfortable the moment is for her. Later, after she says, "They don't make these shrimp like they used to," she pointedly drops the shrimp back onto a plate. And at the end of the scene, right before Fran says, "Jeff Darling," she allows Sheldrake take her hand and kiss it. Each of those movements physically marks a specific beat.

Pay attention when you watch movies to when actors sit or stand or cross a room and you will see that their movements are almost always on beat changes. Think of the scene from Chapter 4 when Sarah's increasing anxiety causes her to retreat from Frank several times. Each of those withdrawals is movement on a beat change. So too is the moment when she stops walking before she asks Frank why he wants to move back east. In that case, since the characters are already moving, it is stasis that marks the beat change.

Camera movement is another way to mark beat changes. I mentioned in Chapter 4 that a push-in can signal a significant moment in the action, and some directors use this technique all the time. Steven Spielberg is one of them. Since I've already mentioned *E. T. The Extra-Terrestrial* in a previous chapter, I'll stick with that film. When Elliot meets E.T. for the first time, for example, he takes several steps forward, a look of awe on his face, as the camera simultaneously pushes in on him. Elliot's physical action, combined with the camera movement, which ends in a closeup, marks his realization that he has discovered an amazing creature.

Always look for these kinds of opportunities when you are blocking both actors and the camera. Look for them in the editing room as well. As also suggested in Chapter 4, don't overuse your closeups. Cut to them when a change in emphasis will mark an important beat change.

If you want to study more recent examples of actor and camera movements on beat changes, I suggest you watch *If Beale Street Could Talk* (2018) by Barry Jenkins. It includes *tour-de-force* instances of both techniques. The opening scene alone is a master class. But other scenes worth studying are when Trish announces to her family that she is pregnant, when Trish and Fonny visit a warehouse loft and the scene immediately after that one when they joyfully walk down a street together and then separate, which leads, as mentioned in Chapter 5, to Fonny's first encounter with the police officer who will send him to jail.

In any case, returning to the scene we are analyzing now, once Claire knocks on the door, Chad opens it. What does he learn? He learns that Claire has unexpectedly dropped by. His beat is this:

K: Claire is at my front door
E: Surprised

He doesn't get to play an action because Claire jumps in with "Hey, stranger." Her beat is this:

K: Here he is, he's wondering why I'm here, moment of truth
E: Nervous
A: Play it down, like it's no big deal

If Claire's hesitancy is played up at the start of the scene, then it only makes sense for her to downplay her unexpected presence on Chad's doorstep when he finds her there. She could of course be more forceful:

K: Here I am, he can't avoid me now
E: Emboldened
A: Press him on why he is avoiding me

Her line "Hey, stranger" would allow for this. But, as will become clear in a moment, it's too soon for her to play that beat; it's too early for her to put him on the spot. So, I'm going to stick with Claire playing it down, which she does because she's nervous. This is better for the scene's outcome anyway. Allowing Claire to become anxious again right after she resolves to knock on Chad's door would further underscore her concern that her own behavior might contribute to or hasten the end of their relationship.

What does Chad now know? He still knows he wasn't expecting Claire. We're still dealing with his first beat, the one that Claire cut short. But in addition to knowing that he wasn't expecting Claire, Chad also knows that he is avoiding her. That is why he hasn't called. The beat is this:

K: Claire is at my front door; I wish she weren't here
E: Surprised, pressured, annoyed
A: Scold her

That's a strong response but the dialogue allows for it: "Claire, I really can't come out to play right now. I'm preparing for this important audition." All of us, when we were children, probably knew a kid we didn't want to play with, and that is how Chad is treating her. That is how he is appraising Claire's presence in light of his character's concerns.

Chad could tease Claire instead of scold her, and that could be tried out in rehearsals too, but a strong response is probably required in order to set up Claire's next beat. As indicated in her dialogue, she's a bit flustered at first: "No, I wasn't, I mean, I was on my way home and I thought I'd just stop by to say hello." For that to work, Chad probably has to overtly express dismay, all the more so because Claire is lying. She did not stop by on her way home. She came from home. That is established in the previous scene. So, she is choosing to cover her tracks. Her beat, then, is this:

K: Chad is not pleased to see me (what she feared)
E: Embarrassed, foolish, flustered
A: Make an excuse

But then, as Claire talks, she becomes more direct and states her purpose: "It was a bit strange the last time we saw each other." The beat is this:

K: Don't make an excuse, this isn't all in my head
E: Renewed determination
A: Justify why I'm here *or* stand up for myself

None of this is very mysterious, the dialogue is helping us along, but Claire has two beats and I want both of them. The appraisals of characters are always changing and you should never miss opportunities to capture those shifts.

So, what has Chad, or the actor playing Chad, just learned? He's learned exactly why Claire has come over. This is an important piece of new information for his character. Always put yourself in the character's shoes. Get inside their head. When Chad opens the door, he knows Claire has popped by unexpectedly, but he doesn't know why she has done that. Now she has revealed why she's come over: to talk about what happened last night.

This is why I didn't want Claire to put Chad on the spot earlier with her line "Hey, stranger." There has to be a specific moment, a single moment, when Chad discovers Claire's purpose; otherwise, the scene is repeating itself. So, this should be the moment when he figures out what she wants. His beat is this:

K: Claire has come over to talk about last night
E: Cornered
A: Play dumb

Chad could also reassure Claire with his line, "Last night? It wasn't weird last night," and it should be tried out both ways when the scene is rehearsed, but either way, whether Chad overtly reassures Claire or does so indirectly by playing dumb, he's expressing the same basic sentiment: "What are you talking about? There's nothing wrong."

And that serves Chad's scene objective, which is to convince Claire that she is overreacting, to make her believe that she's imagining a problem when there is no problem. In fact, this is the moment he adopts that objective. Prior to this he doesn't know what's going on. Now he knows what's going on and how to deal with the situation. So, this moment is begging for some movement in the blocking to mark the change.

If we look at the written scene, it indicates that Chad comes outside and closes the door right before he scolds Claire ("I can't come out to play right now") but that creates a problem. Again, put yourself in the character's shoes. If you were Claire and you were concerned about whether someone still had feelings for you, and if, when you went over to their house, they shut you out while also expressing annoyance that you even came over, then you would have the answer to your question: they aren't interested in you anymore. So, if the scene is blocked as written, it will be over as soon as it begins. Once Chad shuts the door, Claire can leave brokenhearted.

There is an old saying: "Never play the end at the beginning." But if I have Chad step outside and close the door while he plays dumb or reassures Claire, then he is doing something else entirely. He is giving the impression that he is willing to talk about last night, that he is coming outside to have a private conversation with her (in a previous scene it is established that Chad has several roommates, plus if we put two and two together, he may have someone else inside the house, another reason he doesn't want to get into it with Claire right now).

So, if shutting the door is moved from Chad's first beat to this beat, it will not only physically underscore his adoption of a scene objective, it will reassure

Claire and thus keep the scene going. Again, if you just mechanically shoot a script, you may not get the story.

In any case, this revision to the blocking does not mean that Chad's action will or should be wholly successful. Claire can accept that he is coming outside to talk and still believe that he is not being forthright. What she says is this: "Okay maybe it wasn't weird. But you haven't called and I thought maybe something was wrong." In other words, whether it was weird or not, there is still the issue of his unkept promise: The beat is this:

K: Chad is not being honest
E: Disappointed
A: Accuse him avoiding

What has Chad now learned? That Claire is going to persist. His line is "Claire, I just woke up an hour ago." His beat is this:

K: She's not going to let it go
E: Frustrated
A: Dismiss her suspicions *or* set her straight

What has Claire now learned? First, Chad's explanation – he just woke up – is, on its surface, a reasonable one. Second, his action, the way he would deliver the line, reveals that he is irritated. These are significant new pieces of information for Claire. She entered the scene concerned that her plan could backfire, and now it seems like it is backfiring. Moreover, it may be that Chad is right, that it is all in her head, that she is overreacting. Her beat is this:

K: I shouldn't have done this, he's right, I'm overreacting
E: Regret
A: Apologize

Claire's line is "Ugh, I know, I feel like such an asshole," but her action is to apologize. Alternatively, the beat could unfold like this:

K: I'm overreacting, he's right, everything is fine
E: Relief
A: Mock myself, admit I'm behaving foolishly

The beat could even unfold like this:

K: He's making excuses, he's still avoiding
E: Anger
A: Assure him I'm not stupid

In other words, she could deliver the line sarcastically. And this third version is tempting because it would allow Claire to stand up to Chad. The problem, though, is that it has no "after," in Uta Hagen's sense. Chad's next line is "You're not an asshole, sweet Claire," after which Claire says, "No, I know. Um. Well, I'll let you work on your audition." In other words, there is nothing in the dialogue to indicate that Claire is challenging him. We may not want her character to be so self-deprecating, but that's who her character is.

The second version of the beat might not work either, but for a different reason. If Claire decides that everything is fine and feels relief, then she can go home knowing all is well. The scene of course indicates that she doesn't leave, so we should try out the beat in rehearsals, but the first version most clearly raises the stakes. If Claire believes she shouldn't have come over and feels regret, then she still has reason to wonder if everything is okay between them.

But whether Claire expresses regret or relief, the actor playing Chad now has a new piece of information: he has succeeded in getting her to believe she is overreacting. The question is this: how should he feel about that? His line, again, is "You're not an asshole, sweet Claire." One way to play that is this:

K: I've placated her
E: Relief
A: Reiterate that all is well

Or it could be played like this:

K: I'm gaslighting her, she feels bad
E: Guilt
A: Reassure her, be kind, make amends

Again, adjustments are always based on the knowledge of characters, what they believe about the situation. That is primarily what you need to talk about with actors during rehearsals and on set. Both versions could work, but the second version is more complex. It would reveal that Chad has mixed motives. It would be easy to portray him as just a jerk, but maybe he should regret misleading Claire. In a later scene he does come clean and apologize, so planting a seed for that here would help set that up.

If Chad does feel guilty, that makes this another big beat change. A student of mine who directed this scene had Chad put his arm around Claire after he delivered the line and lead her forward to sit down on the steps with him. That was a great way to physically mark the beat change, though it somewhat works against Chad's desire to wrap up their encounter quickly. Still, I remember it because I think it worked. Not everything in a story has to be completely logical.

What does Claire now know? Her line is "No, I know. Um. Well, I'll let you work on your audition … Maybe we'll do something tonight?" She is hesitant. Her beat is this:

K: Is he being sincere or is he teasing me?
E: Encouraged but wary
A: Test him

This scene is quite simple, but actually the writing is sharp. By having Claire try to make plans with Chad, the writers have introduced a concrete way that Claire (and the audience) can determine how Chad feels about her. Claire's tactic also introduces a twist, at least for Chad. He clearly didn't see it coming and is caught off guard: "Yeah, but I … think I want to stay in tonight, I've got this throat thing." Chad thought he had attained his objective, but apparently not. His beat is this:

K: I didn't expect her to ask this
E: Surprised, trapped
A: Evade, make an excuse, lie

What does Claire now know? It needs to be decided whether she believes Chad or not or if she is uncertain. Her line is "Throat thing? Are you sick?" If she believes him, her beat is this:

K: Chad is not feeling well
E: Concern
A: Express my concern, be solicitous

If she doesn't believe him, her beat is this:

K: He's lying
E: Slighted
A: Challenge him, call him on his lie

But if she is uncertain, her beat is this:

K: Is he really sick or is he trying to brush me off?
E: Worried, uncertain
A: Press him for more information

As to which version is best, it also needs to be decided when Claire should realize the truth. The outcome of the scene is that they are not a couple anymore. The question is, when does Claire know that. Again, stories progress according to the changing knowledge of characters. So, if Claire believes Chad is lying, then this is the moment when she realizes he's not interested in her anymore, which may be too soon. That won't be clear until the scene is rehearsed, but the third version – uncertainty – would surely keep the scene going. Delaying outcomes is typically advantageous. It keeps the audience interested.

Moreover, the script indicates when the turning point should occur. A bit later, after Chad grudgingly agrees to meet Claire the following night, it says that she doesn't speak and a long silence follows. So, that is supposed to be the moment she realizes the truth. Again, never be married to the script, but don't ignore it either. So, it's probably too soon for Claire to find out.

At the same time, if it does turn out during rehearsals that the Claire should figure out the truth in this moment, then it may be that some of the remaining dialogue needs to be trimmed. In some cases, scene analysis and rehearsals help you to realize cuts you can make, but I don't want to consider any cuts until I finish analyzing the scene and rehearse it.

As to the first version of the beat – Claire believes Chad – this would also delay the scene's outcome, but it would do so in a way that worries me. If Claire accepts Chad's excuse, she may come off as overly naïve. But believing him could work and so it would be worth trying out in rehearsals. For now, though, I'm going to assume that the third version – uncertainty – is most productive.

If Claire is uncertain and does press Chad to elaborate, then what would Chad learn? His line is "No, I'm fine … I just … I'm sorry, I just want to feel good for my audition." He struggles at first, then he gets to the point. It's two beats:

K: Claire is pressing me for details
E: Flustered
A: Find a plausible way out

Then, as he stalls, he finds that way out:

K: Claire is being unfair, if I have an audition then she should respect that
E: Frustrated, pressured
A: Insist that she please be reasonable and support me

The scene never clarifies whether Chad has an audition or not. Perhaps he does, or perhaps it is another excuse he is making up. But even if he is lying – and the audience can decide for themselves – that doesn't mean he can't commit to the deception. Lies only work if we treat them as true, which can include becoming defensive if other people challenge them.

Still, the beat could be played even more forcefully:

K: Why won't Claire stop? I just need her to leave
E: Angry
A: Accuse her of being a nuisance

But if played that way, then this would be the moment when Claire realizes the truth. It would be the turning point in the scene that leads to its outcome. But again, the script indicates that her moment of realization comes later. Moreover, Claire's response – "No, it's alright, maybe tomorrow night?" – suggests that Chad shouldn't react from anger. Claire's beat, then, is this:

K: He's right, I'm being unfair
E: Sorry
A: Assure him I understand, back off and offer another option

What has Chad now learned? His line is "Yeah, tomorrow night would be okay." But he can't mean it because this is the last opportunity the scene provides to play the turning point. How Chad delivers this line, then, matters a great deal. I would say his beat is this:

K: Claire is unrelenting
E: Exhausted, exasperated
A: Grudgingly and resentfully acquiesce

In other words, he stops hiding his feelings. That makes this an important beat change. My student who had the characters sit down for the previous part of the scene had the actor playing Chad stand up before he delivered his line, which drove the truth home to Claire:

K: It's over
E: Broken hearted
A: Lose hope

And because Claire loses hope, an awkward silence follows. In this instance, inaction marks the beat change, which eventually leads Chad to say, "Claire?" His beat is this:

K: Claire is hurt, she may fall apart
E: Regret but also impatience
A: Gently nudge her towards leaving

What has Claire now learned? Her line is "Yeah, so I'll call you tomorrow night," but obviously she doesn't mean this. She knows it's over. Her beat is this:

K: I look foolish
E: Humiliated
A: Pull myself together, save face, pretend everything is fine

At this point, things get mildly complicated because the next two lines of dialogue are callbacks. When Chad asks Claire out for the first time they agree to meet "not tomorrow night but the night after." However, since Chad can't remember what day of the week it is, he is confused as to what night that is. When Claire helpfully provides that information – "Thursday night" – he jokingly calls her a genius and adds, "I could have just said Thursday night."

So, in this moment, when Chad says, "Thursday night," it needs to be decided whether he knows he's making a reference to that moment. Claire certainly knows she's doing that when she replies, "God, you're a genius, I could have just said Thursday night," but Chad may not initially be aware of the connection. If he is aware, then one way to play the beat is this:

K: Claire knows it's over, it really is over now
E: Sorry for her, but also wistful
A: Reminisce

But if he is only inadvertently making a reference to that night, then his beat is this:

K: Claire knows it's over but is playing along
E: Sorry for her, but relieved
A: Play along too, confirm the "plan"

Trying out both versions, and even other versions, in rehearsals would be the only way to confirm which works best. And again, this would entail talking through with the actor what their character believes about the situation. This is always a discussion because you want to allow actors to express their own ideas about their character. Actors will also analyze the script, so the goal is to reach agreements about what characters are actually thinking and feeling moment to moment in a scene.

As to Claire's next line, "God, you're a genius, I could have just said Thursday night," which is an intentional callback, there are multiple ways it can be delivered. If Chad does reminisce then Claire may reminisce too. Or she may be encouraged by his wistfulness:

K: There is still a chance
E: Hopeful
A: Flirt, playfully tease him

Or she may dislike that he becomes wistful:

K: Chad doesn't get to feel regret
E: Resentment
A: Mock or ridicule him *or* dismiss his feelings

Alternatively, if Chad simply confirms the "plan," then the beat may just be an extension of Claire's previous beat – saving face:

K: Keep it up, don't let him know how I feel
E: Still humiliated
A: Make a joke

It won't be clear how this part of the scene should play out until it is rehearsed. A turning point is typically the most difficult part of scene to get right, so this isn't surprising. But whether Claire reminisces, flirts, mocks or jokes, Chad's next beat, "Goodbye Claire," is unambiguous:

K: There's nothing more to say
E: Impatient
A: Send Claire on her way

And Claire's next beat, "Bye," is also unambiguous:

K: Time to go
E: Resigned
A: Give in

The script then says, "They kiss, almost like they have to." Perhaps this is just a continuation of both of their previous beats: Chad sending Claire on her way and Claire giving into that. But if Claire lingers, not wanting to let go, and if Chad then initiates the kiss goodbye, then there are two more beats, which could be effective. The first beat is Claire's:

K: Is this really it?
E: Heartache, yearning
A: Forestall the inevitable

Followed by Chad's:

K: She's hanging on
E: Sympathy
A: Ease her pain

Or, if it feels wrong to give him a tender moment here at the end, his beat could be this:

K: She's still not leaving
E: Frustrated, irritated
A: Acquiesce again

Either way, Claire now walks away. But what is she thinking as she does so? If we think back to the beginning of the scene, I suggested that the outcome would be more effective if, at the outset, Claire is worried that her own behavior could contribute to the end of the relationship. So, while she's walking away, maybe she's thinking that it's her fault:

K: I screwed up; I came off as needy
E: Regret, anger
A: Blame myself

In the next scene, Claire is alone in her car, expressing frustration, but that beat, as mentioned in Chapter 2, can be played here. She can silently express frustration as she walks away. Now, there is no reason to believe that the scene's outcome is Claire's fault. There is nothing wrong with expecting someone you are in a relationship with to be honest. But Claire seems to believe that it may be her fault and the actor must act on the character's beliefs, not their own.

And that's the end of the scene. To be clear, I don't consider any of the beats in this score to be written in stone because rehearsals, once again, are a process of discovery. But what I've created is a plan that is a strong starting point for a rehearsal. Also, I chose a specific tone: pathos. The scene could also be handled comically. You might try, therefore, as an exercise, to analyze it that way. Several of my students have directed quite funny versions of this scene. This is possible because, in the scheme of things, the drama is fairly low stakes and so can be easily mocked.

But whatever tone you are going for, when you analyze a scene, the questions are the same:

1. What has the character just learned?
2. How does that make them feel?
3. What does their emotion compel them to do?

And when you direct actors, when you adjust how they play a beat, if you focus on their character's knowledge, then the emotion and action will follow. At the same time, don't forget that acting is reacting. If you want to change one actor's performance, oftentimes it's a matter of changing the other actor's performance. Let's return to two beats early in the scene:

K: Claire is at my front door; I wish she weren't here
E: Surprised, pressured, annoyed
A: Scold her

K: Chad is not pleased to see me
E: Embarrassed, foolish, flustered
A: Make an excuse

As discussed, Claire's beat is probably only possible if Chad truly scolds her. So, if I were rehearsing or shooting this scene and decided that the actor playing Claire was not sufficiently flustered, I would have to consider the possibility that the actor playing Chad is not getting her to that place, in which case I would adjust him and not her.

This approach is very useful when shooting coverage. Let's say the camera is on the actor playing Claire. In that case the actor playing Chad, since he'd be off-screen, would be free to modulate his performance in all sorts of ways, including playing some beats over the top if that will help the actor playing Claire respond the way I think she should.

And this brings me to another point: if actors know you are planning to shoot singles, then they almost certainly won't give you their best performance in the master shot. They will save that for their coverage. This isn't to say you shouldn't give adjustments while shooting a master, but don't waste time, or wear the actors out, especially if it is a very dramatic scene, trying to achieve perfection in a master.

And if you are shooting a oner, be very clear about that. I was once talking to an actor about what it was like to work with a particular famous director, and one story they told me was about how the director walked up to them after a take and said, "Just to remind you, this shot is the only shot we are shooting for this scene." The message was clear: give it your all now because you won't have another opportunity.

Communication is always key. If you remember that, all should go well.

But do rehearse your script before you shoot it.

Notes

1 In the case of action scenes – fights, chases and the like – the primary goal of rehearsals might be choreography, safety, even establishing camera positions, and not determining, or primarily determining, the intentions of characters.

2 Using scenes to set the stage for future story events is a hallmark of mainstream films, including most indie films, which aim to tell stories that are comprehensible, unified and emotionally resonant. If your interests lie elsewhere, what I cover in this chapter should still be relevant because films that seek to produce different, even opposite effects – uncertainty, ambiguity, disunity, emotional distance – typically do so by subverting mainstream techniques.

3 For a concise and excellent discussion of truthful responses and other basic acting techniques, see *A Practical Handbook for the Actor* (Vintage Books, 1986), in particular Chapter 3.

4 If the insult never takes place – let's say that the first actor ends up delivering their line in teasing way – then the second actor must respond to being teased and not respond as if they have been insulted, which would not be a truthful response. It is up to actors to perform a scene according to how it actually unfolds, and it is up to you to shape a scene so that it unfolds the way you need it to.

5 Playing against emotions can be interesting because disconcerting. The "grief dance" performed by Laura Palmer's father Leland in *Twin Peaks* is, if you know that show, a remarkable example. This is to some degree culturally specific, dance may play a role in some cultures' grieving rites, but in its context, Leland's behavior in response to his daughter's murder is out of bounds and disturbs every character in the scene, and us as well.

6 Chad and Claire scene is from *Some Girl* by Brie Shaffer & Marissa Ribisi.

12 Obey the Rules of Engagement

Now it is time to head to set. This is when all of your preparation comes to fruition. The goal, however, is not to mechanically execute a plan. The reason I have been encouraging you to exhaustively prep your project, and match its scope to your available resources, is so that you gain time on set to be imaginative and open to creative possibilities.

If a line of dialogue isn't working, or if an actor has a solid suggestion for something their character might do or say, or if a better shot presents itself, then go ahead and make a change. The goal is to always be making your film better. The creative process does not stop until the film is done. And then it starts all over again on your next film.

At the same time, don't start changing everything. Doing that will cost you precious time. Presumably, you've spent months writing your script, analyzing it and developing a visual plan, so be on the lookout for improvements, but also trust what you have.

Where you must methodically follow a plan, however, is in terms of how the work is organized. Production has a structure that is based on long-established and reliable procedures. These are what I am calling *the rules of engagement*. As I've said before, making a film is an uphill battle and if you want to win that battle, then work your way through each shoot day in a disciplined and organized way.

What follows is a description of how to do that. It assumes, as I said at the start of this book, that every crew member is qualified to be on set. If you are heading out with a DSLR, some bounce boards and a few compact LED lights, then yes, most everybody can handle that without a lot of training. In fact, that is the typical scenario in many summer filmmaking programs, and it is a great way to make a film. But if you are heading out with more than that, then *hands-on training* is required. This is what your school provides and this book is not substitute for that. No one should attempt anything that they have not done at least once in a class under the supervision of an instructor or that they have not learned how to do while crewing on other films.

What I am mostly going to describe is the process for shooting an interior scene, one that begins with blocking, lighting and shooting a master, followed

DOI: 10.4324/9781003169864-12

by coverage, though as stressed in Chapter 4, you are not required in every case to shoot a scene that way. The process is the same for exterior scenes. When you shoot exteriors, it is often the case that set dressing plays a less significant role, and if you are relying on the sun then lighting may be minimal, but otherwise the procedures for organizing the work are the same.

Call Time

If, as in the example at the end of Chapter 10, the call sheet indicates that the shoot day begins at 6:00am, then that is when the shoot day commences. This is true even if an actor or a crew member is late, or if you are late, or if the truck is stuck in traffic and no equipment is available. It is true no matter what. If call time is 6:00am, then that is when the clock starts ticking and by 6:00pm wrap must be complete. If your instructor says a shoot day is shorter than twelve hours, then that is what you must work with.

Breakfast

Breakfast should always be set up and available an hour before call. Again, it is up to the producer to ensure that this happens, though they may delegate this responsibility to a PA who can come in early and then leave early.

Duties of the AD Prior to Call

As discussed in Chapter 10, the AD determines where gear will be staged, where props and set dressing will be staged, where makeup and wardrobe will be situated, where actors will go when they are not working, where crafty and breakfast will be set up, etc. Their first duty, then, is to communicate this information to everyone who doesn't already know it, but needs to know it. If this information is not disseminated, a location can quickly become an obstacle course.

To expedite this, breakfast can be a working meal (if your instructor approves). This means that once people get their bagel or Danish, the DP can start giving instructions to the camera and G&E crews, makeup and wardrobe can be directed to where they will set up (art should already know their staging area since, once again, sets are always dressed in advance) and, if crew are up for this, they can start unloading gear. Also, since everyone must report to the AD when they arrive to set, this is when, as I've said, the AD gets signed appearance releases and crew deal memos from anyone who has not already signed one.

And while the AD is not a traffic cop, they should make some effort to ensure that cast and crew park where they are supposed to park. Finally, the AD reviews the day's production plan, yet again, with the director, DP and producer.

The AD Calls the Shoot

Assuming, again, that call time is 6:00am, then at exactly 6:00am the AD clearly, but calmly and respectfully, announces: "We're on." Once the AD does that, all phones should be shut off and everyone must get to work.

Safety Meeting

The first thing up at the start of each shoot day is a safety meeting led by the AD. This means, as I said in the Preface, that before you head to set your department must provide you with safety training. My students are required to pass both a written exam and a practical exam. And our safety manual is over 300 pages. Thus, covering the topic in any kind of detail is beyond the scope of this book. It is the responsibility of your department to provide safety training, just as it is their responsibility to train you in lighting, camera and sound.

That said, the AD must, in the first place, be sure that everyone is wearing proper attire. Flip flops and sandals, for example, have no place on a movie set. There is too much heavy gear involved and if you drop something or slam a toe into a gear case or a length of dolly track, well, you get the idea. And people who will be working with hot lights must have appropriate gloves.

Next, the AD communicates to cast and crew where all the exits are, where everyone will gather for a head count if the set does have to be evacuated for an emergency, where the first aid kit and fire extinguishers will be stored, and they make people aware of any unique hazards at the location (think again of my former classmate falling into a pool).

If there will be special rigging, the gaffer and key grip outline potential safety issues associated with that rigging. If stunts or weapons are involved the responsible department heads review all the relevant safety protocols with crew and cast. And people are reminded not to place equipment in front of exits and to always leave open pathways to those exits. This means, first and foremost, that whenever a piece of equipment is no longer being used, or working, it should be returned to the staging area.

The best way to approach safety is to always ask yourself, no matter what you are doing, "What are the worst things that could happen while I'm doing this?" and then, "What are the worst things that could happen to someone else down the line?" If it seems obvious, for example, that someone could trip over a cable you just ran, then rig a runner over it or tape it down. If you set up a C-stand, put a cut-open tennis ball on the end of its protruding arm so that no one walks into it. If you climb a ladder, make sure someone spots you. In short, use common sense.

When it comes to safety, consequences are almost always foreseeable, no one is invulnerable, rules matter, and resigning yourself to an unsafe situation should never be an option. Always alert the AD to any safety concerns you might have.

Full Blocking Rehearsal

Once the safety meeting is over, the next thing up is always a full blocking rehearsal of the first scene on the schedule. A blocking rehearsal, again, is when the director works out with the actors how, when and where they will move during a scene.

A full blocking rehearsal means blocking the entire scene from start to finish, not just the action for the first shot, which in some instances might only cover part of the scene. Even if the director has rehearsed on location and the blocking is set, it still needs to be shown to the crew. There is nothing to light or shoot until everyone knows what the blocking is.

If the director has not rehearsed on location, which is common, and needs time to block with the actors prior to showing the action to the crew, then the crew can continue to busy themselves with quietly unloading, staging and building equipment. However, the DP should stay with the director and actors to help ensure that the action is staged in such a way that it does not present them with time consuming or even insurmountable lighting problems and to make certain that the most visual and interesting aspects of the location will be visible when the scene is shot. Even when the blocking has been set in advance, the DP should be invited weigh in on it.

Again, much of this will have been discussed during tech scouts, but things have a way of changing on the day you finally shoot a scene, in part because the actors weren't there during tech scouts, so a fluid approach is required.

Setting Marks

After the blocking is set, the actors walk through the scene, starting and stopping, so that the 2nd AC can set marks for each of their positions. Marks are made with paper tape (or sometimes with chalk for exterior locations) and should be T-shaped. This indicates to actors exactly where to place their feet (one on each side of the T). Each actor's marks should be made with a different color tape. If actors are going to sit down at any point during the scene, then the positions of chair legs are also marked so that if a chair is accidentally moved it can be easily be returned to its original position.

Marks should be exact but are always preliminary since small adjustments may be made to them later to accommodate lighting and/or the camera. But once the positions of actors and furniture and even props have been marked (the art director/on-set dresser handles this), the set is now hot. This means that everyone must be careful not to bump into things or move anything around.

Establish Continuity

Once the scene is blocked, and marks have been set, it is important to establish the continuity of the action. It is not enough for actors to hit their marks, they must consistently hit them at the same moments each time the scene is run.

This is true of every action actors perform. If, for example, it is established that an actor sits down before they deliver a certain line of dialogue, then they must consistently sit down before delivering that line. Alternatively, if right before they stand they pick up something, say a notebook, then they must consistently pick up that notebook before they stand. They can't sometimes pick it up before they stand and other times pick it up after they stand. Nor can they sometimes pick it up with their left hand and other times pick it up with their right hand.

If you are not scrupulous about such matters, then actions won't match in different shots, and that will limit your cut points in the editing room.

Therefore, always take a few minutes to establish the continuity of the action. The script supervisor simply talks through the action of the scene, pointing out to actors when they did what and how they did it. If you don't have a script supervisor, which is sometimes the case on student productions, and you are directing, then you can handle this. And if, while establishing continuity, you tweak the action a bit, that's fine, so long as the actors stick to the changes.

This is also when you establish the continuity of props, if the actors are already using them. Sometimes you block without props and actors only pretend to eat or drink or pick up something. But if props are involved in a scene they will at some point be brought in, and once they are, their placement must be precisely established. The script supervisor takes photographs of where props should be placed at the start of each take and where they should be by the end of each take, but the on-set dresser can also handle this.

Frame Up the Shot

Next, the DP and director frame up the first shot with the camera. This is done with the actors and again, adjustments to marks can be made as the shot is set. Take some time to frame up the first shot and every shot. The DP can handhold the camera so that various adjustments to size, height and angle can be tried out. Don't hesitate to try out different focal lengths as well.

Once the shot is set, the 1st AC then measures focus for every actor and sets focus marks for the lens.

Lighting

With the shot set, lighting begins in earnest because the DP can usually get some lighting started much earlier than this. The DP always gives the AD a solid estimate for how long lighting will take. But since, with a master, the entire scene must be lit, don't be surprised if they ask for 45 minutes to an hour. As I've mentioned many times, it will almost always be one to two hours before you shoot your first take. But once you get going, things will move more quickly because the adjustments made to lighting in coverage shots are typically not complex, at least not until you turn around.

In any case, at this point, stand-ins can be used to light the scene. A stand-in is simply someone who stands in for an actor. On a professional production, these people are paid and stars often have a person who regularly stands in for them during lighting, someone who resembles them in terms of height, skin tone and hair color. But on a student shoot, a stand-in is anyone who happens to be available: a PA, the boom op, an extra, etc.

Makeup and Wardrobe

Now the actors go to makeup and wardrobe. Unless elaborate makeup or costuming is involved, don't bring actors in early to go through makeup and wardrobe before blocking. That will only leave them to sit around and wait while the scene is being lit. They will likely finish in makeup and wardrobe before lighting is complete, but this still gives them something to do for at least part of that time. If a scene has been prelit, then in that case actors might be brought in early for makeup and wardrobe.

Review the Shot List

Once the first shot is set, and lighting has begun, and the actors have been sent to makeup and wardrobe, the director, DP and AD pause to go through the shot list. They do this in order to:

1. Make any needed revisions to it based on how the blocking actually turned out.
2. Definitively settle on the shooting order of shots.
3. Assign a priority to each shot so that everyone is clear on which shots can be cut if the production falls behind schedule.

Again, these issues are all discussed during prep, but they should be revisited on set once the blocking is finalized. Let's quickly review. In this simple floor plan, the shots are numbered, as they should be, in shooting order:

Scene 2: INT. TRAIN CAR - NIGHT

The reason this is correct shooting order, again, is because shots 1, 2 and 3 can be taken without any crew or gear, except for the camera, having to be repositioned. But beginning with shot 4 the camera is now looking in the opposite direction, and by the time shot 5 is up, everything that was behind camera – both crew and gear – will now be on camera and so will have to be relocated to the opposite end of the train car. It is also likely that shot 5 will require additional lighting since it is the reverse of shot 1. Again, this is called turning around.

In terms of priority, shots 1, 3 and 4 – the master and singles – are most important. The reverse master, shot 5, is probably next in importance since it is seems intended to underscore a reversal in the story. This leaves shot 2 as least important. But this is always a juggling act. If a crew were to fall behind while shooting shot 1, they would know to skip shot 2 and move directly to shooting the singles. But if they were to fall behind while shooting either the two shot or the singles, then shot 5 would be cut. So, even after you prioritize shots, add-itional flexibility is often required.

Never doggedly stick to a shot list when you fall behind schedule because that will likely only keep you behind schedule. You may believe you'll catch up while shooting the next scene, but if you don't, and if you again refuse to cut shots, then by the time you get to the last scene of the day, you may be forced to cut shots you truly can't live without.

Again, avoid trying to shoot more than three scenes a day. And as was discussed in Chapter 10, assign a specific amount of time to shoot each scene (just under four hours in the example I covered in that chapter), and unless you get ahead of schedule, which does sometimes happen, stick to those timings.

Video Village

If the director and script supervisor are using a monitor, the 2nd AC is responsible for setting this up. It must be placed where it is not in the way of the crew and does not block any exits. For this reason, when shooting in cramped locations, it is often the case that the monitor is set up in a different room than the one the action is being photographed in. The camera might, for example, be in the kitchen with the actors while the director watches on the monitor in the living room. When shooting day exteriors, it is often necessary to rig flags above and on both sides of the monitor to keep sunlight off the screen, in which case the 2nd AC gets help from the grip crew.

The Director Keeps Rehearsing

At this point, if you are the director, you either stay on set to rehearse the shot with stand-ins if there is, for example, a camera move, or you leave set to work with the actors. You can direct actors while they are sitting in a makeup chair, or while they are eating crafty, or while they are reclining on a couch resting. Directing actors, as I've stressed, is mostly about talking through the scene with them. And actors don't need to be up on their feet going through the blocking in order to run lines.

Still, you can always bring actors back to set to run the scene again if you want, but that will almost certainly slow down lighting. So, if you want to run the scene again, do so elsewhere and just approximate the blocking. In any case, never over rehearse a scene. It wears actors out. If the performances are close to where you want them, leave the scene alone and make final adjustments once you start shooting.

If you are not rehearsing with the actors, don't forget about them. If lighting is taking a while, go say hello to them from time to time. Don't pester them, they may enjoy the downtime, but don't abandon them either. Use your best judgment. For this reason, when you are the AD, give the actors regular updates on when you expect to call them to set.

The DP Stays Focused on the Shot

The DP should not set up lights. The temptation to do this is often strong, but the DP should stay focused on making the frame better. This includes lighting, but it also includes set dressing. The DP works closely with the art department to get props and set dressing into each frame. Again, shots in movies are typically busy with set dressing, which can be placed in both the background and fore-ground of shots.

In particular, when you are the DP, pay attention to what is sometimes called breaking up backgrounds. This means not having uniform backgrounds in shots. You can avoid this by carefully positioning set dressing, but how you position actors matters as well. As I've mentioned many times, windows and doorways add depth to a scene, but when using these as backgrounds, especially in coverage shots, don't place the actors directly in front of them. That will create a uniform background. Instead, offset the actors so that the window or door frame is visible. This breaks up the background, as in this shot from *Jerry Maguire*:

Note as well the framed artwork on the right side of frame, which fills in what would otherwise be a blank wall, and also note the wall sconces on the left side of frame, which add additional depth to the hallway. In reality, such a narrow hallway would not likely have wall sconces, so they were almost certainly put there by the art department.

Again, lights that are visible in a shot are called practical lamps and it is difficult to have too many of them since they are visually interesting. Practical lamps are also often used to motivate the key or backlight on an actor (in this case, in the master, a table lamp is established as providing Renée Zellweger's key), but the sconces are simply there to make the image more complex.

The DP also takes time during lighting to rehearse any focus pulls or camera moves with stand-ins. Even simple pans and tilts should be rehearsed. This saves time later during shooting.

Finally, if the DP is rehearsing with stand-ins, the AD ensures that the sound mixer uses this as an opportunity to rehearse placement of the boom. The DP helps the boom op get the boom as close as possible to the actors without it intruding into frame. This is done by allowing the boom to enter frame during rehearsals so that it can then be backed off to a point just above the frame-line.

The Art Department Stays Focused on Set Dressing

The art department's work is always preliminary because it is almost always the case that as you set up shots, set dressing needs to be repositioned. This is why, as just discussed, the DP works closely with the art department.

For this reason, it is essential that there be an on-set dresser, someone who did not stay up half the night dressing the set, and so can be on set throughout the shoot day to move props and set dressing around, as well as add items that are not already being used. As mentioned in the chapter on budgeting, a typical approach to set dressing is to have a lot of items on hand to use. Many more items than you think you need because that provides choices on set.

Sound Stays Focused on Sound

Again, the sound mixer must eliminate as much noise as possible at a location. Air conditioning units and refrigerators should be shut off during takes. If a generator is being used, it must, as I've stressed, be placed as far away as possible. The sound mixer also insists that windows be closed during takes. And if the actors' feet aren't visible in a shot, then the mixer asks the director if it would be okay for the actors to take off their shoes. There is nothing wrong with footsteps except when a loud heel click lands on a word in a line of dialogue. The same is true of scenes in which actors are eating: knives and forks should be put down between lines of dialogue, not in the middle of them. This is true of anything that actors pick up or put down. The goal is to record clean dialogue tracks, and the time for the sound mixer to work these things out with actors and the director is during the final camera and sound rehearsal, discussed below.

The AD Facilitates the Work of the Crew

The job of the AD is to expedite the work of the crew.

This means keeping the set quiet so that crew members who need to communicate with each other can do so easily. It also means giving the DP regular updates on how much time they have left to light, based on their estimate. This doesn't mean badgering the DP, but it does mean keeping them informed.

If the DP has fallen behind and needs more time to light, then the AD settles on a new time with them to start shooting. A good AD never allows open-ended deadlines. At the same time, if the DP is behind schedule, then the AD ensures that they have all the help they need. If someone isn't working and can help with lighting, then the AD assigns them to help, so long as that person is qualified.[1]

The AD also monitors safety throughout the day and does not allow anyone to do anything that is dangerous. Likewise, they are mindful of the location and ensure that crew are careful not to damage property as they move gear around and set it up. For example, when shooting in a house or apartment, don't place light stands and C-stands directly on floors as this typically leads to scratches and marks. Tape the bottom of each leg on each stand, or use tennis balls, and lay down paper or plastic runners in all high-traffic areas.

The AD also makes sure that actors and crew are where they are needed when they are needed. This means knowing where every cast and crew member is at all times. No one should leave set for any reason, even to go to the bathroom (called 10-1 and 10-2 for, I hope, obvious reasons), without telling the AD.

Additionally, the AD runs interference for the director. Only department heads interact with the director, to ask questions, to seek approval, etc.

And, most importantly, the AD ensures that at any given moment at least one of three things is happening: Blocking. Lighting. Shooting. As I said at the start of this book, that is the structure of every production and if you are not involved in one of those three activities, you are not making a movie. If it is not possible to shoot because of, say, a camera problem, then the director blocks the next scene. And if, after that, it's still not possible to shoot the current scene, then the DP and gaffer begin lighting the scene just blocked, assuming of course that it does not take place in the same room as the current scene.

Other Duties of the AD During the Shoot Day

Along with the producer, the AD manages the location. In addition to ensuring that property is not damaged, this means dealing with the owner, neighbors, police (if they arrive), and gawkers.

How to deal with location owners is covered in Chapter 8 but, again, always be respectful and up front with them about everything you plan to do. The AD can even review with the owner the plan again at the start of the shoot day. Also, if any part of a location is off limits to cast and crew, it is up to the AD, and the producer, to enforce that, otherwise the location agreement is being violated.

In terms of neighbors, in addition to complaining about parking, they also sometimes complain if a shoot is noisy, especially if it is a night shoot. So be as quiet as possible. This is another reason to get walkies. If you have them, then no one needs to shout.

Alternatively, neighbors are sometimes noisy, which can make it difficult to record sound. When that happens, negotiate. You have no control over what other people do, especially on their own property, so the AD or producer must be respectful and polite and come to an agreement that works for both parties.

As to the police, this is why you always get a shooting permit if one is required. If you don't have a permit and a police officer happens by, or if a neighbor calls the police, then you're in trouble. But if you have a permit, then you're good to go, even if a neighbor has complained. In that case, just promise to be as quiet as possible, and to move any vehicles that might be causing problems for residents, and get on with the shoot.

You are most at risk when shooting in public areas: a street, a park, a beach, etc. This is because there is no hiding what you are doing: making a film. So, always have a permit if one is required. Several of my students have had their productions shut down over the years while shooting exteriors because they didn't have a permit. As discussed in Chapter 8, the producer secures permits and if they have to leave set, they hand off any relevant paperwork to the AD.

As for gawkers, this is really only an issue with exterior scenes, and it's just a matter of keeping them out of your shots. When you are the AD, invite them to watch, but place them where they will be out of the way, or have a PA do this.

When shooting exteriors, it is also typical for the AD to strategically place PAs (or any crew they can get their hands on) just outside the frame of each shot so that during takes they can prevent people passing by from talking or entering the frame. Anyone who is not supposed to be in a shot but walks into a shot is called a bogey and bogies are bad because they often look at the camera, usually directly into the lens.

In some situations, though, as when shooting on a busy city street, there may be little you can do to prevent people from entering your shots, and you just have to go with it. You may even want them in your shots as atmosphere. But place signs announcing that filming is taking place so that anyone passing by knows that if they continue on, they may end up in a movie. And add in big letters: Please Don't Look at the Camera!

Finally, the AD blocks extras. In the industry, a director cannot speak to extras due to union rules. But in general, it is always best if the AD blocks extras because this frees up the director to work with the actors and DP. In addition to positioning background extras, the AD can have other extras cross through the frame during takes, typically in the foreground but also in the background of a shot.

Call the Actors to Set

Once lighting is complete, and the camera crew has shot a color chart, the AD calls the actors to set. This shouldn't happen unexpectedly. The AD should give the actors a ten-minute warning.

Wire the Actors for Sound

Once the AD has given the ten-minute warning, this is when the sound mixer gets the lavaliers, or wireless mics, on to the actors. This is called wiring them for sound. The reason the mixer doesn't do this sooner, or much sooner, is because it can lead to problems: mics slip out of their clips, transmitters fall off and crash to the floor, etc. For this same reason, the sound mixer retrieves wireless mics and transmitters from the actors whenever there is downtime, either between camera setups or scenes. Never let actors walk around all day wired for sound.

Camera and Sound Rehearsal

There is an old saying, "If you shoot it, it's not a rehearsal." The implication is that if you shoot the first take of a shot without first rehearsing it, there will be problems, and that is a waste of time (and in the old days, a waste of film stock too). So, always rehearse the first take of any shot before you shoot it.

The AD announces, "Quiet on set, rehearsal is up."

The first rehearsal can be a slow walkthrough, but as soon as possible the actors run the scene at regular speed and the camera operator, focus puller, boom operator and dolly grip (if there is a dolly move) try to keep up.

However, don't run the scene again and again. Instead, start and stop for technical directions. These might include asking an actor to walk or sit down more slowly because the camera operator or focus puller can't keep up with them, or it might mean asking an actor to not lean down so far when they pick something up because they are going out of frame.

There are an infinite number of possible technical directions, but my advice, if you are directing, is to let the relevant crew members give these directions. I sometimes hear people say that no one but the director should talk to the actors but, practically speaking, if there is, for example, a focus pull, it is not the director, but the 1st AC, who must make it work, so let the 1st AC work it out with the actor. Likewise, if the dolly grip can't keep up with an actor, then let the dolly grip and DP help that actor find a reasonable speed at which they can walk. These are not performance directions; they are technical directions.

Regarding sound, as mentioned, the DP helps the boom op position the boom. Even if boom placement has already been rehearsed, it should be checked again now. And, as was also discussed above, actors are encouraged to not make noises that interfere with dialogue, though this should always be run past the director first. Likewise, the sound mixer should never to tell actors how loudly to speak. That is a performance issue. If the sound department is having trouble with levels, then they should let the director know that.

But please rehearse every shot before you shoot the first take. This is true even when shooting singles. Oftentimes, with coverage shots, you are using longer lenses, so even small movements, say an actor leaning forward just an inch or two, may require minute focus pulls that should be identified and rehearsed. Even if these have already been rehearsed with a stand-in, they should be rehearsed again because the actor will almost certainly move differently.

Last Looks

Once every aspect of the shot has been rehearsed, the AD asks the director and DP if they are ready for a take. If the answer is yes, the AD announces, "We're going for a take."

Then they say, "Last Looks." This cues Makeup to handle final touch ups on the actors.

Clear the Eyelines

Right before shooting any take, the AD clears the eyelines. This means ensuring that no crew member, hanger-on or gawker is standing or sitting in a place that puts them directly in any actor's line of sight. That distracts actors. To be clear, it is not necessary to keep crew out of an actor's peripheral vision, but in terms of where any actor is directly looking during a take, they should only see the other actors they are playing the scene with.

Picture is Up

Now it is time to shoot a take. The AD says, "Quiet on set. Picture is up."

This means that everybody stops what they are doing, stands or sits in place, and does not move or talk again until the take is complete. If there are crew not on set, the AD's directive must be communicated to them as well. People in another room or outside by the truck can, if they don't know picture is up, ruin sound on a take by talking or making other noises. This is again where walkies come in handy.

The Slate

Shots on the slate are **not** numbered according to your shot list. They are numbered according to the scene number. If you are shooting, let us say, Scene 5, then the first shot you shoot, the master, is numbered 5; the next shot you shoot, say a two shot, is 5A; the shot after that, say a single, is 5B; on and on. In other words, you simply number each consecutive shot by adding the next letter in the alphabet to the scene number.

You do this even when shots are dropped. Let's say the just-mentioned two shot has to be cut because the production is behind schedule. In that case, the single would now be 5A and not 5B. If you still designated it 5B, the person creating dailies will be left to wonder what happened to shot 5A and might conclude, with some panic, that it wasn't offloaded from the camera card and is lost (there will be camera reports, or logs, which you will learn how to fill out in your cinematography classes, but in my experience, people rarely look at them).

The 2nd AC updates the slate but the script supervisor, or AD, always confirms that it has been updated correctly. In cases when you don't have a 2nd AC, the AD can slate takes.

The Script for Shooting Takes

INT. MOVIE SET - DAY

The 2nd AC gets into position with the slate and the DP frames it up. (The DP must always clearly frame up the slate so that it can be read in the editing room later; the shot and take number must be visible.)

The 2nd AC begins with the clapper on the slate open. (If they don't do this, then later when you are scrubbing through footage to synch sound to picture, it will difficult to find the moment when the clapper actually closed to mark synch.)

                    ASST. DIRECTOR
          Camera ready?

                    DIR. PHOTOGRAPHY
          Ready.

                    ASST. DIRECTOR
          Sound ready?

                    SOUND MIXER
          Ready.

                    ASST. DIRECTOR
          Roll sound.

The sound mixer puts the audio recorder into record mode and confirms that they have done so.

                    SOUND MIXER
          Speed.

The AD verbally slates the take.

                    ASST. DIRECTOR
            Scene 5, Take 1. Roll camera.

The DP or 1st AC puts the camera into record mode and confirms that they have done so.

> DIR. PHOTOGRAPHY
> Speed.

> ASST. DIRECTOR
> Mark it.

The 2nd AC claps the sticks. They do this loudly if it's a wide shot and the boom is far away, or they do it not so loudly if the boom is closer. In the case of closeups, if the slate is close to an actor's face, the 2nd AC or AD announces, "Soft sticks," and then the clapper is softly closed.

The 2nd AC clears frame and the DP resets the frame to its first position for the shot. It is important when you are directing to give the DP time to do this. They will verbally confirm when they are ready.

> DIR. PHOTOGRAPHY
> Set. (Or "Frame.")

The director pauses for several seconds to collect their thoughts and focus their attention.

> DIRECTOR
> Action.

The actors play the scene. The director stays by the camera or the monitor to watch the take. If the action goes smoothly, the director waits until the action is complete, then ends the take.

> DIRECTOR
> Cut.

Camera and sound cut and verbally confirm this.

> DIR. PHOTOGRAPHY
> Camera cuts.

> SOUND MIXER
> Sound cuts.

The AD provides final confirmation, including over their walkie.

> ASST. DIRECTOR
> That's a cut.

> DIRECTOR
> Great. Thank you everyone. That
> was fantastic.

This script goes back to the days when all filmmaking was analog. Since the camera and reel-to-reel audio recorder, known as a Nagra, were both mechanical devices, their motors had to get up to speed once they were turned on, and that is why the sound mixer and DP say "Speed" (or "Sound speeds" and "Camera speeds") to confirm that they are recording. The terminology has simply stuck.

As to why you run sound first and verbally slate takes before running the camera, that is because back in the day audio tape was cheap while film stock was not (and still is not). But in the digital age, it is still worth running sound first so as not to prematurely fill up camera cards and so as to limit how much footage you have to scrub through in the editing room.

Problems, Problems, Problems

As indicated in the script above, when you are directing, always say something positive and encouraging after you call "Cut." Do this no matter how disappointed you feel about a take. It keeps up morale. Then, after giving praise, you can give notes. After that, crew can bring up any issues they encountered during a take. Perhaps the 1st AC buzzed focus at some point, or maybe the boom briefly dipped into frame, or maybe there was a continuity problem.

When such problems occur, take a moment to actually fix them. Don't just shoot another take and hope they don't happen again. If there was a focus problem, then 1st AC rehearses that focus pull again. If the boom dipped into frame, then the DP helps the boom op find the frame line again. And if there was a continuity problem, the script supervisor not only points out to the actor that they performed an action at the wrong time or in the wrong way, but they also ask them to rehearse the action as it should be played. (When you don't have a script supervisor, the AD pays close attention to continuity during takes.)

At the same time, please remain positive. If after every take all people do is harp on what went wrong, it gets depressing. Moreover, the director decides if a problem really is a problem. If the AC buzzed focus for a moment during, say, take 5 of a shot, and if the director knows they have that moment in focus in every other take, then they may not care. So, avoid what might be called the doom and gloom approach to shooting takes. Perfection is not required in every instance.

When to Cut Takes and When Not To

Obviously, when you are directing, you cut a take when the action the shot is covering reaches its end point. But don't cut to soon. Always silently count to five before calling cut. The reason to do that is because scenes often end on a pause, a moment of reflection when the characters are still processing what has happened, and you want that pause.

At the same time, you are not required to let every take run its course. If an actor misses their mark and the DP can't adjust because a light stand will be in frame, or if that actor is now blocking the camera's view of another actor, called stacking up, then either keep rolling and ask the actor to go back and hit their mark, or cut the take and start over again.

If an airplane is flying overhead and ruining audio, either keep rolling – the sound mixer or AD says, "hold for plane" – or cut the take and wait for the plane to pass, which is usually the better course of action since planes often take a long time to pass by. For this reason, when dialogue is involved, always give your sound mixer the authority to announce during a take when there is a plane or a helicopter or a lawn mower or whatever, because they will likely hear such noises long before you do.

Lastly, if an actor's performance is not what you want, either keep rolling and give that actor some direction or cut the take and direct them. My own preference is for talking during takes because every time you cut, it means going back to square one. Moreover, whenever you cut, that is when the makeup person wants to run in for a touchup, or when the sound mixer wants to change batteries, or when the gaffer wants to tweak a light. All of that is fine and good, but it robs you of momentum. So, if you can help an actor by giving them an adjustment, then my advice is to speak up and not cut the take. Your voice can be cut out later in the editing room.

But either way, don't waste time shooting footage you know you can't use.

Shooting Another Take

If the director wants another take, the AD says, "First positions everyone, we're going for another take." And at that point everyone and everything – actors, crew, camera and props – goes back to first positions and another take is done, once again following the script above.

Moving On

When you are directing, once you feel you have a good take or, more likely, that you have several takes with good material that can be pieced together in the editing room, then it's time to move on to the next shot. Unless you are covering a scene in a oner, then no take needs to be perfect. So long as you know that across all the takes you've shot you have at a few good versions of every moment in a scene, then you're done.

This is where a script supervisor comes in handy, even if they are no more skilled at matters of screen direction and continuity than anyone else on set. Part of their job is to keep notes on every take, and if you share with them what you like and dislike about each take, then they will have the information you need in order to decide when you can move on.

When you are ready to move on the AD announces, "Moving on."

Then the AD names and describes the next shot for the cast and crew, for example:

"We're going in for coverage. First up is Annie's closeup."

And now the process begins again: the shot is framed up, the DP provides an estimate for how long it will take to adjust the lighting, the shot is rehearsed, on and on.

Shooting Coverage

Coverage, again, means shooting closer views of the same action you shot in the master. In Chapter 4, I discussed ways to selectively use coverage, but once you do go in for coverage, don't be selective anymore. Each coverage shot should be used to cover all of the action that it is capable of covering. If, for example, you are shooting a single for a dialogue scene, then don't use that single to cover only one or two lines. You may think that you will just let the remainder of the dialogue, which you maybe consider less important, play out in the master or a two shot when you cut the scene together, but that is a really bad version of cutting in your head. If there are moments in a scene that require special emphasis, then, as also discussed in Chapter 4, add a push-in to them and/or shoot two or more differently sized singles.

In short, don't use coverage shots to capture select bits of action piecemeal. Doing that throws actors off their game and unnecessarily limits your options in the editing room. So, once you go in for coverage, commit to it and use each shot to cover all of the action that it is capable of covering.

In any case, once you go in for coverage, a new set of challenges arises. These have to do with eyelines, off-camera lines, entrances and exits and overlapping action, all of which must also be rehearsed – along with focus, boom placement, etc. – before any coverage shot is taken.

Set the Eyelines

Whenever you shoot a coverage shot that is meant to be cut with a reverse angle on another actor or actors, then the eyelines in both shots must match. This is typically not an issue with master shots, though it can be, but it is almost always an issue with coverage shots. Eyelines are set by the script supervisor, but they can also be set by the DP.

Eyelines concern where exactly an actor is looking in a frame at someone or something that is offscreen. In the first place, if an actor was, for example, looking screen-right at someone or something in the master, then in their coverage shots, they must still be looking screen-right at that person or object, unless you are purposely crossing the action line for aesthetic reasons. But screen-right is everything from the center of a frame to the right edge of that frame, and this presents a wide range of possibilities.

Moreover, a frame has a vertical axis as well as a horizontal axis, and this raises the issue of how level an actor's eyeline should be. Based on the action, an actor might also need to be looking up or down. But again, this presents a wide range of possibilities. How far up? How far down?

Additionally, an actor may have multiple eyelines, either because there are multiple actors or objects they are looking at off-screen, or because an off-screen actor or object has more than one position during a take. There may, for example, be an eyeline for when the off-camera actor is standing, and another eyeline for when they sit down.

This all sounds very complicated, but it need not be. Just respect that some precision is required. The most important factor is how close the lens is to the action line or 180-degree line. The closer the lens is to the action line, the "tighter" an eyeline will be. The eyelines in these two coverage shots are tight because they are close to the lens:

The young boy is looking only slightly screen-right and a little bit up while Tom Cruise, who is taller, is looking only slightly screen-left and a little bit down. Because of this, they appear to be looking at each other. Perhaps Cruise's eyeline should have been tilted down a bit more, but the difference is minimal, so their eyelines match.

Registering the correctness of eyelines is largely intuitive. This is because in real life we are attuned to other people's gazes. We often attend to what other people are looking at. And this innate ability to follow another person's gaze to its target makes it easy to set eyelines. You feel it when they are right. So, trust me when I tell you that if you just take 30 seconds or so to set each eyeline before shooting a coverage shot, you will get them right. And as Cruise's eyeline attests, there is always some room for error.

These eyelines, on the other hand, are not tight:

The actors are looking much farther screen-right and screen-left than in the previous example, but that is because the camera in both shots is more off-axis, which is to say further out from the action line. For this reason, if either actor's eyeline were closer to the lens (or farther away) they would not appear to be looking at each other.

Again, screen-right and screen-left are just starting points. It is about determining how far screen-right or screen-left an actor should look, as well as how level their eyeline should be. Jack Lemon, the actor on the right, has his head tilted up, but his gaze is still level, as it should be given that the other actor is also sitting.

But do note that Jack Lemon's eyeline is still high. Strictly speaking, he appears to be looking at the top of the other actor's head, and that actor (Fred MacMurray) appears to be looking at Jack Lemon's neck. This reveals again that there is always some room for error. It is most likely because Jack Lemon's eyeline is level that we don't notice the discrepancy. But if his eyeline followed the tilt of his head, and he were thus were looking up, we would certainly notice that.

Mark the Eyelines

In the case of tight eyelines, it is usually the case that the AC sets an off-camera mark that the on-camera actor then looks at to keep their eyeline consistent once it has been set. This is because when an eyeline is close to the lens, there is often not enough room next to the camera for the off-camera actor to stand or sit there. Typically, a mark is a piece of colored tape affixed to the matte box on the camera, or to a C-stand or even a wall, depending on how close the eyeline is meant to be to the lens (in the case of multiple eyelines, multiple marks are set).

When eyelines are not tight, though, the on-camera actor typically gets to look directly at the off-camera actor because the off-camera actor doesn't need to be placed right up against the camera. In the second example above, it is likely that when each shot was taken, the on-camera actor was able to look directly at the off-camera actor.

Off-Camera Lines

This brings us to off-camera lines. Always have the off-camera actor(s) play the scene with the on-camera actor(s) because actors feed off each other's performances. Again, acting is reacting. So even when actors can't look at each other, they still play the scene together, though the off-camera actor(s) should be placed as close as possible to the tape mark(s) that the AC set.

Entrances and Exits

When an actor enters a coverage shot, they should enter clean. This means they begin completely out of frame so that they are entering a clean or empty frame. Likewise, when an actor exits a coverage shot, they should clear frame completely, once again providing a clean or empty frame. This is true whether or not they are entering or exiting through a door. No matter where an actor is coming from or going to in a scene, try to begin and end with an empty frame.

These are called clean entrances and clean exits. And, again, screen direction matters. If within the same scene an actor is going to exit one shot and enter another, then when you shoot those two shots, the direction of the actor's movement must remain consistent (unless, again, you are purposely crossing the action line).

Let's say that the actor exits the first shot on the right side of frame, or screen-right. In that case, they should enter the next shot from the left side of frame, or screen-left. That may seem counterintuitive, but it keeps them moving left to right. Consistent screen direction is required whenever action is continuous.

To better illustrate this, let's return to some of the storyboards from Chapter 4. In all four panels, Martin is walking screen-right, which means that the direction of his movement is consistent from one shot to the next.

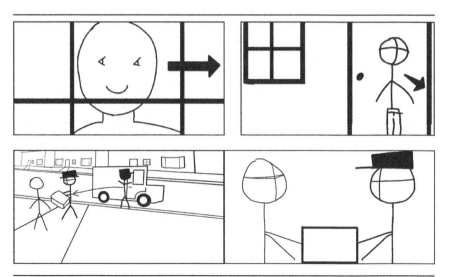

However, as with eyelines, screen-right and screen-left are only starting points. How close to the lens an actor should enter or exit a frame matters as well, and this is determined, once again, by the position of the lens in relation to the action line. If the lens is close to the action line, then the actor enters or exits the shot close to lens. If the lens is off-axis, then depending on how off-axis it is, that will determine the angle at which the actor should enter or exit the shot. The panels above clearly illustrate this because the camera is placed at a different angle in relation to the action line in each shot.

Overlapping Action

One advantage of clean entrances and exits is that they provide overlapping actions across different shots. Let's say that in a wide shot a character walks into an office and stops to look at their boss who is sitting behind their desk. Then let's say that after that pause the character walks forward and sits down across from their boss to have a conversation.

Now let's also say that in addition to the wide shot we also want to shoot a single of the character's initial pause, the one that happens when they enter the office, and that we also want to shoot another single of their action once they sit down in the chair.

When we shoot the first single, if we get a clean entrance at the start, or head, of the shot, that will provide us with multiple cut points in the editing room. We could, for example, cut from the wide to the single before the actor enters frame and pauses, or we could cut to the single when they are already partially in frame, or we could cut to the single when they have paused but are still settling into place, or we could cut to the single when they have completely settled. And since we won't know on set which of those edits will work best, by shooting a clean entrance, we give ourselves all those possible cut points in the editing room.

Likewise, if we get a clean exit at the end, or tail, of this first single, then we again give ourselves multiple possible cut points to get out of the single and back into the wide shot so that the audience can see the character cross the room to the chair where they sit down.

In terms of the second single, let's assume for the sake of argument that we can't get a clean entrance, maybe because there is a light or a C-stand in the way, some obstacle that is preventing the actor from cleanly entering frame and sitting down at the desk. In that case we still want to provide some overlapping action. To do that, it is fine to begin with the actor already in frame so long as we shoot the action of them sitting down. This is called sitting into closeups. Even if the actor rises up only a few inches off the chair before the director calls action, and then they sit down in the chair, that will provide additional cut points in the editing room.

If we don't do this, then when we are editing we might be forced to stay in the wide shot until the actor sits down and completely settles before we can cut to their single. But with even minimal overlapping action, we will have the option to change shots as the actor sits down. Such cuts, called match-on-action cuts, allow you to get into your coverage shots more quickly, which gives you more control over the pace of a scene.

Moreover, as this example demonstrates, clean entrances and exits also apply to master shots. When the character first enters the office in the wide shot, they would enter from out of frame. In the editing room this would give us the option of beginning on a pause before the action of the scene commences. This pause might also be needed to give the character time to get to the office if, in the previous scene, we saw the character make the decision to go see their boss, after which they exited frame on their way to the boss's office.

And this brings me to the other advantage of clean entrances and exits: they can be used to manage time. If an actor, let us say, is going to cross a large room in two different shots (or walk from one office to another), then by allowing them to cleanly exit the first shot and cleanly enter the next shot, we can use those two empty frames in the editing room to keep the actor off-screen just long enough to plausibly account for the time it would take them to cover that distance. At the same time, audiences have become accustomed to time jumps, so don't be afraid to use them, but still shoot clean entrances and exits to be safe.

Room Tone

Once all shots for a scene have been completed, the sound mixer records one minute of room tone. This is ambient sound specific to the location. Keep in mind, though, that room tone has limited utility. While it can often be played underneath an entire scene to smooth out shifts in ambient noises, it is not good for plugging gaps in the audio. Let's say that you did, as director, talk during a take. That will need to be cut out in the editing room. But that will leave a gap in the production track that needs to be filled. What you need to fill that gap is audio from the same take. This is another reason why I am encouraging you to pause before calling "Action." That pause, along with the pause at the end of takes, provides ambient sound specific to each take.

No location has a single ambient soundscape. For example, if when you shoot a closeup it is rush hour and then when you turn around to shoot the other closeup it is no longer rush hour, those two closeups are not going to sound the same. Even different parts of the same room sound different depending on where lights are placed, where windows are, where people are located, etc. This further explains why room tone has limited utility. But it also demonstrates that if room tone is to have any utility at all, then it must be recorded while everyone who was on set during shooting is still on set and before any lights are shut off (perhaps this is not an issue with LED lights, but it certainly is with tungsten or quartz halogen units).

After room tone is recorded, the AD announces what is up next, whether the next scene, or lunch, or wrap. But whatever is up next, even if it is lunch, everyone stays focused. Completing a scene is not an invitation for everyone to scatter.

Next Scene

Assuming you are moving on to a new scene, then the entire process repeats: the action is blocked, marks are set, continuity is established, the first shot is framed up, lighting commences, the DP gives the AD an estimate for how long this will take, the shot list is reviewed, video village is set up, the director keeps rehearsing with the actors and/or the camera, the DP stays focused on the shot, art stays focused on set dressing, sound stays focused on sound, the first shot is rehearsed before it is taken, on and on.

DIT

Ideally, it is during the gap between shooting scenes that the camera cards are offloaded and backed up by the DIT. They must know what editing software is going to be used because this determines how data and metadata must be structured on each drive. If the DIT is also the editor, they may even start creating dailies and proxies and synching sound. As this implies, the sound mixer must turn over the sound cards so that these can be offloaded and backed up too. This is true even if the DIT is only in charge of data management and won't be creating and synching dailies.

Lunch

Six hours after call time, you must break for lunch. The AD announces this. Lunch should be, at minimum, 45 minutes, which begins after the last cast or crew member gets their food in the catering line (the AD monitors this and times lunch). The goal, however, is to allow an hour for lunch, so unless you are behind schedule, allow an hour.

Car Scenes

It is dangerous to handhold a camera inside a moving car. In the event of an accident, it could become a deadly projectile. The same is true of a boom pole, though you can use wireless mics on the actors or instead tape those mics to the dashboard, or to visors or to the backs of seats. There are also rigs for attaching boom mics to cup holders, consoles, etc. But never have a DP handhold a camera in a moving car. I know this is done, but I think it's a bad idea.

My advice, then, if you plan to shoot a car scene, is to mount the camera outside the car on what is called a hostess tray, which can be safely clamped to almost any vehicle door. However, never mount a camera on the driver's side door since that will significantly obstruct the driver's view. The same is true if you use a hood mount to get a shot through the windshield. So, please don't do either of those things. Alternatively, you can rent a process trailer to tow the car, in which case you can shoot from almost any angle as well as position lights outside the car, but process trailers are expensive to rent and require a professional driver.

In order to use a hostess tray, you need your instructor's approval. You also need approval from the underwriter of your department's production insurance policy. Lastly, depending on what roads you plan to shoot on, you may have to hire a police escort. If shooting permits are required in your area, the permit office will let you know if police assistance is required. Otherwise, check with local law enforcement because what you don't want to do is head out with a camera mounted on a car and then get shut down by a passing police officer. Always play by the rules.

When you shoot with a hostess tray, since no one can operate the camera, you'll need a wireless monitor. You'll also want a lead vehicle to drive in front of the picture car. This way, the actor driving can act and not have to worry about when to make turns, when to go straight or when to pull over and stop. They simply follow the lead vehicle's lead. You'll also want walkies so that people in the lead vehicle can communicate with people in the picture car. But if you have a wireless monitor, wireless mics and walkies, then the director can easily direct from the lead vehicle and even talk to actors during takes.

As to lighting, meet with your cinematography instructor to work out a plan. But there are many compact, battery-operated lights that can be safely mounted inside cars. That said, don't use any equipment you don't know how to use. This includes the hostess tray. If no one on your crew has used one before, then hire a professional grip with the requisite experience.

What if it Rains

With exterior scenes, if it rains, you shoot anyway, unless it's pouring. On professional productions they often have what are called rain locations. These are interior sets they can move to if an exterior location gets rained out. But they sometimes rent those locations for weeks at a time. If you can work out having a rain location, then do so; otherwise, you must do what every low-budget filmmaker does: shoot in the rain.

When it does rain, gear must be protected. If lights are involved, then a flag wrapped in a heavy-duty plastic garbage bag, or with a plastic tarp grip-clipped to it, is rigged over every light. Position these flags at a slight angle so that water flows away from the lights. The camera and monitor must also be covered. The camera should be fully wrapped in plastic, with only one cutout for the matte box and another for the view finder, as can be seen in the set photo below.

Shooting a night scene in the rain. Note that clear plastic is used to protect the camera. This makes it easy to see its controls and the fluid tripod head.

The production must also provide canopies so that cast and crew can get out of the rain during periods of down time between camera setups, or when the production breaks for a meal. Part of the AD's job is to monitor weather reports and to know in advance when it is going to rain. Sometimes, of course, they will be caught off guard, but if the AD knows it's going to rain, and they don't prepare by alerting all department heads, precious shooting time will be lost.

Wrap

By the time you reach the 12-hour mark, wrap must be complete. If you will be shooting at the same location the next day, then depending on your deal with the location owner, wrap might be quite simple. I once shot at a friend's house for four days straight, and except for the last day when we had to wrap out the location, we ended each day by simply covering the camera with a sound blanket, turning off our lights, enclosing the set with yellow caution tape and going home. However, keep in mind that the DIT needs time at the end of the day to offload the camera and sound cards. Thus, even when wrap is minimal, you might not be able to shoot right up until the last minute. At the same time, if the DIT is assigned a later call time, or if they are only coming to set at intervals, then they can take the cards home and deal with them there.

But when you wrap out a location, by the time you reach the 12-hour mark, the truck must be loaded and locked and everybody should be free to go home. For this reason, wrap typically needs to start at least 30 minutes before the clock runs out, and in some cases even earlier than that. One way to expedite wrap is to start it while you are still shooting. If you only have one or two shots left with no major lighting changes, then G&E can start quietly wrapping gear the DP no longer needs. Art can also typically begin wrap early.

Finally, if the production is SAG signatory, while the crew is wrapping, this is when the producer and AD complete the actors' time sheets and ensure that they approve them.

What About the Gear

If you are loading out all of the gear from a location, then as I've stressed, it must be protected against theft. The DP and/or AC take the camera and lenses home (alternatively, they can be stored in a secure camera room or equipment locker at school), and the truck is either parked in a production parking lot with 24-hour security, or, as my students often do, it is backed up against the wall of a building.

As to who should drive the truck, be careful about this. If someone is not comfortable doing it, especially if a five-ton has been rented, then they shouldn't do it. They may get into an accident only because of their lack of confidence. Pick someone with experience or who at least has no misgivings about it. It is not difficult to drive a truck (I helped put myself through college by driving a truck one summer) but that said, it is not the same as driving a car.

Don't Despair

Life on set can be difficult. The hours are long, the work is hard and if you are moving from one production to the next, as my students often do, it can become profoundly exhausting. I am never surprised, therefore, when one of them breaks down. I broke down in film school once. I walked the entire length of campus bawling. But in addition to working too hard for too long, I also wasn't taking care of myself. And that leads to trouble.

During production, you have to get enough sleep; you have to eat right; you have to take time to wash dishes, do laundry and clean your apartment. If you don't do these things, you will almost certainly start to feel sad, frustrated and overwhelmed.

For this same reason, stay connected to the people who matter most to you; only seeing your classmates for weeks at a time, no matter how much you like them, can leave you feeling alienated from other relationships in your life. So, pacing yourself and carving out time for the people you care about, and who care about you, is important.

But there are other emotional pitfalls in production.

One of these is personality clashes, which do sometimes occur given how much time you and your classmates spend together. My advice is twofold: don't let other people get inside your head but don't get inside other people's heads either. It usually takes two to tango and there are typically two sides to every story. If someone is upsetting you, it's likely you are upsetting them too. Always think through what you might be contributing to the conflict. Adjusting your behavior might adjust their behavior.

As to processing conflicts, or talking them through, be careful: people typically aren't grateful when you point out to them what you consider to be their shortcomings. Moreover, they will almost certainly return the favor and unless you are truly willing to listen to what they have to say, then it's probably best that you don't say anything. Keep in mind that student shoots are short. The reason we work to resolve conflicts in our personal and professional relationships is because those are long term. Yes, you may be in school with someone for several years, and they with you, but you won't always have to work together.

Still, some conflicts are unacceptable. If you or someone else on a production feels marginalized or harassed in any way, whether this has to do with race, gender, sexuality, ability, age, whatever, tell your instructor so that they can take appropriate action. But that is a last resort. The goal is to create inclusive environments on sets. Be mindful and embracing of differences. Encourage your department to provide diversity training if they don't already.

Anxiety is another problem during production, but unfortunately it is par for the course. The only solution is to manage it. Don't, for example, get into the habit of beating yourself up. Almost everybody arrives to set each day with some nagging doubt only to leave with some nagging regret. The DP wishes they had operated more adeptly on a shot. The sound mixer wishes they had insisted that the generator be placed farther away. The gaffer suddenly realizes how they could have more efficiently executed a lighting setup that cost the production time. The director wishes they had shot one more take of a particular closeup. On and on.

So be it. That's life. Be kind to yourself and move on. The way to do that is to imagine what you might tell a friend if they had the same doubt or regret you do. It would probably be something kind and comforting and encouraging. So, practice self-compassion and tell yourself what you would tell a friend if they were in the same situation.

But be compassionate with others as well. Don't hold people to a standard that even you might not be able to live up to. Student production is especially anxiety inducing because everybody is still learning. The problem, though, is that you can become so focused on what others don't know, or what you think they don't know, that you forget you are still learning too.

This is especially true when directing. It is easy to think when it's your film that you are doing everything right and only others are doing things wrong. I have certainly believed that at times on my own films. But it is *never* true. Speaking frankly, and from experience, the person most likely to undermine your film is you. This is because you have the most control – over the script, over casting, over performance, over how everything is shot – so whether or not you shoot a good film is mostly up to you. Other people are going to make mistakes on your production, but so will you. This isn't bad; mistakes are how we learn. Along with our successes they contribute to how we become proficient at filmmaking. It is a sometimes painful process, but an unavoidable one.

I'm not saying that it's never the case that someone isn't giving 100%, but as somebody who went to film school and has been teaching at a film school for more than two decades, I can tell you that in my experience the vast majority of students give their all on every production.

At the same time, if somebody truly isn't carrying their weight, and they have been assigned to your production as part of a class, meaning you can't part ways, then in that case you should talk to them. You may discover they are going through something and that actually you can help. People get depressed all the time during prep and production, especially if they are making their own film while also crewing on other people's films, and that affects performance. Never assume that somebody is just slacking off. There may be more to it. In fact, that's how to begin such conversations: "Hey, what's going on, is everything okay?"

I also think it is a good idea to hold a debriefing session for every production once it wraps. Have your instructor present and talk about how the next production can be better than the one that just wrapped. Since many student productions are in short order followed by another, this can be very helpful. The issues you discuss will often be quite simple: "We all need to remember to tell the AD when we are leaving set," or "Everybody needs to stay off their phones unless we are on a meal break," or "Let's always return equipment to the staging area when it's not working." Speaking in general terms like that, and avoiding accusations, maintains trust within the group, which leads to more constructive outcomes.

The goal is for each shoot to be more efficient and productive than the one before. If that is happening, then everyone is learning. But nobody needs to be shamed in order to achieve that.

Finally, remember that production shouldn't just be a slog; it should also be fun. I have many fond memories of crewing on my classmates' films. You will too. And more than that, you are building lasting relationships. Next time you go to set, or to class, take a moment to look around. As a colleague of mine likes to point out, some of the people you see will still be amongst your closest friends 30 years from now. Longer than that hopefully.

So, hang in there, have fun, work safely, and learn a lot.

Good luck shooting your film. You're ready to do it!

Note

1 No one without training should be allowed to set up lighting and grip equipment, as there is always a certain amount of danger involved, as when one of my students incorrectly set up a 650 Fresnel on the gobo arm of a C-stand and that arm eventually swung loose, bringing down the lighting unit on someone's head, which resulted in their getting several stitches. (If all of that is Greek to you, then don't set up G&E gear on a shoot.)

Afterword (Postproduction and Beyond)

If you're reading this, then presumably you've shot your film. Congratulations! I hope it went well and that this book helped you and your collaborators through the process. The goal now is to maintain momentum and transition to editing your film as quickly as possible. Shooting a film is only one part of the process – the shortest part, in fact – so don't delay postproduction which will, in many cases, take months to complete. This book is about prep and production, but I will conclude with a few thoughts about postproduction. My goal is not to provide a comprehensive guide to the process, only a general overview of it.

Dailies

If dailies were not created during production, then get to work creating them and after that synch them. You want to review what you shot as soon as possible, taking notes as you go. Do this no matter how anxious you feel about having to watch your footage. Fear of dailies is common, but you have to push through that fear and get to work. Also, be sure to add a LUT when you create dailies; reviewing footage in log is distracting and can even leave you feeling discouraged because the image is so flat and washed out (in fact, some people, when they first encounter log, actually think that a terrible mistake has been made).

When you watch dailies, start fresh because what you thought were the best takes on set may not in every case be the best takes. Also, be on the lookout for the best moments in each take. Even if a take has many problems, it may still contain material you can use (assuming you shot coverage). Take a copy of the shooting script and next to each bit of action and dialogue jot down every shot and take that includes what could be a useful version of that action or dialogue in the edit and then circle the ones you think are strongest. If you had a script supervisor on set, you will have their notes too, but your footage provides the more perfect record, so don't treat those notes as the final word on anything.

Editing

My advice is to cut your own film. While I have a number of times throughout this book mentioned the possibility of working with an editor, you won't learn very much if you don't have to grapple with your own footage. Since story problems in your script will remain problems in the editing room where they will finally have to be solved, and since any deficiencies in the footage you shot will also have to be overcome, you won't become a better director, or writer or editor, unless you have to rely on your own ingenuity to resolve those issues. For this reason, even if you are working with an editor, get in the editing room with them every time they cut. Simply turning over footage and periodically reviewing cuts is not how it's done.

Assembly. The first cut should match the script. Include every scene you shot and within each of those scenes keep all the action and dialogue. You have to see what you have before you start chipping away at it. For this reason, don't worry about how long the first pass at the film is. You can begin by simply stringing your masters together, then you can go back and start adding coverage shots. Avoid spending too much time finessing cuts, though. An assembly is a rough version of the movie. The goal, again, is to just see what you have so that you can get feedback on it from your editing instructor and classmates. If you are working with an editor, they can create this cut on their own, but once it is complete, you should get directly involved.

First Cut. Once you've received notes, you can begin shaping the film. My advice is to focus first on scenes that most excite you. Some of what you shot is certainly wonderful and if you start there, you will sustain that excitement. Trim what you can from these scenes – cut into them as late as possible and get out of them as early as possible – and work hard to include the best moments from your coverage. But, again, don't finesse every cut because when you edit out of order, as I am suggesting, you won't have a clear sense yet of how each scene fits into the whole.

Next, turn your attention to problematic scenes. If you truly hate how a scene came out – this does sometimes happen – then delete it to see if the film can work without it. If it can't, then put some effort into creating a workable, not flawless, version of it because perfection is not the goal yet. What you want to achieve with this pass is a watchable, though still probably overlong version of the film, one that is at least beginning to play like a movie.

Fine Cut. This is a tight, polished version of the film with temp music (though not every film requires score or songs). You work towards a fine cut over the course of several cuts or more. How many cuts depends on the footage you have, the story problems you are or are not encountering, your tenacity, and the time you have available to edit. But as you work towards a fine cut, there are a number of issues to consider.

First, don't overtell the story. As discussed in Chapter 2, we all include extraneous scenes in our scripts and while I encouraged you to identify and remove these from your shooting script, you will almost certainly discover that you still shot a scene or two you don't need. The purpose of scenes, as discussed in Chapter 11, is to make the rest of the story possible. Any scene which doesn't do that, or which over motivates what follows such that it is redundant, should go, no matter how painful it might be to do that. Holding onto a scene because you like how it was shot, or because the location was expensive, or because cutting it will mean that an actor you like will no longer be in the movie, or for any other irrelevant reason, will only hurt the film.

At the same time, tell the story. If people can't follow the narrative, or if they are confused about any of its basic premises, then you have to solve those issues. For instance, I had a student who made a movie about a brother and sister, both young adults, who visit their childhood home, but everyone who watched the film assumed they were a couple because at no point was it established that they were siblings. The filmmaker knew they were siblings, but they failed to communicate that to the audience. Never forget that while you know everything there is to know about your story, the audience only knows what you reveal to them.

One way to solve such problems is by adding new, off-camera lines of dialogue. If you shot coverage, then it is usually easy to insert such lines; so long as an actor is offscreen, or the camera is on their back, they can say anything. It's simply a matter of recording it.[1] In the case of the film just mentioned, you can imagine any number of off-camera lines that would effectively establish the relationship between the characters. Most dialogue is to some degree expositional, so don't be afraid to use it that way. You might protest that you would rather not hit the audience over the head, but unless your aim is to deliberately confound the audience, which is a legitimate artistic goal in some instances, there is no reason why you can't be explicit.

This is why you also shouldn't be afraid of title cards and voiceover if using them will make your film more understandable. Hollywood filmmakers use these devices all the time. Think of the scroll at the beginning of every *Star Wars* movie. If you pay attention, though, you will notice that many films begin with such overt exposition, even if this is just a literary quote that spells out the central theme. But the number of films that begin with title cards which establish the locale, or the time period, or the basic narrative premises, should not be underestimated.

The same is true of voiceover. People often believe that if you introduce voiceover it must run through the film, but many films use it only in the opening moments, like title cards, to get the audience up to speed. *The Apartment*, discussed in Chapter 11, begins with a two and half minute voiceover that not only establishes the film's central premise – in order to gain a promotion, an accountant is allowing executives at his company to use his apartment for their extramarital affairs – but also its central theme, which is that corporations diminish the humanity of those trapped within their power structures. Then, after that, we never hear voiceover again.[2]

Restructuring a film can also sometimes make its story more comprehensible. This is difficult to pin down because every story is different, but now that you have all of your scenes on a timeline in an editing program, it is easy to move them around and to even consider where new scenes might go that could fill in holes in the story. Shooting new scenes during the later stages of editing is common, so don't rule out that possibility. On my first feature, we shot two new scenes and added six title cards to fill in confusing gaps in the plot. These gaps were intentional – we were creating an episodic plot with big time jumps – but audiences didn't like the approach; they did, however, like the new approach and no one has ever said to me that the title cards are uncinematic because, again, people prefer to understand a film rather than be confused by it.

Still, even if some parts of your film are confusing, other parts probably are not and could even stand to be more subtle. This is particularly true of dialogue. Just as we include unnecessary scenes in our scripts; we also include unnecessary dialogue. The goal with scenes, again, is to earn their outcomes, but you want to do that as efficiently as possible, especially with short films. If a line of dialogue, which should be thought of as an action or a beat, is not contributing to a scene's outcome, or if it is overcontributing to it, then cut that line. In the scene between Chad and Claire that I analyzed, the possibility that it contained extraneous beats came up more than once. The time to identify and cut such beats is during script analysis and rehearsals, but editing provides one more opportunity to do so (again, assuming you shot coverage). My advice is to go too far when deleting lines of dialogue and then work your way back from there.

Also, as a general rule, cut for performance. This means giving it priority over other considerations. For example, it is often better to live with a continuity problem if using a particular take will strengthen an actor's performance. It won't matter much if an actor's head or hand is suddenly in different position when you cut from, say, a two shot to an over-the-shoulder or a single, if what you gain is a more effective dramatic or comedic beat. There are limits, of course, and you must discover these through trial and error, but continuity, by itself, won't tell the story. Only the beats that earn the outcomes of scenes can do that.

This is why you must shape beats in the editing room just as you did during script analysis and rehearsals. Don't, for the sake of speeding up the film, cut out the emotions that motivate each character's actions. As I've stressed, this will make performances seem mechanical. Viewers want to see characters processing what is happening and emotion expressions are, once again, how actors portray that. This means that as you are editing, you have to anticipate what the audience wants to see. Don't endlessly ping-pong back and forth between characters, but don't linger on the wrong character either. Whenever a character learns something important, you probably want to cut to their reaction.[3] Again, you know everything about your story, including what characters are thinking, but the audience only knows what you reveal to them.

This is why it is important to screen your film for others, whether in class or on your own. At the same time, not all audiences are equal. Friends and family who have an emotional stake in your success may let you off the hook for story problems that your professors and classmates won't, and you need to keep that in mind. At the same time, your classmates are going to see problems other people won't. I mentioned above that small violations of continuity are tolerable if it means you can build a better performance, and just because your classmates see those violations doesn't mean that untrained eyes will. It's always a balancing act and, in the end, you must rely on your own instincts and judgments.

At the same time, always be open to other people's instincts and judgments. If someone suggests a way to recut something in your film, try out their note. Relying on your powers of divination to predict how and why a revision won't work closes off possibilities. Until you try out a note, any objections you might have to it are largely speculative. Likewise, don't give up on scenes that you find to be naggingly problematic. Just because you decide a scene is unsalvageable, doesn't mean it is; it likely only means that you can't see how its problems might be solved. In such instances, meet with your editing instructor to get specific advice on how to rework the footage.

Another approach is to let someone else cut the scene. On my second feature, for example, I despised a certain scene and wanted to reshoot it, but the producer wouldn't even entertain that possibility until I first let her take a pass at it with the editor. I went to the movies while they recut the scene and when I returned, it worked. I have several times seen this exact scenario play out amongst my students. One of them is ready to give up on a scene, or even on an entire film, but then they let another student take a stab at it, and that student's fresh perspective allows them to significantly rework the footage. Never underestimate the power of editing. Many films are saved in the editing room, so keep plugging away.

Finally, at least for this brief overview, as you get closer to a fine cut, it's a good idea to review dailies again. When you think a scene is close to being finished, go back and look at all the shots you took for that scene again. Takes, and moments within takes, that you initially dismissed may suddenly be relevant to how the scene actually turned out. If so, try swapping those takes. This won't always lead to a better scene – perhaps your first instincts were right – but you won't know that until you try, and I have more than once improved a scene by reconsidering material that I initially rejected.

Locked Picture. The process outlined above is infinitely more complex than my short account indicates. Respect that and rely on your editing instructor's expertise to help you get to locked picture, which is the final version. This means that no additional picture changes will be made. While you are editing, you can slug in missing scenes, shots and VFX (for example, an image on a TV or computer screen), but until all of those elements are included, you cannot lock picture and start sound. Beginning sound work before locking picture will force you to keep revising that sound work to match changes in the picture track, which is a waste of time and energy.

Sound Work

Dialogue Edit. This is done to clean up dialogue tracks. A clean dialogue track contains only well-recorded dialogue. Anything that is not well recorded and which cannot be made to sound acceptable by the application of digital audio filters and other frequency manipulations, must be replaced. In some cases, this will mean re-recording dialogue, called ADR, though in other cases the bad audio in one take might be replaced with good audio from another take or from several other takes that are stitched together. In many instances, a dialogue editor will provide both options, and the final decision on which audio to use will be made during the final mix. If ADR is recorded, this is also when new, off-camera lines of dialogue you've written will also be recorded, though you may be surprised to discover that some of the temp lines you recorded will actually be good enough for the final mix. Still, every off-camera line should be recorded again on an ADR stage and cut in before final decisions are made.[4]

All of this work is done outside the software that was used to cut picture, typically in Pro Tools, though other software options are available. That said, dialogue editing begins while you are cutting picture. If there are noises you can remove from dialogue tracks in the editing room, then remove them. There is no reason for viewers to hear a horn honk, a dog bark, a motorcycle zooming by, or any other extraneous sounds. Also, if an actor, let us say, loudly put down a fork on a word in a line of dialogue, then get that word from another take and try to cut it in. If that doesn't work then, as just discussed, try cutting in the audio of the entire line from another take. You could, of course, simply change takes, but sometimes we like the picture track from one take but the audio track from another, and you'd be surprised how often the two can be matched. It is also often possible to remove distracting lip smacks and unwanted breaths from dialogue while editing picture.

In sum, start cleaning up production sound in the editing room. Once you've taken a pass at a scene, stop, go back, and fix any sound problems, including sound problems you created while editing. These might include dropouts, pops, abrupt level changes, synch issues, etc. If you don't do this, then when you screen the latest cut for people, they will be repeatedly distracted by these problems and you may end up getting more notes on sound than on picture, which is not helpful.

SFX Editing. This also begins during picture editing. If, for example, we're supposed to hear a phone ringing or someone knocking on a door, then put those sounds in as you are cutting because they are part of the story. Presumably, your school provides access to a sound-effects library, but sound effects can also be found online. You should also add ambiences along the way: traffic, wind, rain, crickets, birds, etc. Some of these might be relevant to the story but even when they are not, they make scenes feel like they are actually happening in the real world, and they also help to smooth out, or cover up, ambient shifts in the dialogue tracks. Again, you want notes on the story, not on sound problems, when you screen your film for people.

As with dialogue, final SFX editing is done outside of the editing software that was used to cut picture. This begins with a spotting session. This means going through the film and identifying what sound effects are needed and where they are needed. In the first place, when dialogue is recorded, mics are positioned for that, so most of the other sounds that get on a production track are often badly recorded. These include things like footsteps, doors opening and closing, keys being picked up or put down, etc. These sounds either need to be replaced or augmented. For example, an actor may put on a jacket during a scene, and perhaps some sounds associated with that are on the production track, but over those you might add what are called clothes rustles. If you listen closely to movies, everything makes a sound. This is because when a story world is too quiet, it can begin to feel strange.

Many of these types of sound effects are recorded live, which is called foley. A foley artist creates sound effects in real time as they watch the movie on a monitor in a foley stage. They may create footsteps by walking in synch with a character on screen. If that character is walking in the woods, they may put dirt and leaves and twigs on the floor and walk in place on those. If an actor pours a glass of water, the foley artist pours a glass of water. If an actor taps a pencil on a desk, the foley artist taps a pencil. In my last short, there is a scene of a character delivering newspapers, and the foley artist even recorded the sound of each paper leaving the actor's hand as he tossed them, even though no such sound was on the production track. Again, every action in a film typically has an associated sound effect.

In addition to simply replacing or augmenting sounds on the production track, there is sound design. This names more artful uses of sound effects. For example, in the film just mentioned, after the character finishes their paper route, they go home to their tiny, empty apartment. They are a lonely person at the bottom of the economic ladder and to underscore that, we added a series of loud car-bys as well as a muffled, but blaring, television playing in another apartment. A car-by is, as its name suggests, the sound of a car driving by, and we were able to find ones of cars zooming by at high speeds. The goal was to give the impression that the character lives in an old, noisy building situated close to a busy boulevard or highway. But then, when the character receives a devastating phone call, we slowly faded out, or dialed down, these other sounds to draw attention to the conversation. After that, we faded in a melancholy music cue.

Music. Working with a composer also begins with a spotting session. This means watching the film together and identifying all of the places where you both think score would be appropriate. It's up to you to know what type of score you want, and how you want it to work in the film in terms of both mood and tone, so be very clear about all that with the composer. Still, don't expect their first pass at the score to be perfect. You may remember that I allowed $1000 for the score in *Orbiting*, and one reason I did that is because scores often go through several iterations, and some cues may be reworked many times. Scoring a film is typically a protracted process and at some point, you may even go to the composer's studio to work with them. A score is not something that is simply written, recorded and delivered.

For this reason, it's best if the composer begins by composing only a few cues for significant scenes so that you can then discuss with them if they are on the right path. After that, continue to review and discuss cues as they are created. After that, when you are both happy, the score can be recorded. Finally, the composer should not deliver the score as a single track. They should provide what are called stems. One stem, for example, might include piano, another guitar and another percussion. This way, the music can be further manipulated during the final mix.

Final Mix. This is the fun part. You get to sit on a mix stage and listen to your movie. As this implies, you need to be there the entire time. The mixer may make a preliminary pass at the dialogue without you, but otherwise they want to make adjustments in real time with you. It is never the case that you just turn over your sound files and walk away (the mixer will tell you exactly what you need to deliver to them). Still, if after the mix is done you later have misgivings about the level on a particular music cue or sound effect or line of dialogue, then email the mixer and they will usually make the adjustment on their own, but otherwise you need to be present and involved. Finally, be sure to get both stereo and surround-sound files of the mix.

Final Color and Output

Color. As with the sound mix, you want to be in the color suite as the film is being graded, even if the adjustments you expect to make are simple. The time to make decisions about things like bringing down highlights, crushing blacks, desaturating some colors while making other colors pop, is while the film is being colored. As mentioned in the chapter on budgeting, your DP may be the colorist, but if they are not, they should still be present to provide input.

Output. To post your finished film online, you need only match the final mix to the final color output in a professional editing program and then export it, which is called printing. Talk to the colorist first, though, about what settings to use because different video hosting sites compress video in different ways.

If you are exporting for a theater or a festival, get their exact specs (codec, bit depth, file size, etc.), so that you can tailor the print to what they want. And if you need to create a DCP for a festival, they may, as I've said, dictate who can create it.

Timeline

It is always good to give yourself deadlines. Your department almost certainly expects you to complete your film by a certain date. Just take that date and work backwards from there, creating a timeline for post, one that includes specific dates for when each step – assembly, first cut, fine cut, picture lock, dialogue edit, SFX, music, final mix and color – will be complete. Be reasonable about each deadline. For example, you're likely not going reach picture lock in a few weeks or even a month. If you are screening cuts in your editing class, there are going to be lags between those screenings because other students also have to screen, and that alone will delay the process. But that aside, the goal is to spend serious time cutting the best film you can. This is especially true with a first film. It takes experience and practice to learn how to edit and so first films often take the longest to cut, ten weeks or more in my experience.

As to post sound, keep in mind that you won't always have control over every aspect of it. Even if you cut your own dialogue, foley and SFX, you probably won't be mixing the film, and at that point, mixing the film is subject to the mixer's schedule. This is also true of score and color. So, anticipate delays. Talk to fellow students who have already completed a film because they can give you reliable information on how long it takes to complete each phase of postproduction.

A postproduction timeline for *Orbiting* is included in the online resources for this book. Use it as a template for your own timeline. But again, get input from people with more experience, including your instructors and the postproduction staff in your department.

Afterwards

Festivals. As mentioned in the chapter on budgeting, these are typically not career changing. Most festivals are regional affairs with little to no influence outside their geographical areas. But it is still fun to screen at them. As to more prominent festivals, ones that have a national and even international reach, these are incredibly difficult to get into. In part, this is because they invite many films and don't simply select from submissions. There is even a saying associated with this: "Those who play don't pay, and those who pay don't play." This is an exaggeration, but it means that filmmakers who pay the submission fee by submitting online have less of a chance than filmmakers who are invited to submit. This is not meant to discourage you, but my advice is to also focus on smaller festivals because you are apt to get more bang for your submission buck. Also, apply to as many festivals as you can afford to. Rejection is common, so you have to really get your film out there.

Online. After festivals, consider making your film publicly available online to see what happens. Vimeo even provides advice in its help center on how to position your film to potentially be chosen as a Staff Pick, which, while a long shot, would gain you some exposure. Short of the Week is another good option, but it does have a submission fee. There are other options, so do your research and talk to classmates about what they have done to get their films out into the world. Finally, I advise you create a website where all of your work is available.

What's next?

The answer is your next film. Keep producing work. And if your goal is to become a feature director, get to work writing a feature script. The industry is not, *per se*, looking for directors. But it is always looking for content. Even if your short garners industry attention, the first question any agent or development exec is going to ask you is if you have script. The same is true if you want to work in television. But as to feature scripts, if you are not specifically writing mainstream commercial material, then consider submitting to screenwriting labs. The lab at Sundance, for example, has fostered a great many successful projects, in part because it is geared towards developing content for the Sundance festival and its market.

At the same time, you need to make a living after you graduate. One reason to crew on as many films as you can while you are in school, and to edit your own films, including being your own assistant editor (creating dailies, proxies, etc.) is to gain job skills. Your goal of becoming a professional director will take years to achieve and in the interim you want to be in the industry working, learning and growing as a filmmaker. Also, if you are in an MFA program, your degree will allow you to apply for teaching jobs, whether adjunct or tenure track. Whichever path you choose, though, whether industry or academic or both, stay in the game and stick with it.

You're on your way. Good luck!

Notes

1 You can temp in any off-camera line by having the actor record it on their phone and then email or text you the sound file. And prior to that, you can just add a subtitle.
2 It is also common to use voiceover and title cards at the ends of films. *The Road Warrior*, for example, begins and ends with voiceover, while *Fury Road* begins with voiceover and ends with a title card. All of this is easier to handle in features because they have time to spare but, that said, you can solve a lot of story problems with these devices.

3 If you can't find an appropriate reaction from an actor to something that just happened in a scene, you may be able to repurpose another one. It doesn't matter what an actor actually reacted to on set; if a particular reaction will work elsewhere in a scene, use it there.

4 Sometimes these new lines won't be off-camera lines but on-camera lines. You may, for whatever reason, want to slightly alter what a character says, and so long as the change is not significant, you can usually cram in the new line without anyone noticing, especially if it is not a closeup.

Appendices

Appendix I: *Orbiting* by Karen Glienke

1 INT. BEDROOM - DAY

   A TV is on, SCI-FI RERUN, no sound.

   TREVOR (32), disheveled, unshaven, watches from his
   desk.

   He tears himself away from the TV and turns to his old
   LAPTOP. He begins typing:

   "The Season of Darkness - Chapter 2"

   "Steve froze as the glimmering Hybrid Orbiter cloud..."

   Letter by letter, he adds "hovered insidiously."

                   MOM (O.S.)
         Tomorrow is too late!

   Trevor cringes, grits his teeth and deletes the last
   word. He types "hysterically."

                    DAD (O.S.)
        I'm not going to be late just so--

                   MOM (O.S.)
        It expires today and we get money
        back!

                    DAD (O.S.)
        So, send Trevor!

                   TREVOR
        Fuck!

   He pounds the delete key. Furiously he types "in a
   cataclysmic, raging convulsion."

The bedroom door suddenly swings open. Trevor turns.
The CAT saunters in. He glumly watches it.

>   MOM (O.S.)
>   I don't want to interrupt his work.

>   DAD (O.S.)
>   His "work" my ass! You just don't think
>   he's capable of using a goddamn coupon!

Trevor stands, grabs his KEYS, but when he hears
footsteps approaching, he ducks behind the bedroom door.

Trevor's DAD (60) enters and looks around. He peers
behind the door to find Trevor.

>   DAD
>   Trevor, we need you in the living
>   room.

2 INT. LIVING ROOM - DAY

Organized clutter. At a work table, MOM (60) thumbs
through a FILE BOX full of COUPONS. Behind her is
a BULLETIN BOARD full of CLIPPINGS, a CALENDAR and
STACKS OF FILE BOXES.

Trevor enters with his father.

>   DAD
>   Your mother needs you to run an
>   errand. The Koops will be here
>   any minute.

>   MOM
>   No, you're busy working on your,
>   your novel.

>   DAD
>   He'll do it!

Mom sighs and gives in.

>   MOM
>   OK, Trev, it's very important
>   that you do this just right. The
>   sale starts today, one dollar off
>   (MORE)

MOM (cont'd)
the price of two, but I have a
two-for-the-price-of-one coupon
that expires today so we pay less
than the price of one, but with
the rebate, okay--

She pauses. Trevor is staring at her calendar: a BIG STAR
and the words "Mid-Summer's Eve coupon expires today."

DAD
Are you listening, Trevor?

TREVOR
Yes, dad.

MOM
I don't know if I can trust him
with this!

DAD
He'll do it!

MOM
OK, Trevor. It's on sale starting
today, one dollar off the price
of two. I have a two-for-the-
price-of-one coupon. It expires
today. And with the rebate, which
specifies "we will reimburse you
the purchase price," and not
minus the coupon, they're paying
us to buy the--

DAD
Hurry up.

MOM
So, you need to get two four-
packs of the Starlight Breeze
Ultra Cleansing, okay? Here's the
$3.50 and here's the coupon.

She hands him the MONEY and the COUPON. It reads:
"Mid-Summer's Eve feminine cleansing douche, 4-pack,
one dollar off when you buy two."

MOM
Okay, you understand what you
need to do?

                         TREVOR
           Yes.

Dad leads Trevor towards the front door. He speaks to
him in a low but insistent tone.

                         DAD
           Trevor, I don't give a damn about
           the douches. But screw this up
           and I'm going to have to pay the
           consequences. You know what I
           mean?

                         TREVOR
           I've got it.

                         DAD
           Screw this up and we're going to
           have a talk. Got it?

Mom pushes Dad aside, thrusting a NOTE at Trevor.

                         MOM
           Here.

It reads: "3rd aisle, 2 boxes Mid-Summer's Eve
Starlight Breeze Ultra Cleansing, show coupon, request
rebate form, GET RECEIPT."

3 EXT. RESIDENTIAL STREET - DAY

Trevor walks, slouching, rock-bottom miserable.

He reads his MOTHER'S NOTE again. Humiliating.

He sticks the note in his back pocket.

4 INT. STORE - FEMININE HYGIENE AISLE - DAY

Trevor stands before a shelf of DOUCHE BOXES. He
selects two, turns and trudges towards the front of
the store.

5 INT. STORE - CASH REGISTER #1 - DAY

Trevor sets down the TWO BOXES and takes the $3.50
from his pocket. He reaches into his other pocket,
then into both of his back pockets.

He pulls out his MOTHER'S NOTE. The coupon is gone.

The cashier, WENDY (25), rings up the first box.

                    TREVOR
          Wait - not both.

                    WENDY
          What?

                    TREVOR
          I have a coupon - for a free one.

                    WENDY
          For a free douche?

                    TREVOR
          Yes.

                    WENDY
          Okay, um, I need to see it.

He pulls out an old, worn WALLET and opens it. It's empty.

                    WENDY
          You need to give the coupon to
          me.

                    TREVOR
          Right. Sorry. Hold on. It must
          have fallen out of my pocket.

He turns to see THREE IMPATIENT CUSTOMERS in line
behind him. Wendy starts to ring up the second box.

                    TREVOR
          Wait. Shit! OK, I can only pay
          for one. But I need both.

Wendy stares, incredulous.

Trevor picks up the two boxes. He squeezes past the
customers and heads back into the store.

6 INT. STORE - FEMININE HYGIENE AISLE - DAY

Trevor retraces his steps. At the end of the aisle, he
sees a small PIECE OF PAPER on the floor.

He runs and picks it up. It is BLANK. He throws it down.

He frantically searches his pockets again.

He sees ANOTHER PIECE OF PAPER on the floor.

He runs and picks it up. It is his MOTHER'S NOTE.

7 INT. STORE - CASH REGISTER #2 - DAY

Trevor stands smiling awkwardly at a different
cashier, LINDA (22). He glances at her NAME TAG.

>   TREVOR
>   Hey... Linda? I know you, right?

She looks at the TWO BOXES and raises her eyebrows.

>   TREVOR
>   Yeah, uh, I need both of these
>   and--

>   LINDA
>   Weren't you just in line over
>   there? I mean, do you have the
>   coupon now?

>   TREVOR
>   Uh, no, but...

>   LINDA
>   So, you want two douches but can
>   only pay for one?

>   TREVOR
>   No, I...

She picks up a PHONE and gets on the P.A.

>   LINDA
>   I need a manager. Coupon check
>   for Mid-Summer's Eve douche for a
>   gentleman here. He needs two but
>   can only pay for one.

Trevor looks around.

There is a LINE OF PEOPLE.

Everybody is staring at him.

He sees a large, heavy-set MANAGER walking towards
him.

8 EXT. BOULEVARD - DAY

Trevor runs with the DOUCHES, the manager close
behind.

Trevor outruns him. The manager gives up, panting.

>   MANAGER
>   Take your damn douches! Enjoy
>   them, you pathetic loser!

9 EXT. RESIDENTIAL STREET - DAY

Trevor is still running as fast as he can.

He glances back as he rounds a corner and runs
straight into SCOTT (32), stylishly dressed, about to
get into a large and imposing BLACK SUV.

>   SCOTT
>   Woah - watch out!

Their eyes meet.

>   SCOTT
>   Trevor Gunderson? Wow man, what
>   are you doing around here?
>   Visiting your mom too?

Trevor hides the DOUCHES.

>   TREVOR
>   Uh, yeah man.

Scott shifts to reveal AMBER (30), equally stylish,
sitting in the passenger seat.

>   SCOTT
>   Trevor, this is Amber.

>   AMBER
>   Hi.

Trevor stumbles backwards, begins walking away.

>   TREVOR
>   Hi. Good to see you, sorry - I,
>   uh, gotta run.

                    SCOTT
          Yeah, uh, give me a call, we can
          catch up.

Scott and Amber watch as Trevor ducks into an alley.

10 EXT. ALLEY - CONTINUOUS - DAY

Trevor slams ONE OF THE BOXES against a fence. He
resumes walking. He picks up his pace, determined.

11 INT. LIVING ROOM - DAY

Trevor rushes in and hurls the BOXES at the desk.

They take a pile of COUPONS with them as they bounce
off the desk and land on the floor.

Trevor storms out.

12 INT. TREVOR'S BEDROOM - DAY

Trevor bursts in. He violently opens his closet and
takes out a SUITCASE.

He starts throwing possessions in it: UNDERWEAR,
T-SHIRTS, paperback NOVELS, an AUTOGRAPHED PICTURE of
Salman Rushdie.

He eyes the TV. An *X-FILES* RERUN. He finds the REMOTE
and turns on the sound. He continues packing, but
more slowly.

Eventually, he sits on the bed, fully engrossed.

13 INT. TREVOR'S BEDROOM - NIGHT

Trevor is asleep. He wakes to the sound of CAR DOORS
and VOICES in the driveway.

14 INT. LIVING ROOM - NIGHT

The sound of KEYS in the front door.

CLOSE ON

The TWO DENTED BOXES and the mess of SCATTERED
COUPONS. The parents enter in the background.

                    DAD
          What's that on the floor?

Mom walks forward.

                          MOM
         Oh, the cat must have knocked
         them over. Is the receipt here?

   She kneels down and shuffles through the mess of coupons.

   Her efforts become more frantic.

                          MOM
            Trevor!

                                          CUT TO BLACK.

Appendix II: Sample Breakdown

ORBITING BREAKDOWN SHEET 1

Scene No.: __1__   Scene: _TREVOR'S BEDROOM_   I/E: _INT_ D/N: _DAY_

Synopsis: _Trevor writes, mom and dad argue off-screen, Dad enters_

Pg. Count: __1 2/8__   Script Pgs.: __1–2__ Location: ___Los Angeles___

CAST	EXTRAS – SILENT BITS	EXTRAS – ATMOSPHERE
1. Trevor 2. Dad		
PROPS & SET DRESSING TV Laptop	**WARDROBE**	**MAKEUP/HAIR**
VEHICLES & ANIMALS Cat	**SPECIAL EQUIPMENT**	**PRACTICAL EFFECTS/VFX** Sci-fi rerun on TV
STUNTS	**PRODUCTION NOTES** Green screen TV?	

ORBITING BREAKDOWN SHEET 2

Scene No.:   __2__   Scene: ___LIVING ROOM___   I/E: _INT_ D/N: _DAY_

Synopsis: __Mom and Dad send Trevor to the store__

Pg. Count: _2 1/8_   Script Pgs.: _2–4_ Location: ___Los Angeles___

CAST	EXTRAS - SILENT BITS	EXTRAS - ATMOSPHERE
1. Trevor 2. Dad 3. Mom		
PROPS & SET DRESSING Work table File boxes Bulletin board Calendar Coupons & clippings Starlight Ultra coupon Mother's note Money ($3.50)	**WARDROBE**	**MAKEUP/HAIR**
VEHICLES & ANIMALS	**SPECIAL EQUIPMENT**	**PRACTICAL EFFECTS/VFX**
STUNTS	**PRODUCTION NOTES**	

ORBITING BREAKDOWN SHEET 3

Scene No.: __3__   Scene: __RESIDENTIAL STREET__   I/E: __EXT__   D/N: __DAY__

Synopsis: __Trevor forlornly walks to the store__

Pg. Count: __2/8__   Script Pgs.: __4__   Location: __Los Angeles__

CAST	EXTRAS - SILENT BITS	EXTRAS - ATMOSPHERE
1. Trevor		
PROPS & SET DRESSING Mother's note	**WARDROBE**	**MAKEUP/HAIR**
VEHICLES & ANIMALS	**SPECIAL EQUIPMENT**	**PRACTICAL EFFECTS/VFX**
STUNTS	**PRODUCTION NOTES**	

ORBITING BREAKDOWN SHEET 4

Scene No.: __4__ Scene: ____STORE – AISLE____ I/E: _INT_ D/N: _DAY_

Synopsis: __Trevor grabs two boxes of Starlight Ultra__

Pg. Count: __1/8__   Script Pgs.: _4_ Location: ___Los Angeles___

CAST	EXTRAS – SILENT BITS	EXTRAS – ATMOSPHERE
1. Trevor		6 shoppers
PROPS & SET DRESSING Starlight Ultra boxes (50)	**WARDROBE**	**MAKEUP/HAIR**
VEHICLES & ANIMALS	**SPECIAL EQUIPMENT**	**PRACTICAL EFFECTS/VFX**
STUNTS	**PRODUCTION NOTES**	

ORBITING BREAKDOWN SHEET 5

Scene No.: _5_ Scene: _STORE – REGISTER #1_ I/E: _INT_ D/N: _DAY_

Synopsis: _Trevor discovers that he no longer has the coupon_

Pg. Count: _1 1/8_   Script Pgs.: _4–5_ Location: _Los Angeles_

CAST	EXTRAS – SILENT BITS	EXTRAS – ATMOSPHERE
1. Trevor	3 impatient customers in line	3 to 4 background shoppers
4. Wendy		
5. Linda (in background)		

PROPS & SET DRESSING	WARDROBE	MAKEUP/HAIR
Starlight Ultra boxes (2)	Retail vests – Wendy & Linda	
Money ($3.50)	Wendy's name tag	
Mother's note	Linda's name tag	
Wallet		

VEHICLES & ANIMALS	SPECIAL EQUIPMENT	PRACTICAL EFFECTS/VFX

STUNTS	PRODUCTION NOTES

ORBITING BREAKDOWN SHEET 6

Scene No.: __6__ Scene: __STORE – AISLE__   I/E: __INT__ D/N: __DAY__

Synopsis: __Trevor searches the floor for the lost coupon__

Pg. Count: __2/8__   Script Pgs.: __5__ Location: __Los Angeles__

CAST	EXTRAS - SILENT BITS	EXTRAS - ATMOSPHERE
1. Trevor		6 shoppers
PROPS & SET DRESSING	**WARDROBE**	**MAKEUP/HAIR**
Blank piece of paper Mother's note Starlight Ultra boxes (2) Starlight Ultra boxes – shelf		
VEHICLES & ANIMALS	**SPECIAL EQUIPMENT**	**PRACTICAL EFFECTS/VFX**
STUNTS	**PRODUCTION NOTES**	

ORBITING BREAKDOWN SHEET 7

Scene No.: __7__ Scene: __STORE - REGISTER #2__ I/E: _INT_ D/N: _DAY_

Synopsis: __Trevor tries again to buy the two boxes of Starlight Ultra__

Pg. Count: __7/8__ Script Pgs.: _6_ Location: ____Los Angeles____

CAST	EXTRAS - SILENT BITS	EXTRAS - ATMOSPHERE
1. Trevor 4. Wendy (in background) 5. Linda 6. Manager	5 customers in line	4 background shoppers
PROPS & SET DRESSING	**WARDROBE**	**MAKEUP/HAIR**
Starlight Ultra boxes (2) Money ($3.50) Phone (P.A.)	Retail vests – Linda & Wendy Linda's name tag Wendy's name tag	
VEHICLES & ANIMALS	**SPECIAL EQUIPMENT**	**PRACTICAL EFFECTS/VFX**
STUNTS	**PRODUCTION NOTES**	

ORBITING BREAKDOWN SHEET 8

Scene No.: __8__ Scene: ___BOULEVARD_____ I/E: __EXT_ D/N: _DAY__

Synopsis: __Trevor runs from store manager_____

Pg. Count: __2/8__   Script Pgs.: _6–7_ Location: _____Los Angeles_____

CAST	EXTRAS – SILENT BITS	EXTRAS – ATMOSPHERE
1. Trevor 6. Manager		
PROPS & SET DRESSING Starlight Ultra boxes (2)	**WARDROBE**	**MAKEUP/HAIR**
VEHICLES & ANIMALS	**SPECIAL EQUIPMENT**	**PRACTICAL EFFECTS/VFX**
STUNTS	**PRODUCTION NOTES**	

ORBITING BREAKDOWN SHEET 9

Scene No.: _9__   Scene: _RESIDENTIAL STREET_ I/E: _EXT_ D/N: _DAY_

Synopsis: _Trevor bumps into Scott and Amber_

Pg. Count: ___1___   Script Pgs.: _7__   Location: ___Los Angeles___

CAST	EXTRAS - SILENT BITS	EXTRAS - ATMOSPHERE
1. Trevor 7. Scott 8. Amber		
PROPS & SET DRESSING Starlight Ultra boxes (2)	**WARDROBE**	**MAKEUP/HAIR**
VEHICLES & ANIMALS Black SUV	**SPECIAL EQUIPMENT**	**PRACTICAL EFFECTS/VFX**
STUNTS Trevor bumps into Scott	**PRODUCTION NOTES** Stunt coordinator?	

ORBITING BREAKDOWN SHEET 10

Scene No.: __10__ Scene: _____ALLEY_____ I/E: _EXT_ D/N: __DAY__

Synopsis: _Trevor smashes a Starlight Ultra box on a fence_____

Pg. Count: __1/8__   Script Pgs.: __8__ Location: ___Los Angeles_____

CAST	EXTRAS - SILENT BITS	EXTRAS - ATMOSPHERE
1. Trevor		
PROPS & SET DRESSING Starlight Ultra boxes (2) Backup boxes	**WARDROBE**	**MAKEUP/HAIR**
VEHICLES & ANIMALS	**SPECIAL EQUIPMENT**	**PRACTICAL EFFECTS/VFX**
STUNTS	**PRODUCTION NOTES**	

ORBITING BREAKDOWN SHEET 11

Scene No.: __11__   Scene: __LIVING ROOM_____   I/E: __EXT__ D/N: __DAY__

Synopsis: __Trevor throws both Starlight Ultra boxes at the calendar_____

Pg. Count: ___1/8___   Script Pgs.: __8__ Location: __Los Angeles_____

CAST	EXTRAS – SILENT BITS	EXTRAS – ATMOSPHERE
1. Trevor		
PROPS & SET DRESSING Work table File boxes Bulletin board Calendar Coupons & clippings Starlight Ultra boxes–dented	**WARDROBE**	**MAKEUP/HAIR**
VEHICLES & ANIMALS	**SPECIAL EQUIPMENT**	**PRACTICAL EFFECTS/VFX**
STUNTS	**PRODUCTION NOTES**	

ORBITING BREAKDOWN SHEET 12

Scene No.: __12__   Scene: _TREVOR'S BEDROOM_   I/E: _INT_ D/N: _DAY_

Synopsis: _Trevor packs a suitcase while he watches TV_

Pg. Count: __3/8__   Script Pgs.: __8__   Location: _Los Angeles_

CAST 1. Trevor	EXTRAS - SILENT BITS	EXTRAS - ATMOSPHERE
PROPS & SET DRESSING Suitcase Laptop TV Remote Paperback novels Photo – Salman Rushdie	**WARDROBE** Underwear Socks T-shirts Etc.	**MAKEUP/HAIR**
VEHICLES & ANIMALS	**SPECIAL EQUIPMENT**	**PRACTICAL EFFECTS/VFX** *X-Files* rerun on TV
STUNTS	**PRODUCTION NOTES** Green screen TV?	

ORBITING BREAKDOWN SHEET 13

Scene No.: __13__ Scene: <u>TREVOR'S BEDROOM</u> I/E: __INT__ D/N: __NITE__

Synopsis: <u>Trevor has fallen asleep in front of the TV</u>

Pg. Count: __1/8__ Script Pgs.: __8__ Location: __Los Angeles__

CAST	EXTRAS – SILENT BITS	EXTRAS – ATMOSPHERE
1. Trevor		
PROPS & SET DRESSING	**WARDROBE**	**MAKEUP/HAIR**
Suitcase	Underwear	
Laptop	Socks	
TV	T-shirts	
Remote	Etc.	
Paperback novels		
Photo – Salman Rushdie		
VEHICLES & ANIMALS	**SPECIAL EQUIPMENT**	**PRACTICAL EFFECTS/VFX**
		X-Files rerun on TV
STUNTS	**PRODUCTION NOTES**	
	Green screen TV?	

ORBITING BREAKDOWN SHEET 14

Scene No.: __14__   Scene: __LIVING ROOM__   I/E: __INT__ D/N: __NITE__

Synopsis: __Mom and dad return and find the boxes on the floor__

Pg. Count: __4/8__   Script Pgs.: __8–9__   Location: __Los Angeles__

CAST	EXTRAS – SILENT BITS	EXTRAS – ATMOSPHERE
2. Dad 3. Mom		
PROPS & SET DRESSING Work table File boxes Bulletin board Calendar Coupons & clippings Starlight Ultra boxes–dented	**WARDROBE**	**MAKEUP/HAIR**
VEHICLES & ANIMALS	**SPECIAL EQUIPMENT**	**PRACTICAL EFFECTS/VFX**
STUNTS	**PRODUCTION NOTES**	

Appendix III: Sample Budget

Draft Budget (Date)   *Orbiting*   4-day shoot: Los Angeles

Acct	Description	Amount	Units	X	Rate	Subtotal	Total
1000	**CAST**						
1002	Principal Cast						
	Trevor	4	Days		125	500	
	Dad					0	
	Mom					0	
	Wendy					0	
	Linda					0	
	Store Manager					0	
	Scott					0	
	Amber					0	500
1004	Perks & Adjustments		Allow		150	150	150
						Total 1000	**650**
2000	**PRODUCTION STAFF**						
2002	Producer						0
2004	Assistant Director						0
2006	Production Assistants						0
2008	Gas food, parking		Allow		100	100	100
						Total 2000	**100**
2100	**EXTRAS**						
2102	Featured Extras						0
2104	Atmosphere						
	Shoppers at store	1	Days	6	75	450	450
						Total 2100	**450**

Acct	Description	Amount	Units	X	Rate	Subtotal	Total
2200	**ART DEPARTMENT**						
2202	Production Designer						
	Prep, Shoot, Wrap						0
2204	Art Director						
	Prep, Shoot, Wrap		Flat		250	250	250
2208	Purchases and Rentals						
	Starlight Ultra boxes	50	Boxes		4.72	236	
	Scott's SUV	1	Days		125	125	
	Trevor's bedroom		Allow		250	250	
	Living room		Allow		150	150	761
2210	Meals - prep		Allow		50	50	50
2212	Gas - prep		Allow		25	25	25
2214	Loss & Damage		Allow		50	50	50
						Total 2200	**1136**
2300	**WARDROBE**						
2302	Costumer						
	Prep only	4	Days		100	400	400
2304	Purchases & Rentals						
	Trevor		Allow		50	50	
	Mom		Allow		150	150	
	Dad		Allow		50	50	
	Wendy		Allow		25	25	
	Linda		Allow		25	25	
	Store Manager		Allow		50	50	
	Scott					0	
	Amber					0	350
2306	Meals	4	Meals		10	40	40
2308	Gas		Allow		25	25	25
2310	Cleaning & Repairs					0	0
						Total 2300	**815**

Acct	Description	Amount	Units	X	Rate	Subtotal	Total
2400	**MAKEUP & HAIR**						
2402	Makeup Artist						
	Shoot	4	Days		150	600	600
2404	Kit Fee		Flat		50	50	50
						Total 2400	**650**
2500	**GRIP & ELECTRICAL**						
2502	Gaffer						
	Prep	1	Days			0	
	Shoot	4	Days			0	
	Wrap	1	Days			0	0
2504	Key Grip						
	Prep	1	Days			0	
	Shoot	4	Days			0	
	Wrap	1	Days			0	0
2506	Grips & Electricians						0
2508	G&E – school						0
2512	G&E Rentals		Allow		200	200	200
2514	Expendables		Allow		100	100	100
2516	Loss & Damage		Allow		100	100	100
						Total 2500	**400**
2700	**CAMERA**						
2702	Dir. of Photog.						0
2704	1st Assistant Camera						0
2706	2nd AC						0
2708	DIT						0
2710	Camera - school						0
2712	Lenses - school						0
2714	Shoulder Rig	4	Days		20	80	80
2716	Doorway Dolly	4	Days		20	80	80
2718	Shoot Drives	2	8TB		200	400	400
2720	Expendables		Allow		50	50	50

Acct	Description	Amount	Units	X	Rate	Subtotal	Total
2722	Loss & Damage		Allow		200	200	200
						Total 2700	**810**
2800	**PRODUCTION SOUND**						
2802	Sound Mixer w/Gear	4	Days		300	1200	1200
2804	Boom Op						0
2806	Expendables		Allow		50	50	50
2802	Loss & Damage		Allow		100	100	100
						Total 2800	**1350**
2900	**TRANSPORTATION**						
2902	15' Rental Truck						
	Prep	2	Days		33	66	
	Shoot	4	Days		33	132	
	Wrap	2	Days		33	66	264
2904	Damage Waiver	8	Days		14	112	112
2906	Mileage	200	Miles		1.10	220	220
2908	Gas		Allow		50	50	50
						Total 2900	**646**
3000	**LOCATIONS-CATERING**						
3002	Site Rentals						
	Trevor's House					0	
	Streets					0	
	Store - UCLA					0	0
3004	Safety Officer						
	Regular	8	Hours		25	200	
	Over-Time	4	Hours		37.50	150	350
3006	Parking - Store	10	Passes		12	120	120
3008	Shooting Permits	3	Permits		26	78	78
3010	Police (traffic control)						0
3012	Gas - location scouting		Allow		25	25	25

Acct	Description	Amount	Units	X	Rate	Subtotal	Total
3014	Location Supplies						
	Tables, Chairs, etc.		Allow		350	350	
	Walkies	15	Walkies		10	150	500
3016	Catering						
	Breakfast	85	Meals		3	255	
	Lunch	85	Meals		10	850	
	Second Meals		Allow		100	100	1,205
3018	Craft Service Supplies	4	Days		65	260	260
3020	Loss & Damage		Allow		200	200	200
						Total 3000	**2738**
3500	**GENERAL EXPENSES**						
3502	Insurance		Flat		380	380	380
3504	Copying/Printing						0
3506	Office Supplies		Allow		30	30	30
3508	Parking - Prep		Allow		25	25	25
3510	Meals - Prep		Allow		100	100	100
3512	First Aid Supplies		Allow		50	50	50
3514	Perks & Adjustments		Allow		100	100	100
3516	Casting						
	Casting Director					0	
	Water, crafty etc.		Allow		50	50	50
						Total 3500	**735**
	Total Production						**10,480**
5000	**EDITORIAL**						
5002	Editor						0
5004	Additional Drive		Allow		200	200	200
5006	Titles						0
5008	Editorial Meals						0
						Total 5000	**200**

Acct	Description	Amount	Units	X	Rate	Subtotal	Total
5100	**SCORE & MUSIC RIGHTS**						
5102	Composer		Flat		1,000	1,000	1,000
5104	Music Rights						0
						Total 5100	**1000**
5200	**POST PRODUCTION SOUND**						
5202	Dialogue & ADR	30	Hours		20	600	600
5204	Foley & SFX	40	Hours		20	800	800
5206	Foley artist						0
5208	Mix – school						0
						Total 5200	**1400**
Acct	Description	Amount	Units	X	Rate	Subtotal	Total
5400	**COLOR & DCP**						
5402	Color		Allow		500	500	500
5404	DCP		Allow		100	100	100
						Total 5400	**600**
	Total Postproduction						**3200**
	Total Production and Postproduction						**13,680**
	Contingency (10%)						**1368**
	Grand Total						**15,048**

Index

Made in the USA
Las Vegas, NV
15 June 2023

73428876R00151